JESUS FOR EVERYONE

ALSO BY AMY-JILL LEVINE

The Bible With and Without Jesus: How Jews and Christians Read the Same Stories Differently (coauthored with Marc Z. Brettler)

Short Stories by Jesus: The Enigmatic Parables of a Controversial Rabbi

The Gospel of Mark: A Beginner's Guide to the Good News

Signs and Wonders: A Beginner's Guide to the Miracles of Jesus

The Good for Nothing Tree (coauthored with Sandy Eisenberg Sasso)

Witness at the Cross: A Beginner's Guide to Holy Friday

The Difficult Words of Jesus: A Beginner's Guide to His Most Perplexing Teachings

100 Sheep: A Counting Parable (coauthored with Sandy Eisenberg Sasso)

The Kingdom of Heaven: 40 Devotionals

Sermon on the Mount: A Beginner's Guide to the Kingdom of Heaven

A Very Big Problem (coauthored with Sandy Eisenberg Sasso)

The New Testament: Methods and Meanings (coauthored with Warren Carter)

Who Counts? 100 Sheep, 10 Coins, 2 Sons (coauthored with Sandy Eisenberg Sasso)

The Gospel of Luke (coauthored with Ben Witherington III)

The Marvelous Mustard Seed (coauthored with Sandy Eisenberg Sasso)

Entering the Passion of Jesus: A Beginner's Guide to Holy Week

Who Is My Neighbor? (coauthored with Sandy Eisenberg Sasso)

Light of the World: A Beginner's Guide to Advent

The Pharisees (coedited with Joseph Sievers)

The Jewish Annotated New Testament (coedited with Marc Z. Brettler)

The Misunderstood Jew: The Church and the Scandal of the Jewish Jesus

The Meaning of the Bible: What the Jewish Scriptures and the Christian Old Testament Can Teach Us (coauthored with Douglas A. Knight)

AMY-JILL LEVINE

HarperOne
An Imprint of HarperCollinsPublishers

JESUS FOR EVERY-ONE

NOT JUST CHRISTIANS

All scripture translations, unless otherwise indicated, are by the author.

KJV: *King James Version*, used under public domain.

NJPS: *New Jewish Publication Society*, used under public domain.

NRSV/NRSVUE: *New Revised Standard Version Bible*, copyright © 1989 National Council of the Churches of Christ in the United States of America. Used by permission. All rights reserved.

HarperCollins books may be purchased for educational, business, or sales promotional use. For information, please email the Special Markets Department at SPsales@harpercollins.com.

FIRST EDITION

Designed by Yvonne Chan

Library of Congress Cataloging-in-Publication Data has been applied for.

ISBN 978-0-06-221672-4

24 25 26 27 28 LBC 5 4 3 2 1

In memoriam
Elizabeth A. Clark
David Campbell Sim

CONTENTS

INTRODUCTION
MEETING JESUS IN HIS TIME AND OURS

J **ESUS IS FASCINATING.** The stories he told, his arguments with fellow Jews, even the way the Gospel writers variously describe his teachings and his works, are packed with challenge, insight, and a fair amount of humor. This material is more than the stuff of ancient history. Jesus's teachings can help us negotiate not only everyday hassles, but also global problems. My point is not that Jesus solves everything by sunset; he obviously did not and so does not. My point is that his stories, and stories about him, can help us get through the day and even help us sleep better at night, by prodding us to ask the right questions, consider various options, and recognize that while our conclusions will necessarily be tentative, we *must* do the work. We cannot be "the light of the world" if we put our heads in the sand.

As the Gospels present him, Jesus helps us think about economics, slavery, ethnicity/race, health care, sexuality, and politics—topics covered in the chapters of this book. To get the help we need, we do well to understand how Jesus and the Gospels fit within their historical contexts: Jesus was a Galilean Jew living under Roman domination in the early first century CE; the Gospels were written decades later, outside Galilee and Judea and after the Romans destroyed the Jerusalem temple in 70 CE. What Jesus might have sounded like to a Galilean stonemason sometime in the late 20s can be quite different from what his words, packaged into a Gospel narrative, sounded like to an enslaved woman in Ephesus seventy years later.

The import of the stories does not stop with the history of either Jesus or his first-century followers. The Gospels are not just historical documents; they are also sacred writings—scripture—to countless people. Consequently, our interpretations cannot be restricted to what they meant to their original audiences, whether Jews in Capernaum or gentile disciples in a house church in Antioch. Believers in Jesus as Lord, that is, people eventually called "Christians" (not a term either Jesus or his first followers used, or even knew) will also ask, "What does this text mean to me today?" or "What does it mean to my community?" The answers necessarily differ across time and place. A twelfth-century monk will respond differently than a soldier in a World War I foxhole or a poll watcher in twenty-first-century Miami. Conscientious readers will also find different meanings for themselves: if a text means the same to us when we are six years old and then when we are sixty-six (I speak personally here), something has gone wrong, and it hasn't gone wrong with the text. Were the text to mean only one thing, then preachers would be out of business and biblical studies professors should find another career.

In his classic book *When Religion Becomes Evil*, Charles Kimball notes, "Authentic religion encourages questions and reflection at all levels. When authority figures discourage or disallow honest questions, something is clearly wrong."[1] The point holds for pastors and priests, religious educators and academics, parents and caregivers. Next, failing to question makes the text irrelevant, since the failure presumes either that the text has nothing to say about today's issues or, conversely, that we should be reduced to playing a version of first-century Bibleland. Questioning does not signal a lack of faith; failing to question signals this lack, since it abdicates our responsibility for engaging with the text. Plus—and let's be honest about this—failing to question makes the subject under discussion boring.

Granted, teachings by and about Jesus can frustrate. When we want a straight answer, Jesus sometimes offers an enigma. He rarely answers a question directly. To a lawyer's question, "Who is my neighbor?" (Luke 10:29), Jesus tells what we call the Parable of the Good Samaritan (Luke 10:30–35), which does not answer the lawyer's question. Instead, Jesus asks a different question: How do neighbors act?[2] When asked by a scribe which of the traditional 613 commandments is the most important (Mark 12:28), Jesus offers not one but two: love of God (Deut. 6:5) and love of neighbor (Lev. 19:18). Like politicians today (so much so that he appears to have invented media training), Jesus answers not the questions reporters ask; he speaks to the issues that he thinks are important.

* * *

Jesus's sayings can be and have been interpreted in multiple ways, which is why he gets cited by all sides of political issues. Is "Render therefore unto Caesar the things which are Caesar's; and unto God the things that are God's" (Matt. 22:21 // Mark 12:17 // Luke 20:25, KJV) an exhortation to pay one's taxes, since the government deserves its cut, or is it a sly way of saying that the emperor gets nothing, since all things belong to God (see Ps. 24:1)? How do we square "Do not resist an evildoer. But if anyone strikes you on the right cheek, turn the other also" (Matt. 5:39) with "the one who has no sword must sell his cloak and buy one" (Luke 22:36)? Is Jesus the poster child for the Second Amendment,[3] or should we take him seriously when he talks about loving enemies rather than killing them (Matt. 5:44 // Luke 6:27, 35)?

Too often Jesus is silent about major issues. When I want a condemnation of what I see as social sins—slavery, sexism, xenophobia—he says nothing directly condemnatory. At times, his words threaten to exacerbate those problems. Instead of rejecting the institution of slavery, he tells his followers to act as if they were themselves enslaved. In terms of gender, I would have appreciated seeing a few women among the inner circle of twelve disciples. Regarding positive relations with foreigners, "don't go to the gentiles" (see Matt. 10:5b) is not a great start.

And yet, narratives that seem to ignore problems or to leave those problems in place should prompt us—and they do prompt me—to reread. Good readers interrogate what is missing as well as what is present; good theologians bring the text into conversation with issues that did not appear on the first-century radar. When we read carefully, we can find that the text consistently prompts new insights.

This engagement of ancient literature in light of present context is how we Jews traditionally read our scriptures, for all texts require interpretation. The commandment "the seventh day is a Sabbath to the LORD your God; you shall not do any work" (Exod. 20:10, NRSVUE) requires defining "work"; different Jews, in different locations and at different times, defined the term differently. Thus, we Jews generally do not place on our cars the bumper sticker I have seen in Nashville: "The Bible says it; I believe it." It would be great if someone would market an alternative: "The Bible says it; let's discuss it." Traditional Jewish readers would begin with, "What does the text say in Hebrew, and in the targums, the ancient Aramaic paraphrases?" We ask what commentators, from the early rabbinic period through the Middle Ages to modern readings, have said. We preserve, even celebrate, different interpretations.

Once we have more or less determined what the text says, we then assess, and so we take our place as interpreters. For example, rab-

binic texts, dating to the early first centuries CE, debate whether God
was culpable in Cain's murder of Abel (yes) or whether "an eye for
an eye" should be taken literally (no). These readings then open to
discussions of capital punishment (not for Cain, who although guilty
of murder receives not a death sentence but a mark of protection)
and of compensation for permanent physical injury (with consid-
erations of pain, medical expenses, loss of work due to injury, etc.).
When Jesus says, "You have heard that it was said, 'eye for an eye
and tooth for tooth.' And I say to you, 'Do not resist the evil [one].
But whoever strikes you on [your] right cheek, turn to him even the
other'" (Matt. 5:38–39), he is not doing away with Torah. Rather, he
is changing the subject. There's a huge difference between losing an
eye and enduring a backhanded slap meant not to maim but to hu-
miliate. Refusing to resist evil means allowing evil to continue: this
would be both stupid and malevolent. Reading Jesus through rabbinic
lenses, I see his comments as opening such questions as, under what
circumstances—personal humiliation, social protest, etc.—is turning
the other cheek appropriate, and when is resistance essential? What
form should such resistance take?

Jesus, good Jew that he is, offers his own opinions on laws concerning such matters as divorce and oath-taking; other Jews disagreed
with him (which Jesus would have expected). Jesus forbids divorce,
period; other Jews would have accepted the legality of divorce but
then debated the circumstances under which it can be granted. Jesus
forbids taking oaths (cross my heart, it's there in the Sermon on the
Mount: Matt. 5:34–37); other Jews debated what kind of oaths one
could take, and the circumstances under which an oath can be an-
nulled. Through the centuries a number of Jesus's own followers disagreed with him, or at least with what they took to be the meaning of
his statements. Some have rejected his statements on divorce; others
have no problem swearing on a Bible in a court.

I disagree with him too on such matters as economics and slavery, gender roles, and language concerning disability. We always start with our own perspective, and from that perspective we put ourselves in dialogue with the text. Here's my perspective: I am a woman, a Jew, at one time the Sara Lawrence-Lightfoot Associate Professor of Religion at Swarthmore College, and now both University Professor of New Testament and Jewish Studies emerita at Vanderbilt University and the Rabbi Stanley M. Kessler Distinguished Professor of New Testament and Jewish Studies at Hartford International University for Religion and Peace. Otherwise put, I'm a Jew who teaches the New Testament to anyone who is interested—undergraduates and divinity students, priests and pastors, rabbis and imams.

Whether my disagreements with Jesus come from my own readings of the scriptures of Israel (what Christians call the Old Testament, Jews call the Tanakh, and people attempting—but failing—to find a neutral term call the Hebrew Bible), from my academic training, from my personal values, or from a combination, I cannot determine. But disagree I do, and in my conversations with the text, again, I find myself asking better questions and becoming more empathetic to views not my own. This is something we all can do when we engage with the texts about Jesus—we can question, we can disagree, and we thereby can become both better individuals and better neighbors.

I was not raised on the "Bible says it, I believe it" diet. I was raised with the meat of asking questions and the fruits of skepticism (I'll stop the culinary metaphors lest we get indigestion). In discussing with my mother what I learned in school, she would often ask, "How do you know that?" Were I to say, "I heard it from my teachers," my mother would respond, "How do they know that?" She wanted me to find the evidence and not simply take someone's word. I do the same now to my students, such that one of them gave me a mug embossed with, "How do you know that?"

Disagreeing with a parent or teacher, even disagreeing with the divine, is part of the Jewish tradition. Abraham debated with God as to whether destroying the city of Sodom was the righteous thing to do given that it might have had fifty, or even ten, righteous people in residence. What a good question to ask before bombing a city. Rachel complained to God about being infertile. Moses had more than one debate with God, and Job filled his eponymous book with them. The Psalms of Lament, such as Psalm 22, which begins, "My God, my God, why have you forsaken me?" and which Jesus, according to Matthew 27:46 and Mark 15:34, cried out as he was dying, are protest psalms. Disagreement with God is part of the system. Even what we call "petitionary prayers," prayers that ask for something, are types of complaints (e.g., "Your kingdom come . . . give us this day our daily bread"), since they show dissatisfaction with the way things presently are.

I think Jesus encourages such discussion, in part because he does not spoon-feed his audiences. At times he is direct: to the commandment against murder, he issues another commandment, this one against being angry (Matt. 5:22). He wasn't kidding. But he also treats his followers with enough respect to allow them to draw their own conclusions. That concern for drawing conclusions is, for example, how parables function. The world is messy, and while assessing biblical texts can help sort some of the mess, most of the mess will continue until the Messiah comes or comes back, until we blow ourselves to smithereens, or until we finally learn how to turn swords into plowshares, or weapons into wind farms. To presume that all we need to do is read the Gospels and we'll have peace on earth, universal health care, and ecological renewal is fantasy, not fact. However, to read the Gospels and think about them might move us a little farther away from the smithereens option.

Ironically, Jesus was anticipating a version of the smithereens option. As comments in the Gospels, the writings of Saul of Tarsus (i.e., St. Paul), and the book of Revelation indicate, some people thought that the end of the world as we know it was on the horizon. It seems to me that Jesus was preparing his fellow Jews to live as if the *'olam ha-ba*, the "world to come," or in his language the "kingdom of God," were coming, quickly, and indeed as if they already had partially entered it. He warns, "Woe to those who are pregnant and to those who are nursing infants in those days!" (Matt. 24:19 // Mark 13:17 // Luke 21:23), since these conditions will make enduring the end times even more difficult. His view, as we'll see in Chapter 5, is one that downplays marriage and children in favor of singleness and celibacy.

Today, I read these words and think, Woe to you who are nursing, when there is a lack of baby formula and affordable prenatal and postnatal care; woe to you who may have ectopic pregnancies or be carrying a fetus with fatal abnormalities or be pregnant and in need of chemotherapy for your cancer and cannot receive medical help. The setting has changed, and so has the significance of the words. But the words themselves remain prescient and pragmatic. They also form a prompt for preachers: What will be the sermon based on these passages?

My point is not that Jesus is either mourning or celebrating the demise of *Roe v. Wade*. Because Jesus lived in a different time and place than ours, "What would Jesus do?" or "How would Jesus vote?" are not the right questions (in Nashville, where I live, WWJD bracelets are sometimes taken to mean not "What Would Jesus Do?" but "We Want Jack Daniels!"). Jesus did not live in a democracy, did not confront late global capitalism, never studied Marxism or neo-liberalism, and did not have social media to distribute, or distort, his message. Jesus made no pronouncements about the Second Amendment, the Affordable Care Act, NAFTA, school vouchers, vaccinations, or masks. He does not speak about abortion or homosexuality, gender-affirming care, or artificial insemination.

This book reframes that question—"What would Jesus do?"—by asking, instead, how a historical approach to the stories of and by Jesus, coupled with awareness of how these narratives have been understood over time, helps us see better what matters in his world, and ours. This book asks how Jesus and the Gospels can help us get through the minefields of today's culture wars in such a way that we bind up wounds rather than blow up bodies.

IMAGINING AN AUDIENCE

This book was originally titled *Jesus for Atheists*. I wanted to reach people who had rejected religion as theological oxycodone: it makes us feel good at first, but in the end it threatens to rob us of independence, community, and life. But the more I worked on these chapters, the more I realized that that title, although provocative and probably commercially viable, was wrong.

I want to speak to atheists, but also to agnostics, to deists and theists, to the seekers who want a social justice Jesus, to the baptized who now reject Christian identification, and to Jews who might be curious about, or even prejudiced against, one particular first-century Galilean Jew. I want to speak to people who have concluded that since we cannot prove Jesus existed, then he was probably fictional, like Hercules, William Tell, Ned Ludd, or Betty Crocker.[4] And as some skeptics correctly note, there's no body.[5] I also imagine in this audience Muslims, Hindus, Wiccans, and others for whom the New Testament might be unfamiliar.

Much of my work involves engaging with Christians across the spectrum: liberal Protestants, Evangelicals, Pentecostals, Roman Catholics, Latter-day Saints, and Mennonites, as well as with Messianic Jews and some Unitarians. For readers who worship Jesus (if you are still with me)—whether identifying as Christians or as Messianic

Jews—be assured: historical study, or historical study the way I engage it, should not challenge faith commitments; rather, understanding Jesus in his historical context should enhance such commitments. It is not my role, as either a Jew or a biblical scholar, to tell people what to "believe" about Jesus. Belief is not a matter of history, for the existence of God and the divinity of Jesus can neither be proved nor disproved on the basis of scientific analysis.

Nor is belief, at least as I understand it, a matter of reading the Bible as objective history. First, there is no such objective reporting: we determine what to mention and what to ignore, what to highlight and what to relegate to the background. The same event can be reported on Fox News and MSNBC with very different takeaways. Then we who hear these reports have to interpret them. There is also always my mother's question, "How do you know that?"

Belief is also not a matter of connecting the dots, so that if we read what Christians call the Old Testament correctly, we'd see proof that Jesus fulfilled prophecy. For every text that Christians claim points to Jesus, Jews have alternative readings and secular biblical scholars a host more.[6] Belief is not initially a matter of logic or intellect; it is initially a matter of the heart. We know some things because we have assessed the evidence; other things we know because our heart tells us they are true.

The Gospels are not objective reports: they are written by insiders or "evangelists," a term that literally means "good newsers." Their authors, followers of Jesus, write to encourage their audiences to understand his teachings and actions in particular ways. Thus, each evangelist tells a distinct story. The evangelist we call Luke—the names Matthew, Mark, Luke, and John are not part of the earliest texts; the authors were originally anonymous—opens by remarking that while others have told the story of Jesus, he will do it better. Since Luke likely was familiar with Mark's Gospel and probably Matthew's as well,[7] this assessment shows that the New Testament books display internal critique. We have the Gospel writers' individual takes, and they do not always agree. That observation does not make the Gospels error-ridden failures; it makes them stories of Jesus played in different keys on different instruments. The baseline—teaching, healing, controversies, crucifixion, resurrection—remains the same.

My historical approach does not presume that all words and deeds the Gospels attribute to Jesus are things Jesus said or did. We do not have access to him directly; we have only the memories, and memories of memories, of those who knew him as resurrected Lord. Eyewitness testimony, or earwitness testimony, is notoriously inexact. Memory is fragile and easily influenced by external factors. And, as I assure my fundamentalist students as they navigate historical-critical approaches, even were we to determine that the Gospel writers recorded exactly what happened, we still need to interpret: Why did the writers tell this story but not that one? Why did they use different words to tell the same story? What difference does the narrative context make in how we understand a verse? What are the various ways the Greek can be translated? Again, all texts require interpretation.

My job as a teacher is to introduce my students to the major scholarly understandings of the New Testament, the Roman and Jewish worlds in which the figures lived and the texts took shape, the narrative worlds the texts create, and the world in front of the text, that is, the way the texts have been interpreted over time and place. It is also to help them find their own interpretation, whether in advancing a historical or literary argument or in finding their own reading by answering, "What does this text mean to me?" I do not require them to agree with any theory or conclusion presented, but I want them to know these theories and conclusions. And if they disagree, I want them to be able to articulate why.

Responding to a child who has questions about a biblical passage with the comment "if you ask questions, you'll be led into temptation" is not helpful. To dismiss a question is to disaffect the questioner. When already disaffected young adults learn in the college classroom that the Gospels have contradictions, that a single text can be read in multiple ways, that Jesus was not a feminist, or that passages in the New Testament condone slavery, they feel misled by their pastors and priests. The church thus loses both credibility and congregants.

Ironically, my historical approach has helped a good many people *remain* in church. Weird as it is, when Christian students find their faith failing, they often come to me, the Jew. If I, as an outsider, can find enormous value in the Gospels, they can too. Readers who believe Jesus to be divine and the New Testament to be the inspired Word of God should also, if they are faithful to Christian teaching, see Jesus as fully human. That means he lived in a real time, in a real place, and amid real people who heard his teaching and reacted to it. Knowing this historical context, this *Jewish* context, can then help them better understand and appreciate Jesus.

For disaffected Christians who no longer believe in the Gospels as infallible records, the historical approach allows them better to appreciate the distinctions among the texts. It shows them the value of interpretation, and it allows them to wrestle with texts they find difficult. For those who have been harmed by church teachings, and church members who promulgate those teachings, biblical interpretation can be a means of recovery, of fighting back, of reclaiming the text from those who use it as a bomb rather than a balm.

I also want to address those who see themselves as "spiritual but not religious" as well as members of the two fastest-growing religious groups today: the "nones," those who have no affiliation, and the "dones," people who have given up on the church, broadly defined. Churches are hemorrhaging members for numerous reasons: sexual abuse crises ranging from the Roman Catholic Church to Southern Baptist settings; the impression of hypocrisy, where the clergy speak of care for the neighbor and the stranger but do nothing to support either; the politicization of the pulpit, where the good news is not from the Bible but from the latest poll. Further, many are leaving because they are bored. The stories of Jesus sound to them like fairy tales, banal platitudes, or irrelevant discussions.

For the spiritual but not religious and for former Christians who reject church affiliation, creedal recitation, and forms of fundamentalism that restrict inquiry and imagination, encountering Jesus in his historical context can reawaken the importance of community, the benefit of ritual, and the significance of scripture and so of history.

I am also dedicated to introducing Jesus to Jews. Jesus was a Jew; more, much of the New Testament is part of Jewish history. At the time the Gospels were written, there was no formal separation between what came to be known as "Judaism" and "Christianity." Jesus, all the Marys (Mary his mother, Mary Magdalene, Mary the sister of Martha, Mary the mother of John Mark, etc.), Peter and Paul, etc., are all Jews, and none denies that Jewish identity. The authors of the Gospels of Matthew and John are likely to have been Jews, and the same case can be made, although it is not as strong, for the authors of Mark and Luke.

Reading the Gospels as part of Jewish history allows us Jews to recover parts of our own tradition, comparable to reading the Dead Sea Scrolls, the first-century Jewish historian Josephus, and the first-century Jewish philosopher Philo of Alexandria. Studying the Gospels in their historical context and understanding how they have been interpreted over the centuries also helps us combat antisemitic New Testament interpretations, of which there are many. Finally, such study helps us to hone our ethical values, definitions of justice, and ability to see the multiple readings a text may prompt.

GETTING THE CONTEXT RIGHT

Far too often, the Jewish context of the New Testament stories is misunderstood. A number of my students, let alone people who write to me, regard Jews and Judaism as static. In their view, nothing much changed from Abraham to Moses to the Pharisees to Mrs. Goldberg down the street. Worse, from the Pharisees to Mrs. Goldberg, if not starting with Abraham, that context is painted in noxious colors.

To misunderstand Judaism is to misunderstand Jesus. Years ago I wrote *The Misunderstood Jew: The Church and the Scandal of the Jewish Jesus* (the subtitle was necessary lest readers think the book was autobiography). Like that book, this one offers corrections to popular, but erroneous, stereotypes of Jesus's Jewish context. For example, it's time to stop the canard that the Old Testament (a perfectly good term for the Christian Bible, Part I) is a bad text, so anything Jesus is an improvement. For example, professional atheist Richard Dawkins avers, "Well, there's no denying that, from a moral point of view, Jesus is a huge improvement over the cruel ogre of the Old Testament. Indeed Jesus, if he existed (or whoever wrote his script if he didn't) was surely one of the great ethical innovators of history."[8] Such a claim misrepresents the earlier scriptures, with their commands not only to love one's neighbor (Lev. 19:18), but also the extension of this commandment: "the alien [we might also translate 'immigrant' or even 'migrant'] who resides with you shall be to you as the native-born among you; you shall love the alien as yourself, for you were aliens in the land of Egypt" (Lev. 19:34, NRSVUE); it ignores Jesus's dependence on these earlier traditions as well as his own teachings about hellfire, which make what happens at Sodom and Gomorrah a walk in the park. Conversely, it was Jesus who announced regarding the people in Capernaum, "But I tell you that on the day of judgment it will be more tolerable for the land of Sodom than for you" (Matt. 11:24).

One variant on the "bad Old Testament" stereotype is the claim that the tradition was just fine until the Pharisees got hold of it. In this false construction, the Pharisees were legalistic, elitist, money-loving, xenophobic, misogynistic, purity-obsessed hypocrites who resisted Jesus's liberalizing teachings and arranged his death.[9]

The only Pharisee from whom we have extant writings is Paul of Tarsus, and Paul speaks with no small amount of pride of his Pharisaic training: "If anyone else has reason to be confident in the flesh, I have more: circumcised on the eighth day, a member of the people of Israel, of the tribe of Benjamin, a Hebrew born of Hebrews; as to the law, a Pharisee" (Phil. 3:4b–5, NRSVUE). Paul sees nothing wrong and everything right with being a Pharisee, and he never forsakes his Pharisaic identity (Acts 23:6). We do not have to make Judaism look bad in order to make Jesus look good.

Some Christians today view Jesus not as divine Lord but as social justice warrior. Problems arise, however, when this yearning for a moral exemplar imbues Jesus with *unique* qualifications, for this claim to uniqueness is in fact a theological claim. If Jesus is the only Jew seen to care about health care, the plight of the poor, and the dangers of church-state relations, then he, in effect, drops down from heaven rather than draws from his Jewish roots.

When Jesus is seen as "radical," associating with "outcasts" and/ or as "transgressing" social concerns, more than likely the context is a false and poisonous depiction of Jewish practice and belief. For example, in a recent op-ed in the *New York Times*, published the day before Christmas and titled "The Forgotten Radicalism of Jesus Christ," Peter Wehner finds Jesus to be "truly radical and radically inclusive" because he "shattered barrier after barrier."[10] How so? Wehner notes, for example, that Jesus never criticizes the Samaritan woman for having five husbands. We'll return to this conversation in Chapter 5; for now, it is necessary to mention that only because we do not know the circumstances of her situation, there may be nothing to criticize. She was not stigmatized, shunned, nor otherwise shamed by her community, since they are more than willing to trust her impression that she had found the Messiah. It is Wehner who judges the woman, not Jesus. Then we read, "Jesus, a man, was talking earnestly to a woman in a world in which women were often demeaned and treated as second-class citizens"; the problem: for a man to speak with a woman, or a woman with a man, was neither illegal nor unexpected. Or, "He touched lepers and healed a woman who had a constant flow of menstrual blood, both of whom were considered impure," as well as gave sight to a blind man, even though, in the author's view, such people were thought to be "worthless and useless." The rest of the article continues in this vein.

I published a rebuttal, together with biblical scholars Marc Z. Brettler (Duke University), Candida Moss (University of Birmingham, UK), Paula Fredriksen (Hebrew University of Jerusalem), and Margaret M. Mitchell (University of Chicago), in the *Daily Beast*—because the *Times* would not accept a response to an op-ed. In "What the *New York Times* Gets Wrong About Jesus," we detailed Wehner's multiple errors, and then we concluded: "In the name of inclusivity and the need for humility and self-criticism about one's own myopia, Wehner has demonstrated precisely such myopia vis-à-vis Jews, both of Jesus' own time period and today. He yanks Jesus out of his historical context and ignores the only Scripture—what the church calls the 'Old Testament' and the source of the 'radical teachings' of the imago dei and of social justice—Jesus and his disciples followed. That's not good news, whether for Jesus or for his modern-day followers."[11]

Other Christians find the Jesus of history too spooky, too kooky, or too Jewy and so strip him of his Jewish markers. They see him as rejecting Sabbath practice rather than debating with other Jews about how one honors the Sabbath and keeps it holy. That debate is not a rejection, but a loud affirmation. They see him rejecting the practices of ritual purity and even suggest that his program was one of replacing purity with compassion or purity with forgiveness (as if these are opposites) when in fact he reaffirms the purity laws by *restoring to purity* those who are impure: by healing a man suffering from a skin disease, by drying up a woman with a vaginal or uterine hemorrhage, by raising a corpse to life.[12] They see him as rejecting Jewish identity in favor of a universalism in which ethnicity is trumped by Christian identity, even though he restricts his mission largely to Jews.

The claim that universalism is better than particularity is a claim those in the majority make: it is the idea that "everyone should be like us." Jesus, Paul, Peter, James—they never gave up their Jewish identity. They agreed, as did fellow Jews outside their movement, that the God of Israel is the God of the world. We do better when we think of particularism not as tribalism but as a form of multiculturalism. Further, Jesus and his followers did not sacrifice the particulars of their own Jewish practice and belief on the altars of religious pluralism or a lowest-common-denominator religion. More on this topic when we look at the stories of and by Jesus in relation to Samaritans and gentiles (Chapter 3).

Finally, concerning the view of Jesus as promoting the interests of the "outcast" and the "marginal" (these terms, like "radical," are almost requisite in sermons), care must be taken in defining terms. Cast out of what? Cast out by whom? Marginal to what? When some Christian commentators suggest that Jews regarded people who are blind or deaf, unable to walk, or suffering from osteoporosis as outcasts, worthless, or sinful, they misread the culture.[13] Just as bad, these commentators turn people living with, and sometimes suffering from, disability into at best objects of pity and so deny them their own agency.

Jesus appointed no women among the twelve disciples, refers to God in masculine terms as "father" and "king," and never critiques the institution of slavery. For many who read the Gospels, this apparent lack of consideration for justice issues is unacceptable. The solution: posit a first-century Judaism so misogynist that even by talking to a woman, Jesus invents feminism; posit a first-century Judaism that regarded slaves as chattel and praise Jesus for noticing slaves, healing their bodies, and giving them voice. As we'll see, both of these constructions are incorrect. Nevertheless, we can derive helpful lessons from Jesus's encounters with women and his teachings about slavery. Doing so does not require engaging in antisemitic stereotyping.

Each of the following chapters includes discussion on how misunderstanding the Jewish tradition leads to a misunderstanding of Jesus. My agenda is not to charge people with being antisemitic. Most of the mistakes are based not in bigotry but in ignorance. The result, however—a teaching that maligns Jews or the Jewish tradition—is the same. Were Christians to take more seriously the Jewish context of Jesus and Paul, and to listen more closely to how we Jews understand our own tradition, they'd be better Bible readers, better disciples of Jesus, and better neighbors.

IS THERE ANYTHING LEFT TO SAY ABOUT JESUS?

For those who are tired of the incessant parade of books about Jesus (a parade in which I have occasionally marched), or who are convinced that what is called the "quest of the historical Jesus" is dead, some words of comfort.

Biblical scholars have expended over the past three centuries a great deal of effort in pursuing this quest. The title, which comes from Albert Schweitzer's 1906 book *The Quest of the Historical Jesus*, marks the attempt to get behind the Gospel writers and find the "real" man from Nazareth. If success means consensus, then the various quests have substantially failed.

For a while, we scholars were sanguine that the so-called criteria of authenticity could help us get behind the Gospel writers and behind the oral tradition to Jesus's original Aramaic pronouncements. The criterion of multiple attestation proposes that a teaching or an action found in more than one independent source has a higher claim to authenticity (i.e., Jesus really said it or did it) than something attested only once. This criterion doesn't work, since we cannot determine what sources are independent. Matthew likely used Mark as a source; John likely had access to all three first Gospels—Matthew, Mark, and Luke—called the "Synoptic Gospels" since they "see together" (what "synoptic" means), that is, they tell basically the same story in the same narrative order.

Nor should a single appearance be seen as less, or more, historical. The Parable of the Good Samaritan is only in Luke's Gospel. Perhaps Mark (who never mentions Samaritans) and Matthew (who in Matt. 10:5 has Jesus speak against a Samaritan mission) had reasons for omitting the parable. John has no parables. Something that appears only in one Gospel might even have better claims to authenticity in that, perhaps, the other three evangelists found it disturbing or incomprehensible.

The criterion of dissimilarity suggests that if Jesus says or does something dissimilar to what other first-century Jews were saying or doing, or if the material is dissimilar to what the church proclaimed about him, then it has a higher degree of authenticity. In other words, if it looks weird, it must be historical. This criterion also fails. That the Gospel writers included material suggests that they found it congenial, so nothing in the Gospels is necessarily dissimilar to church teaching. Nor did first- or early second-century followers of

Jesus have creeds in place by which they could check what was chris-tologically appropriate, or, well, kosher. We also do not know enough about first-century Judaism to determine that comments by Jesus are unique (that pesky word again); worse, this criterion strips Jesus of his Jewish identity.

The late, and great, Fr. John P. Meier, whose five volumes of *A Marginal Jew* offered detailed historical-critical studies of Jesus, epit-omized the use of these criteria. In many cases, especially concern-ing the parables, he labels the material *non liquet*, not proved.[14] This is a fair judgment about pretty much everything in the Gospels, aside from generalities such as that Jesus had followers, was known as a healer, disagreed with other Jews on matters of Torah observance, spoke in parables, and was crucified.

Initially, relatively more conservative Christian scholars decried these criteria, since questioning the authenticity of the Gospel claims was suspect. Today, such scholars use the criteria, and (miraculously!) the criteria in their hands prove the authenticity of the Gospel nar-ratives. If there is no disconfirmation, then the approach doesn't work. Consequently, other approaches toward understanding the historical Jesus are needed.[15]

This is not to say that attempting to distinguish what Jesus said or did from what his followers attributed to him is a waste of time. In some cases, it's clear, or at least it's clear to me, that certain events either never happened or did not happen the way the Gospel writers present them. For example, it strikes me as unlikely that Jesus entered the temple and stopped business twice, once at the beginning of his public speaking (John 2:13–25) and again, years later (Matt. 21:12–17 // Mark 11:15–19 // Luke 19:45–48). I think it hogwash (this is the right word!) to claim both that Jesus encoun-tered demons named "Legion" possessing a man in Gerasa and that when Jesus exorcised the man and sent the demons into a herd of pigs, the pigs stampeded into the sea and drowned (Mark 5:1–20 // Luke 8:26–39); and that he also encountered demons named "Legion" possessing two men in Gedara, and where, again, Jesus sent the demons into a herd of pigs, who stampeded and drowned (Matt. 8:28–34). Much more likely, Matthew changed the location (since Gerasa is close to forty miles away from the Sea of Galilee) and increased the miracle by multiplying the number of victims.

Similarly, we can tease out how and why the Gospel writers changed stories. Luke transformed the account in Matthew and Mark of the woman who pours perfume on Jesus's head at the beginning of his last week in Jerusalem into a story of a woman who pours perfume on his feet, well before he begins his journey to the city. Likely John knew the story in Luke 10:38–42 of the sisters Mary and Martha, who never speak with each other, and provided a narrative in which the sisters, although maintaining the same descriptions— Martha serves or, better, "ministers," and Mary sits at Jesus's feet— work together. Matthew's depiction of an encounter between Jesus and a Canaanite mother desperate to obtain an exorcism for her demon-possessed daughter (Matt. 15:21–28) rewrites and augments Mark's story (Mark 7:24–30) of a Syrophoenician woman in the same circumstances. We discuss the reasons why in Chapter 3.

Such changes across Gospels, and they are numerous, do not mean the Gospel writers got the tradition "wrong." Just as children's Bibles, sermons, even translations necessarily interpret the biblical text, so too did the evangelists adapt the materials as they saw fit.

Since the questions of authenticity of words and deeds or even the historicity of Jesus will not be resolved to everyone's satisfaction, and since I doubt that much new is going to be argued, I find it more refreshing to engage in historical imagination and attempt to understand what a text might have meant to an early first-century CE Jewish audience, what it might have meant to a Gospel reader, and what it might mean to readers today.

This approach is also an alternative to another form of the dismissing of the historical Jesus: in this configuration, readers do not deny Jesus's existence; rather, they downplay or even deny the importance of his social context, his embeddedness in time and place. For an increasing number of interpreters, the only worthwhile or even morally acceptable interpretations are those based in the reader's social location or subject position. The question to be asked is only, "What does this text mean to me?" and not "What might it have meant to first-century Galilean Jews?" For some who promote this personal reading, attempts to see how Jesus's words and actions would have been received by a first-century audience are capitulations to white supremacy, sexism, homophobia, elitism, and even antisemitism. Why? Because many of the German and British Protestant founders of what we call the historical-critical method, as educated men of the nineteenth and early twentieth centuries, were elitist, racist, sexist, and antisemitic and because their readings on occasion served to legitimate colonialist and imperialist aims. Further, historical-critical work involves learning ancient languages and rhetoric, learning about Jewish and Roman history, and otherwise having privileged knowledge that others do not have.

Henry Ford said, "History is more or less bunk." Henry Ford was wrong. While the historical-critical approach as put into practice over the past three centuries has had multiple failings, including the inculcation of antisemitic, racist, sexist, ableist, etc., views (again, historians are inevitably influenced by our own subject positions; we can never be fully objective), it is historical criticism that today helps us recover women's history, the history of enslaved individuals, and Jewish history. Indeed, to combat the historical-critical claims of antisemites, Abraham Geiger used their method to recover Jesus the Jew.[16] Granted, his reading was no more objective than that of Christian scholars who saw Jesus as the pristine visionary emerging out of a Jewish cesspool. Today we are generally better aware of the prejudices of previous scholars as well as, at least to some extent, of our own. But the fact that those who initially crafted a method were antisemites does not make the method itself unusable; if it did, we would not be driving cars.

Finally, books on the historical Jesus have gotten predictable.[17] The mythicists, those who do not see Jesus as a figure within history, have had their say; so have the apologists and the secular historians. We've had our various Jesuses, whether wisdom teacher, shaman, apocalyptic prophet, cynic-sage, peasant revolutionary, whatever. New approaches continue—affect theory, memory studies, material production of written texts, neurobiological understandings—and these too have both their benefits and their drawbacks. In some cases, I lose patience in reading fifty pages of method often with its own technical terminology ("jargon"), only to find in the end something that has already been argued, but by another route. In others—such as recent studies of Jesus in relation to purity practices,[18] how the Dead Sea Scrolls provide insight into Gospel material,[19] how Luke's redactional interests help us consider such questions as whether Jesus was literate,[20] how Womanist readings can find new meaning in the parables,[21] how the Gospel of John has reworked material in the Gospel of Matthew,[22] how enslaved people were involved in the production and dissemination of Christian texts,[23] even how people suffering from what the Gospels call "leprosy" lived in the first century[24]—advancement is made.

We cannot prove that Jesus said anything or did anything. We cannot even prove that he existed. But if he did not speak the words attributed to him, then we have to invent someone who did, which just adds another layer to the problem. But we know that the stories of and attributed to Jesus developed initially in a Jewish context in the first and early second centuries CE. And therefore we can attempt to understand what they might have meant to a first-century audience. With this approach we can read the familiar anew. We can determine how the passage fits into the rest of the Gospel, and finally we can see what instruction the passage may have for readers today.

DISCLOSURES

I am not a "believer," as that term is used either in a Christian context or more broadly in the sense of "belief in divinity." And not for lack of interest. As a child, I went to synagogue, a lot: Hebrew School Mondays and Wednesdays, Friday night services, Saturday morning junior congregation, Sunday school. I became a bat mitzvah (literally, a "daughter of the commandment") on a Friday night at Tifereth Israel Congregation in New Bedford, Massachusetts (this was before the conservative movement became egalitarian). I like the idea of the traditional God of the synagogue in which I grew up: the God of kindness and justice, love and compassion. This God sounded like, and even looked like, Rabbi Ziskind, who was the rabbi at Tifereth Israel when I was a child. According to my mother, I once asked Rabbi Ziskind if he was God. The good rabbi responded, "No, but I work for him." That worked for me.

To this day, when I hear the Hebrew of Numbers 6:24–26, "The LORD bless you and keep you; / the LORD make his face to shine upon you and be gracious to you; the LORD lift up his countenance upon you and give you peace" (NRSVUE), I feel that warmth and that peace. I live *as if* there is a God, and I take seriously the idea that all humanity is created in that divine image and likeness. That proclamation, from Genesis 1:27, means we must see in the face of another a divine image. It is easy to look at the face of a newborn, or a loved one, and see something beautiful. It is much harder to look at the face of someone tattooed with a swastika or spouting racist propaganda on social media and still see a divine image. But it is necessary, lest we turn people into demons. When we demonize, we lose a piece of our own humanity even as we grant those who promote bigotry a super-human power.

And yet, I do not take Genesis 1 as a factual report of what happened at the beginning of time. I belong to an Orthodox synagogue—I am at home in the liturgy, the community, the discussions about the Torah reading; I am happy sitting in the women's section—but I do not self-identify as Orthodox. I recite with the rest of the congregation ancient prayers that address God as "our Father" and "our King," but I do not believe in a male God, whether in the role of parent or monarch; I do not believe in a single being who created heaven and earth. But I do find inspirational and renewing the connection prayer gives to history and to community. Apparently, this makes me "religious" (in terms of practice) but not "spiritual" (in terms of belief).

Belief, in the traditional sense, was never there for me—not when I was in Hebrew School, not when I became a bat mitzvah, not after my father died and my mother decided we needed to say Kaddish for him, in the synagogue, morning and late afternoon, during the subsequent year of mourning. The belief did not come when I fell in love with the man who would become my husband or when our children were born. The belief did not come when, following a bout of long-undiagnosed endocarditis, I had heart surgery to replace two destroyed valves. My major worry was that dying would be greatly inconvenient: I had a husband and children to love, students to mentor, books to write, a sweater to finish knitting.

Belief is palpable among some of the members of my synagogue; it is equally evident in the classrooms where I have taught and the countless churches and synagogues I have visited. Ironically, I can deepen the faith, the beliefs of those who begin with theological premises, by showing them wonders in their scriptures, of both Judaism and Christianity, that they had not considered. I can also sit with them, in friendship and love, when they express their doubts. If I, as a nonbelieving Jew, find value in the Tanakh and in the Christian Bible, then how much more so should those who have that spark of belief find value?

*   *   *

Although I am not a Christian, I have, since the age of seven, when a girl on the school bus accused me of killing "her Lord,"[25] been asking questions about Jesus, reading about him, seeing the movies and attending the plays, looking at artistic representations and listening to music about his birth (I love most Christmas carols) and his passion (I love what Bach does with the music; less thrilled with the librettos). I'm fluent in most dialects of Christianity, from mainline Protestant to Evangelical to Roman Catholic (I'm working on various forms of Eastern Orthodoxy and the Church of Jesus Christ of Latter-day Saints).

And yet . . . Jesus the speaker of Jewish wisdom has taught me much, and continues to teach me, about priorities and principles, about how to live and how to love. The human Jesus—storyteller and healer, agitator and sage, dreamer and martyr, failure and yet success—has much to teach us, regardless of our theology or beliefs.

GETTING ON THE PATH

Jesus's early disciples, men and women, called themselves followers of the "way"; the Greek term underlying "way" is *hodos*, as in the word "odometer," a mileage indicator. They were following a particular path that led from the teachings of Jesus to his death to the promise of resurrection and eternal life. Jewish tradition, then and now, speaks of *halakhah*. The term, which comes from the Hebrew word for "to walk," is the path, based in Torah and its interpretations, one follows. There were multiple interpretations, then and now, since all texts, whether narratives or law codes, need to be interpreted. With both *hodos* and *halakhah*, the first move is to get on the path.

In the following pages, we'll see how Jesus's stories and stories about Jesus can help us think about that litany noted above: economics, slavery, ethnicity/race, health care, celibacy, marriage, divorce, and adultery, even politics. For each case, we'll start by locating Jesus in his own historical context: such locating helps us to determine how much material is case-specific and how much is applicable across time and place. Our concern is not to find the one "right" answer, any more than it is to find the one "right" reading of the Bible. The text necessarily opens to multiple readings. Then again, some are better than others.

Each test case begins with a very literal, and therefore not particularly mellifluous, translation of the Greek. Such literalistic translations are designed to help defamiliarize the stories for those who have heard them before, and the literalness can reveal levels of meaning missing in the standard translations. Here and throughout, where I think the Gospel writer has made a personal contribution to the discussion (i.e., it did not come from Jesus), I'll explain why. And where commentators have projected a false view of Judaism in order to make Jesus look good, you can bet I'll flag those problems as well.

The following is a map for the path on which we'll embark. Each of the sections gives an overview of the topics each chapter will cover.

ECONOMICS

Chapter 1 finds us engaging biblical economics. After clearing out the weeds of such incorrect views as "Jews equate wealth with righteousness and poverty with sin", and "Jews argue that poverty is the result of laziness," we turn to comments made by Jesus and stories told by him. We start with Jesus's instruction to the composite figure we call the "rich young ruler." We'll see how Jesus's advice is case-specific rather than generic, how wealth affects individuals differently, and how on the local level, economic redistribution is not only practical, but also commendable.

We then look at two parables. The story traditionally called the Parable of the Rich Fool concerns a fellow who dies with the most money, but who loses rather than wins. The parable leads us to discussions not only of the adage "you can't take it with you," but also to consideration of what we want our legacy to be. The Parable of the Dishonest Manager, or to update, we might speak of the Parable of the Shrewd Chief Financial Officer, often considered the most difficult of all Jesus's parables, appears to commend a rogue who cheats his employer and ropes others into his scheme. Luke, who struggles to find a meaning to attach to this parable, winds up by having Jesus say that one cannot "serve God and mammon." On the other hand, one can use mammon, that is, "wealth," to serve God. The trick is in telling the difference between service and servitude, between appropriate and appropriating use of finances.

The parable also helps us with such questions as whether the end justifies the means, whether finagling with a very wealthy person's finances is less of a problem than doing the same with someone's limited income, and even how debt reduction can be good business practice.

We end this chapter with the story of a widow who gives her last two coins to the temple treasury. Jesus tells his disciples to look at her, but it is up to us to find a takeaway from this sight. Her story provides both guidance and warning about such matters as how we understand those who are monetarily "rich," wealth distribution, legacies, charitable donations, and the victimization as well as the agency of people who are economically insecure.

ENSLAVEMENT

Chapter 2 engages our second topic, slavery, which only now is being addressed in books about Jesus. In November 2022 (2022!), several states voted to remove from their constitutions language that allowed certain kinds of involuntary servitude or slavery. Although the Thirteenth Amendment to the Constitution abolishes slavery, it allows people serving prison sentences to be used as enslaved labor. The vote to remove this language passed in the state where I live, Tennessee, as well as in Alabama, Oregon, and Vermont; it did not pass in Louisiana.[26] Nor can we ignore human trafficking, which continues throughout the globe, or slavery that is still legal in some countries. We cannot afford to ignore the biblical passages that use slavery as an image of fidelity and so threaten to normalize it.

To address slavery, we again start with the scriptures of Israel, where slavery in Egypt and then liberation by the hand of God and through the leadership of Moses become a major, if not the major, marker of identity. We move through a few stories of enslaved individuals in Hellenistic Jewish literature, briefly assess the letters written by and attributed to Paul and those likely written not by him but by his followers, skip ahead several centuries to rabbinic texts to show ongoing understanding of the scriptures, look at Roman laws regarding slavery, and finally come to the Gospels.

In such study, we can better understand why some people, to this day, find the idea of being a "slave of God" freeing, since it proclaims that they have no earthly master, and it is the best way they have for understanding how they want to empty themselves and be vessels for God's will. We'll also see why some people find this image obscene.

Our test cases will be, first, two stories of actual enslaved people in the Gospels: in Matthew 8:5–13 and Luke 7:1–10, Jesus heals the slave of a Roman centurion; in the Gethsemane scene, an enslaved man, eventually identified by name and owner, is injured in the disciples' attempt to prevent Jesus from being arrested. These narratives not only demand we pay attention to those who have no freedom, but also reveal the vulnerability of the bodies of the enslaved. In the first century, enslaved people lived under the constant threat of physical punishment, including torture and mutilation. They lead us, inexorably, both to the cross—since crucifixion was the standard punishment for those owned by others and for rebels against the Roman state—and to Jesus's own scarred and mutilated body.

Next, we turn to enslaved people in parables, including the abused and murdered messengers in the parables of the Wicked Tenants (Matt. 21:33–46 // Mark 12:1–12 // Luke 20:9–10; and the noncanonical Gospel of Thomas 65) and the Great/Wedding Feast (Matt. 22:2–14 // Luke 14:15–24; Gospel of Thomas 64). Talking about the "kingdom of God" and ignoring the enslaved would be comparable to talking about the history of the United States but overlooking the institution of slavery and those it affected.

Finally, the parables of the Wise and Foolish Slaves and the Slave Who Serves as Expected address a difficult if not impossible question: Given what we know today of slavery, can it ever be appropriate to speak of ourselves as "slaves" of God? Whether being "slaves of God" is a model of freedom or whether—considering the history of slavery in the United States and its effects to this day as well as the ongoing issue of human trafficking—any positive view of the term is possible are questions the passages present but do not resolve.

There are no easy answers in this chapter, yet the questions raised must be addressed.

ETHNICITY AND RACE

Chapter 3 addresses yet another issue in the news today: the relationship between insiders and outsiders or, for the Jesus tradition, first between Jews and gentiles and second between Jews and Samaritans. Today these passages are read in terms of ethnicity and/or racial identification.

We start with the biblical antecedents, including examples both of intermarriage between Israelites and gentiles and of attempts to forbid such relationships. We also look at laws regarding the treatment of ethnic outsiders (the Hebrew is variously translated "strangers," "aliens," "immigrants," and "migrants"), including the mandate that they, along with the poor, the widow, and the orphan—that is, the most vulnerable members of society—are to be protected and supported. We conclude this brief survey with the place of the non-Jew in the messianic age.

Concerning gentiles, our test cases include that demon-possessed man in Gerasa, whose exorcism prompts the drowning of thousands of pigs. I think it likely that Jesus was an exorcist (whether demons exist is another matter, but the people of the time certainly thought they did), and thus that people experienced him as exorcising demons. But I also think the story is overlaid with references concerning the horrors of Roman military operations, as the name "Legion" for the demon indicates. Hints in the language of this incident, as well as Matthew's rewriting of Mark's original, even suggest to me that we have here not a historical reminiscence, but an allegory of a cosmic battle: Jesus versus the supernatural powers of Rome. Jesus wins.

Our last story regarding a gentile is one of the more difficult passages in the Gospels: Jesus's encounter with a woman whom Mark calls "a Greek, a Syrophoenician by birth" (Mark 7:26) and Matthew identifies as a "Canaanite" (Matt. 15:22). In Matthew's version, when the woman requests a healing for her demon-possessed daughter, Jesus responds, "It is not right to take the children's bread and throw it to the dogs" (Matt. 15:26). The story offers teachings about ethnic identity, discipleship, and most important, both how those with resources must attend to those without and how those in need can use their own resources to achieve their goals without either violence or abjection.

Regarding Samaritans, who are not "gentiles" (i.e., "pagans"), our test case is the famous Samaritan woman at the well. The scene from John 4, which I think John developed to resemble stories in the earlier scriptures of how the meeting of a woman and a man at a well resulted in matrimony, responds to the commandment Jesus gives his disciples in Matthew, "Enter no town of the Samaritans" (Matt. 10:5b), the absence of the Samaritans in Mark, and Luke's locating the Samaritan mission to the time of the church (see Acts 8). In contemporary terms, John has engaged in spin control to legitimate the Samaritan mission and ground it in the actions of Jesus himself. John 4 raises questions of how much we today are willing to promote pluralism. We might wonder what the Samaritan woman thought when Jesus tells her, "You worship what you do not know; we worship what we know, for salvation is from the Jews" (John 4:22). While the line may not be the best starting place for interreligious dialogue, at least it is honest in refusing lowest-common-denominator religion or the claim that we are all climbing up the same mountain.

Such accounts help us with matters of multiculturalism, which includes preserving one's identity despite pressures to assimilate, viewing the enemy, sharing resources, the legacy of colonialism, and to what extent cross-border conversation requires relinquishing or sharing power.

HEALTH CARE

In Chapter 4 we turn to another hot-button issue: health care. My students, my friends, even strangers on email ask me: If Jesus heals the hemorrhaging woman, why won't he heal my father's prostate cancer? If Jesus raises Jairus's daughter, why won't he raise my daughter? Had I prayed without doubt, would my tumor have disappeared?

We begin by diagnosing the bad approaches that still mar studies of healings in the Gospels, including the incorrect association of sickness and impurity with sin.

Our test cases are, first, the woman suffering from a hemorrhage, who steals a healing from Jesus—here we have a woman proactive on health care. This account not only opens discussion about resources, but also addresses the relationship between disability and shame and the difficulties of talking about ailments that are unique to female anatomy. Given that the woman's story is embedded within the story of the synagogue ruler who begs Jesus to heal his daughter, it also opens the conversation about health care, including how so often those with economic resources receive better, and quicker, care. Jesus disrupts this process.

Finally comes the story of the man suffering from dropsy (edema), which includes the symptom of unquenchable thirst. The account raises the question of whether greed should be understood not simply as a bad attitude, or even as a sin. What happens when we view greed, like those other deadly sins—lust, gluttony, sloth, wrath, envy, and pride—as a disease for which a cure is needed and thus not, or at least less of, a negative but controllable personal trait? If we say "he has greed," then we are better able to address the problem; if we say "he is greedy," then the greed becomes an essential characteristic that cannot be easily removed, if it can be removed at all.

FAMILY VALUES: CELIBACY, MARRIAGE AND DIVORCE, ADULTERY

Chapter 5, on the broad subject of family values, looks at Jesus's comments on divorce, on becoming a "eunuch" for the kingdom of heaven, and on the story of the woman caught in an adulterous relationship.

On matters of sexuality, Jesus's focus is less the identity of the sexual partner than sexual activity, period. He is single and celibate, two states that he finds better prepare him for the inbreaking of the kingdom of God. Given this urgency, regular patterns of marriage and divorce and of procreation take new shape. Attention to Jesus and sexuality even leads us to matters that today would be called "gender fluidity" or the challenging of gender roles: If men are not defined primarily as husbands and fathers, and women are not defined primarily as wives and mothers, what then do we learn about gender roles? Just as Jesus was not a feminist but feminists can find much good news in the Gospel narratives, so Jesus was not a spokesperson for the LGBTQIA+ communities. Nevertheless, his challenge to normative expectations—concerning marriage and family, identifying women primarily through maternal roles, the authoritative role of the father in a patriarchal household setting—provides the opening for people whose sexual or gender identity is a site of discrimination.

The chapter also looks at the view of divorce in Jesus's cultural context and then his teachings regarding divorce (don't do it) and remarriage (certainly don't do it). Here history is helpful, since these teachings appear in an eschatological and idealized context; otherwise put: what we do if we think the world is going to end a week from Tuesday will not be the same as what we do if we think it's got years if not centuries to go.

Next comes celibacy, as it was understood both in Jesus's time (a viable option) and in his own teaching (good, if one has the calling or what might be called the "spiritual gift" [see 1 Cor. 12]). This discussion reclaims the importance of individuals who, whether by choice (e.g., those who have no interest in marriage) or by fate (e.g., those who are widowed and have no interest in remarrying), define themselves as other than primarily a spouse. Again, the stories of Jesus help us shift the discourse from marriage and childbirth to the concerns of individuals, who will have different needs and concerns.

While his statement about becoming "eunuchs" for the kingdom of heaven does not mean that one should be celibate, since eunuchs could and did engage in various forms of sexual expression, it does mean forgoing becoming a father. By extension, the statement calls into question views of masculinity.

The chapter concludes with a discussion of adultery, with attention to the story in John 8 of the woman caught in the act. The story helps us with a sympathetic understanding of why people might commit adultery, what compassionate community support would look like, and how one moves from the act, which has become a matter of public record, into the future. Such discussion in turn helps us with other public accusations, from #MeToo to counterclaims of seduction. There is no quick fix here, but there are, in the Gospels, resources for moving past blame and shame, for accepting responsibility for one's actions, and for putting the brakes on the rush to judgment.

POLITICS

Finally, Chapter 6 addresses politics. For the past few decades, the topic of "empire" was the go-to subject for New Testament studies'

professional meetings and publications. Especially since the begin-
nings of the Gulf War in the early 1990s, New Testament studies
and sermons looked to the Gospels for responses to expansionism,
colonialism, militarism, and cultural imperialism. Thus was born
the anti-imperial Jesus who, zealously, fights the good political fight.
Of course, so this school of thought concluded, Jesus was against
empire, and because he was against empire, the empire killed him.
The approach, while it has much worthwhile to say, is insufficient in
explaining Jesus's death.

After a brief explanation of how Rome came to govern Judea directly (Pontius Pilate) and Galilee via a client-ruler (Herod Antipas),
we look at Jesus's enigmatic comment regarding taxation, "Render
to Caesar things that are Caesar's, and to God things that are God's."
We also look at the so-called triumphal entry, with its hints, as well as
subversions, of military conquest and even, for Luke, an a-triumphal
entry.

The Gospels prompt us to raise the good questions of what our
tax dollars fund, what we want in a leader, and how political gatherings can lead either to constructive action or to destructive riots.
The stories of Jesus can be read as ignoring the Roman Empire (why
challenge something if the world is about to end?), supporting it (by
failing to criticize it directly), and subverting it (by speaking of the
kingdom of God and so denying that the present kingdom has value).
Stories about paying taxes, about public processions, about kings and
kingdoms prove helpful, two millennia later.

*　*　*

This book addresses the passages with which my students struggle;
these are the passages that are worth the struggle. The struggle is
valuable outside of the classroom as well—in churches, in homes
and coffee shops, even in hospitals, courts, and legislatures. We will

never fully mine their meanings, for interpretations will necessarily change over time. We will never fully understand how they functioned in their original contexts, because new information and new approaches will nuance our conclusions. But as the ancient Jewish text Pirke Avot (Ethics of the Fathers) says in regard to Torah, so too in regard to the study of Jesus, "You are not obligated to complete the work, but neither are you free to desist from it" (2.21).

CHAPTER I
ECONOMICS

THE GOSPELS ARE full of stories about money, rich people and poor people, managers and employees and day laborers, those who have and those who need. In this chapter, we look at how the stories of, and by, Jesus open up questions that all people—religious or not—should ask when it comes to how we understand and use financial resources.

We begin with a general discussion of how to approach matters of wealth and poverty in these narratives, including the connotations we bring to each term, the question of whether money in itself is evil, and the popularity today among some sectors of Christianity of what is known as the "Prosperity Gospel." We then turn to our test cases, all of which interrogate how we relate to our possessions, what we do with them, and how some approaches are better investments than others.

WEALTH AND POVERTY

The terms "wealth" and "poverty" come with connotations that nec-essarily skew interpretations, including questions of class, personal responsibility, and systemic economic conditions. For example, "poor" can conjure images of laziness or dependence on the welfare state, and thus poverty becomes associated with moral failure. Conversely, identification of "the poor" can be romanticized with the notice that poor(er) people not only are more generous with charitable donations (they are, proportionally to the extent of their capital), but also are under God's special protection. Thus, it is better to be "poor" than to be "rich."

"Rich" can evoke images of people who are honored or at least followed on social media, a Kardashian or a Trump or an Elon Musk. It can also suggest those who manipulate the market for their own ends, given that "forty percent of all political donations come from the top 1 percent of the 1 percent."[1] "Rich" can describe individuals who use their wealth for the betterment of society such as by investing in education (e.g., some impressions of George Soros) or those who use their wealth to destroy the society some people want (again, e.g., some impressions of George Soros). Being identified as "rich" today can lead to honor or distrust, to praise or condemnation.

The terms "rich" and "poor" also find themselves attached to generalizations about salvation. Jesus predicts the time when "the last will be first, and the first will be last" (Matt. 20:16 // Mark 10:31 // Luke 13:30) since, in this configuration riches pave the path to hell while poverty secures a seat at the heavenly banquet.[2] This view leaves poverty in place rather than addresses its causes or remedies its effects. It fails to recognize that poor people are not exempt from sin, or rich people from benevolence. It also sets up a theologically problematic, and weird, view of cost-benefit salvation: a student once asked me, "How much can I keep in my bank account and still get into heaven?" Had this not been a serious question, I would have said something about adjusting for inflation.

Some readers conclude that, according to Jesus, money is evil and what we own (private property, stuff) interrupts our relationship to God and to others. They quote Jesus, "Lay not up for yourselves treasures upon earth, where moth and rust doth corrupt, and where thieves break through and steal" (Matt. 6:19, KJV; most do not realize that the quote draws on Sir. 29:10–11: "Lose your silver for the sake of a brother or a friend, and do not let it rust under a stone and be lost. Lay up your treasure according to the commandments of the Most High and it will profit you more than gold" [NRSVUE]), that is, donate all to the needy and don't have a bank account. Since money cannot save us, and since we cannot save our money, the only option is to follow Jesus's advice to a fellow the Gospels variously identify as "rich," "young," and a "ruler": "Go, sell what you have, and give to the poor, and you will have a treasure in the heavens, and come, follow me" (Matt. 19:21; cf. Mark 10:21 // Luke 18:22).

Selling what one has and giving to the poor is fine for some, but for those of us with young children, elderly parents, or dependents incapable of taking care of themselves, divesting both endangers those who rely on us and strains social systems by adding more people to the line at the soup kitchen or food bank. Voluntary poverty, designed to show solidarity with "the poor" and to understand better food-and-housing insecurity, risks becoming theological tourism. I find it more ethically appropriate to support those in need rather than to give up my own resources and thereby add to those in need. Further, as my colleagues who work in sociology and anthropology note, types of support that work in one culture (charity, microloans, external advisers, distribution of resources through religious organizations, ethics of care, etc.) may not work in another.[3] There is no quick fix, no one-size-fits-all fix, and perhaps no permanent fix at all. Alluding to Deuteronomy 15:11, "Not will there cease to be needy from among the land," Jesus states, "You will always have the poor with you" (Matt. 26:11 // Mark 14:7 // John 12:8).

Other readers, purveyors of the Prosperity Gospel, insist that God *wants* us to be rich; some exemplify their good news with yachts and jets bought from the donations of the faithful. If you're poor, they suggest, your faith is insufficient. Up the donations, and up your income. The Prosperity Gospel offers false promises even as it deforms biblical teaching; Jesus was many things, but a promoter of wealth was not one of them. For Jesus, and for the Bible, a lot of money is usually an indication of sin and selfishness.

Before we jump into the texts, we first need to divest ourselves of the false stereotypes I've heard, repeatedly, about Jews and money. To do so we look briefly at Jesus's context: what Torah mandates, what the prophets require, what wisdom teaches, and how postbiblical Jewish texts continue the conversation.

Next, we turn to select Gospel examples about money: the story of the rich young ruler, the parables that begin "There was a rich man who . . ." (the news is usually bad for the rich man), and the anecdote known as the Widow's Offering, about Jesus witnessing a poor widow putting all she had, two coins, into the temple treasury. Using a combination of humor and horror, Jesus prompts his audiences, then and now, to ask substantial questions about wealth, poverty, distribution of funds, and social welfare. If we do not pay attention, we are the poorer for it.

DIVESTING OF BAD HISTORY

One thing we can bank on, with interest, is that commentators will contrast Jesus's economics with those of his fellow Jews. Countless commentaries assert that "Judaism" or "the Jews" believed that to be poor is in indication of sin and to be rich is an indication of divine blessing and so of righteousness. Therefore, when Jesus says "blessed are you poor" (Luke 6:20; Matt. 5:3 speaks of the "poor in spirit") or insists that it is easier for a camel to go through the eye of a needle than for a rich person to enter the kingdom of heaven (Matt. 19:24 // Mark 10:25 // Luke 18:25), he transgressed Jewish teaching and shocked his Jewish audience.[4] Nonsense.

To show how pernicious this stereotype is, that Jews equated money with virtue and poverty with sin, I cite from the pages of the well-known evangelical magazine *Sojourners*.[5] The piece first errantly describes the Pharisees as "rich and successful people who lived in fancy houses and stepped over their destitute neighbors who slept in the gutters outside their gates! Proud people who judged, insulted, excluded, avoided, and accused others!"

After mischaracterizing the Pharisees, the article goes on to mischaracterize Judaism by suggesting that "multitudes and Pharisees alike" would have been "shocked" by the idea that the poor and the destitute, the sick and the homeless would be welcomed into heaven.

The article was so wrong that *Sojourners'* readers contacted the editor, who in turn contacted me to make the corrections.[6] Here are four. First, Pharisees are not all rich, and most of them, as far as we can tell, are part of the working class. The one Pharisee from whom we have written records, Paul of Tarsus, was a leatherworker (Acts 18:3).

Second, the first-century Jewish historian Josephus, himself an elite priest and no fan of the Pharisees given their popularity among the people, remarks that they simplify their lifestyle and despise luxurious food (*Antiquities* 18.12). Luke's charge in 16:14 that the Pharisees are "lovers of money" is a commonplace insult. Had the Pharisees been engaging in love of money, it's odd that Josephus, who has no hesitancy condemning people he dislikes, never mentioned this.

Third, regarding the claim of Pharisaic separation and exclusion, the popular explanation that the term "Pharisee" derives from a Hebrew or an Aramaic term meaning "to separate" is a guess; the name may derive from a word meaning "to interpret." If the etymology is from "separate," we need to ask: separate from what? The most likely answer: the holy from the profane, which means extending the sanctity of the temple to the entire people, so they could all see themselves as a "kingdom of priests and a holy nation" (Exod. 19:6).[7] The term "Pharisee" could also suggest being set apart for a special mission, such as Paul, a Pharisee, describes himself as "set apart for the Gospel of God" (Rom. 1:1).

Fourth, and most important, Jews then did not, and Jews now do not, equate personal wealth with righteousness or personal poverty with sin. If we took the time to see what Torah and its interpreters say about wealth and poverty, we would quickly realize both that poverty is not equated with sin and that those with means are enjoined, by commandment and by conscience, to support the poor.[8] When Jesus tells his disciples, "Blessed are you poor, for yours is the kingdom of God; blessed are you who are hungry now, for you will be filled" (Luke 6:20–21), he is not suggesting that poverty is an ideal state. One should no more want to be poor than to be hungry or in mourning or hated, the topics of the other beatitudes. Jesus's point is that, in the ideal community that he not only envisages but also is creating among his disciples in anticipation of the final judgment, the poor will receive needed funds and the hungry will be fed. Consistent with his Jewish tradition, Jesus's blessing of the poor is also an assurance that his followers will do what Torah mandates.

The best way of summarizing Jewish teaching on economics, from the Bible to today, comes from Tevye the milkman known from the stories by Yiddish author Sholem Aleichem, and made even more famous in the musical *Fiddler on the Roof*. As Tevye puts it to God: "You made many, many poor people. I realize of course it's no shame to be poor, but it's no great honor either."

THERE WILL BE NO POOR IN THE LAND, BUT IF THERE ARE . . .

In antiquity, most people would be classified as "poor" in that most could not be assured of retaining the few resources they had. Rarely in the Gospels do we find people who are destitute, such as the poor widow who puts her last two coins into the temple treasury (Mark 12:42 // Luke 21:2) or a woman, suffering from hemorrhages for twelve years, who "spent all her money on physicians" (Mark 5:26 // Luke 8:43).

The death of a spouse, then and now, could lead to a major loss of income; then and now, medical expenses could lead to bankruptcy. A third source of financial insecurity was crime, whether economic exploitation or, literally, highway robbery. The prophet Amos condemned the wealthy who "sell with silver the righteous, and the needy for the sake of shoes" (Amos 2:6). The fellow aided by the proverbial "good Samaritan" was the victim of robbers, who "stripped him, beat him . . . leaving him half dead" (Luke 10:30).

Fiduciary irresponsibility can also lead to poverty, as can famine. Jesus tells a parable about a prodigal who "squandered his property [the Greek can even have the sense of his 'essence' or his 'being'] in dissolute living. When he had spent everything, came a severe famine against that region, and he himself began to be in need" (Luke 15:13b–14). The parable also distinguishes between being foolish and being sinful. Although the prodigal, seeking to place himself back in his father's good graces, plans on telling him "I have sinned against heaven and against you" (Luke 15:18, 21), his comment overstates. Ancient Israelites were not Puritans: to gamble or consort with prostitutes or drink too much alcohol, or what we would call "to party," is not the same thing as to sin.[9] Consequently, the parable says nothing about forgiveness, since at least as far as this prodigal is concerned, no sin was committed. Sin requires forgiveness. Foolishness requires cleaning up the mess or living with it.

As sin requires atonement, so poverty requires a response. The Hebrew term for "righteousness," *tzedakah*, also means "charity"; one cannot be righteous without caring for those in need. Support for the poor is built into the Bible's judicial and agricultural systems. For example, Exodus 23:6 forbids perverting justice when poor people bring lawsuits, and Exodus 23:11 instructs landowners to let the fields, vineyards, and orchards lie fallow every seventh (sabbatical) year "so that that the poor of your people may eat." Deuteronomy 14:22–29 (cf. Deut. 26:12) similarly establishes tithes to support the Levites, the members of the tribe of Levi, since they have no land, as well as immigrants (non-native-born residents), orphans, and widows.

On the economic register, the Bible occasionally overstates the benefits of fidelity. Deuteronomy 15:4 proclaims, "There will be no one in need among you," given divine blessings in the land of Israel. But three verses later, 15:7 states, "If there is among you anyone in need . . ." and goes on to mandate that the people are neither to be hard-hearted nor tightfisted in helping out the neighbor in need. The chapter continues, in v. 11, with a verse already cited, "Not will there cease to be needy from the land." The next line offers the response, "I therefore command you, open your hand to the poor and needy neighbor in your land." Also as noted, this is the verse to which Jesus alludes when, after being anointed with expensive perfume, he states, "For always you have the poor with you." The verse continues, "and whenever you wish you are able to do good to them; but me not will you have. She has done what she could; beforehand she has anointed my body as preparation for burial" (Mark 14:7–8). No divesting here; Jesus approves the one-off extravagance. Perversion of such texts enters when those who are rich insist that since the poor will always be present, the rich can spend what they want on what they want. This is not what Jesus had in mind. He is about to be tortured to death, not to jet off for a vacation in St. Moritz.

Readers will sometimes attempt to escape the Bible's insistence on support for the poor by introducing other matters, especially those that engage the culture wars. For example, one popular view is that Sodom was destroyed because of consensual, nonheterosexual activity. Yet the first biblical commentary on Genesis 19, Ezekiel 16:49, condemns the city because it had "pride, abundance of bread, and quiet tranquility [or prosperous ease]," but it did not aid "the poor and needy." I wonder whether better understanding of the problems in Sodom would lead politicians in my home state of Tennessee to be more concerned with food insecurity than with drag shows. But now I'm preaching.

Among the numerous prophetic concerns for the destitute, Zechariah 7:10 continues, "Do not oppress the widow, the orphan, the migrant, or the poor." The Psalms condemn those who despoil the poor (e.g., Ps. 12:5), and Proverbs 28:11 unmasks the self-complacent wealthy, "Wise in his own eyes is the rich man, but a poor person, understanding, will search [NRSVUE: 'sees through the pose']."

For Wisdom texts of the second century BCE, people who are rich escape condemnation and even receive praise *if* money is not the center of their lives and *if* they behave with righteousness. Sirach 31:8 offers the beatitude, "Blessed [*makarios*, the same term that begins Luke 6:20, Jesus's beatitude, 'Blessed are you poor'] is the rich person who is found blameless and who after gold does not go." Sirach then notes that the rich have the power to transgress or do evil; the blameless do not succumb to the temptation to hoard but provide for those in need.

Some Jews at the time of Jesus participated in the forerunners of today's intentional communities.[10] The Essenes, according to Josephus (*War* 2.127), shared property; the Roman naturalist Pliny the Elder states that Essenes also eschewed money (*Natural History* 5.15.73); and Philo claims that they avoided the trade economy (*Quod omnis probus* 78). In 1 Enoch 91–104, the so-called Epistle of Enoch, the rich are not and cannot be righteous; they are enemies of God. First Enoch 94:8 pronounces, "Woe to you, rich people! For you have put your trust in wealth." The verse sounds very much like Luke 6:24, "But woe to you, the rich, because you have received your consolation."

While rabbinic sources agree on supporting the poor, they disagree on what standard determines the qualification for wealth. B. Shabbat 25b records a discussion among several rabbis who were active ca. 90–135 CE. The text begins by asking, "Who is wealthy?" and continues with various answers. Rabbi Meir responds, "The one content with his wealth." Rabbi Tarfon, reputed to be wealthy himself, answers that the rich person is one who has one hundred vineyards, one hundred fields, and one hundred enslaved people working in them. Rabbi Akiva, known to have been supported in his studies by his wife, the daughter of a very wealthy man who chose instead to live in poverty with Akiva, says, "The one who has a wife beautiful in good deeds." Rabbi Yose ends this discussion with the comment, "The one who is wealthy has a toilet not far from his table." I suspect he was flush. The question of wealth is thus relative, and some answers are better than others. My favorite comment in this genre is from Rabbi Abaye: "We have a tradition that only the one who lacks knowledge is poor" (b. Nedarim 41a).

When we discuss wealth and poverty, we are not, as Rabbi Abaye realized, always talking about economics. That fact means that we have to reevaluate how we understand the terms, and so how we understand what gives rise to wealth and poverty, economic and otherwise.

TAKING AN AUDIT: JESUS WAS NOT A PEASANT, HIS CLOSEST FOLLOWERS WERE NOT DESTITUTE

Many sermons and articles, especially by those who look to Jesus for comments on alleviating poverty, begin with the alternative facts that Jesus was a peasant, that he was destitute, and that his audience was composed primarily of dispossessed farmers and others impoverished by Roman taxation, the temple's tithing, and the Pharisees' rules regarding purity.

First, a peasant is usually attached to the land, as would be an agricultural worker in a feudal system. According to this definition, Jesus was not a peasant. Mark 6:3 says that he was a *tektōn*, a builder, and thus an artisan. The term *tektōn* appears in the Septuagint (the Greek translation of the Hebrew Scriptures, abbreviated LXX), where it describes those who make swords and spears (1 Sam. 13:19; cf. Isa. 44:12) as well as blacksmiths (Zech. 1:20); artisans working with bronze (1 Kings 7:14), silver (Hosea 13:2), and gold (Isa. 40:19; 41:7); and woodcutters (Wisd. of Sol. 13:11, in the deuterocanonical collection or Old Testament Apocrypha). Matthew 13:55 makes Jesus the "son of a *tektōn*," which gets picked up in the second-century Infancy Gospel of Thomas. This later, variously charming and horrifying, text describes in one of the more pleasant episodes little Jesus lengthening a plank of wood that Joseph has incorrectly cut.

Sociologically, regarding Jesus as an artisan rather than either as a peasant or as among the leisured rich makes sense. Artisans are in the best position to move among classes: they can subcontract with those below; they are hired by those above. From this position, Jesus could proclaim good news to the poor as well as instruct the rich about how to create this good news.

Jesus's entourage included a tax collector (called "Matthew" in Matt. 9:9 and "Levi" in Mark 2:14 // Luke 5:17); James and John, sons of Zebedee, a comparatively well-to-do boat owner who had hired laborers (Mark 1:19–20) but who also expected his sons to help with mending nets; and Simon (called "Peter") and Andrew, who may well also have owned a boat (Mark 1:16–18). Peter also apparently owned his own home, since it is at this house that Jesus heals Peter's mother-in-law (Mark 1:29–31). In Mark 6:8–9, Jesus provides missionary instructions to his disciples to "take nothing for their journey except a staff: no bread, no bag, no money in their belts; but to wear sandals and not to put on two tunics." The command presumes they had money to take. In Matthew's retelling (Matt. 10:9), they are not to take gold or silver or copper.

Just as the mitzvot, the commandments, require community members to support each other, so Jesus mandates support among his followers. This is, for example, the point of the Parable of the Sheep and the Goats in Matthew 25:31–46 (if at the final judgment you discover a sheep line and a goat line, get into the sheep line). The sheep, those who are saved from damnation, had fed the hungry, clothed the naked, visited the sick and the imprisoned, and welcomed the stranger, the "other," the "not from their group." Judgment is based on what they did, not on what they believed. Matthew 7:21 neatly summarizes, "Not everyone who says to me, 'Lord, Lord,' will enter into the kingdom of the heavens, but the one doing the will of my father in the heavens."

Other New Testament texts make the same point, with the same sense that the audience consists of people with means. The Epistle of James, which frequently echoes sayings attributed to Jesus in Matthew's Gospel, states, "If a brother or sister ['or sister' is not a gender-inclusive addition to the translation; the words are in the Greek text] is naked and lacks daily food, and one of you says to them, 'Go in peace; keep warm and eat your fill,' and yet do not give to them what is necessary for the body, their bodily needs, what is the benefit?" (James 2:15–16). Similarly, 1 John 3:17 asks, "If any would have the life of the world [i.e., worldly goods] and would see his brother [or sister, not in the Greek] having need, and would close his guts against him [i.e., refuse to help], how does God's love abide in him?" These are very good questions.

THE "RICH YOUNG RULER": SELL ALL YOU HAVE

Our first test case is Mark 10:17–26. To Mark's version, which refers to a "man," Matthew 19:16–26 adds that the petitioner was "young" (Matt. 19:22), and Luke 18:18–27 upgrades him to a "ruler" (Luke 18:18). The man's words prove that he is wealthy. Hence, we have a "rich young ruler." In the context of his story, we can, with some accuracy, interpret Jesus's statements about both divesting and the salvation of the rich. A fairly literal translation reads:

> And while [Jesus] was going out on the road, running toward him and kneeling to him, [a fellow] was asking him, "Good teacher, what shall I do so that I might inherit eternal life?"
>
> And Jesus said to him, "Why do you call me 'good'? No one is good except the one God. The commandments you know: do not murder, do not commit adultery, do not steal, do not bear false witness, do not defraud; honor your father and mother."
>
> And he said to him, "Teacher, all these I have guarded from my youth."

And Jesus, looking at him, loved him, and said to him, "One [thing] you lack; go, whatever you have, sell and give to the poor, and you will have treasure in heaven, and come, follow me."

And being shocked upon the word, he went away, grieving, for he was having many possessions.

And looking around, Jesus says to his disciples, "How with difficulty the ones having possessions into the kingdom of God will go."

And the disciples were marveling at his words.

And Jesus, again answering, says to them, "Children, how with difficulty it is into the kingdom of heaven to go. Easier it is a camel through the eye of a needle to go, than a rich person the kingdom of God to enter."

And all the more were they astounded, saying to each other, "And who will be able to be saved?"

And looking at them, Jesus says, "By people it is impossible, but not with God, for all is possible with God."

Below we look at some of the more important lines—and how they've been interpreted and misinterpreted over the years—to help us gain a better understanding of what Jesus was saying, not only about money, but also about priorities, personal needs, and possibilities.

"Easier it is a camel through the eye of a needle to go, than a rich person the kingdom of God to enter."

I read this translation to a group of undergraduates and asked whether they could identify the speaker. One responded, "Yoda." Wrong.

Equally wrong is the popular claim that ancient Jerusalem had a low clearance gate, such that owners needed to unpack the burdens their camels carried and have the animals bend to enter. Therefore, Jesus is not demanding that rich people divest everything; they need to give away only a few things. This legend translates into the platitudinous teaching that those who donate used toys to Goodwill will find the gates of heaven open to welcome them. Glossing this view, a few of my students add that bending indicates humility. The fact that it is the camel, not the rider, that does the dipping escapes them. Nor are camels known for humility. There is no camel gate; the camel is not going to get through a needle, and according to Jesus, without divine help a rich person will face a very poor afterlife.

Also attempting to mitigate the starkness of Jesus's comments on wealth, a few pastors report that "camel" is a mistranslation based on a scribal error. The Greek *kamelos* means "camel," but a similar word, *kamilos*, means a rope or a cable. Therefore, Jesus was not presenting the impossible image of a camel passing through a needle's eye but the plausible image of a cable passing through a ship's rigging. An ancient Syriac translation offers this alternative, and the *Jubilee Bible 2000* translates Mark 10:25, "It is easier to pass a cable through the eye of a needle than for a rich man to enter into the kingdom of God." Nice try. To see Jesus as issuing the banal teaching that the rich may have a smidge of a problem regarding salvation is to sell him short.

The Babylonian Talmud records several similar sayings designed to express impossibility or absurdity. According to b. Bava Metzi'a 38b, "Rav Sheshet said mockingly [to his opponent], 'Perhaps you are from Pumbedita [the site of a rabbinic academy], where people pass an elephant through the eye of needle [i.e., they engage in specious reasoning]." From a much later Jewish source comes the contrast, "The eye of a needle is not too narrow to hold two friends that agree;

the breadth of the world is not sufficiently wide to contain in its fold two foes" (Shekel Hakodesh).[11]

Were Jesus talking about removing a few packs or promoting humility, the disciples would not have asked, "Who will be able to be saved?" When he says, "By people it is impossible, but not with God," then whatever the subject—camel, rope, elephant—it could not pass without divine aid. The point is impossibility, not inconvenience.

Interpretations that make statements from Jesus less provocative make Jesus less provocative. Jesus well understands the value of hyperbole. Matthew 23:24 has Jesus inveigh against the Pharisees, "You strain out a gnat but swallow a camel!" No one argues that the camel here is really a piece of string cheese.

Some interpreters recognize the impossibility suggested by both Jesus's statement and the disciples' response, but they still try to get Jesus off the hook (another sewing image) by inventing a Judaism that equates wealth with righteousness and poverty with sin. Here's one popular approach from a website titled "Frequently Abused Verses": "Christ's exclamation, 'How hard it is for those who are wealthy to enter the kingdom of God!' (Luke 18:24) would have been a shock to His original audience. As John MacArthur [author of a commentary used by numerous Protestant pastors] explains, 'The idea that wealth was a sign of God's blessing was deeply entrenched in Jewish theology.'" The commentator concludes: "The rich young ruler was a product of the Jewish religious system, and his self-assurance about earning his salvation was a direct reflection of the Pharisees' man-centered legalism."[12]

MacArthur paints an even more noxious, and false, picture of Judaism: "For many centuries the rabbis taught that accumulation of wealth was a virtue . . . They had designed a religious law to protect their selfishness and greed. . . . For Jesus to teach that wealth was actually a serious *barrier* to the kingdom was diametrically contrary to everything most Jews had been taught."[13] There are, of course, no footnotes to support such claims.

This type of reading, which seeks to place a socially aware Jesus amid a clueless Judaism, is based on bad readings of texts. I could, were I so inclined, suggest that all Christians are greedy, given the New Testament's numerous injunctions warning against love of money. For example, 1 Timothy 6:10 insists that "the root of all evils is the love of money" (cf. 1 Tim. 3:3), and Hebrews 13:5a teaches, "Let your lives be free from the love of money, and be satisfied with what you have." All people are faced with temptations to greed and covetousness; Jesus's teachings regarding both are consistent with, not antithetical to, his Jewish context.

The following story, one of many in the Babylonian Talmud (b. Kallah 5.1), counters MacArthur's narrative:

The story begins with Rabbi Tarfon, he of the hundred vineyards, who, although he was very rich, did not give many gifts to the poor. Rabbi Akiva, he of the wife beautiful-in-deeds, said to him, "Master, would you like me to purchase one or two cities for you?" Tarfon, agreeing, gives Akiva four thousand gold denars. Akiva then distributes it to the poor. When Tarfon asks Akiva, "Where are the cities that you bought for me?" Akiva leads him to the *bet ha-midrash*, the house of study. There, he opens Tehillim, the Book of Psalms, and the two read until they come to Psalm 112:9, "He has scattered [i.e., distributed], he has given to the needy; his righteousness stands forever." Then Akiva tells Tarfon, "This is the city I bought for you." Hearing these words, Tarfon stands up, kisses Akiva, and says to him, "You are my rabbi and my friend—my rabbi in wisdom, my friend in right behavior." The story ends with Rabbi Tarfon giving Rabbi Akiva more money to distribute.

Jesus's instruction to the fellow who ran toward him is, really, "sell all you have." Jesus's statement shocks, but not because the Jewish tradition privileged wealth. It shocks because Jesus demands from this would-be disciple total divestment. He wasn't kidding.

"Good teacher, what shall I do so that I might inherit eternal life?"

Both our rich young ruler and the lawyer to whom Jesus tells the Parable of the Good Samaritan (Luke 10:25–29) ask about inheriting eternal life. Both stories open with problematic motives. According to Luke 10:25, the lawyer sought to "test" Jesus; "test" is the same term used to describe Satan's actions in the temptation narrative (Matt. 4:7; Luke 4:12–13), and the verse in the "Our Father" prayer, "Lead us not into temptation," is literally, "Do not bring us to the test" (Matt. 6:13 // Luke 11:4). I also suspect the young man's motives: his address to Jesus as "good teacher" could be fully respectful. On the other hand, the more appropriate title, from those who see Jesus as the ideal teacher, is "lord" (e.g., Mark 1:3; 7:28; 11:3). "Good teacher" sounds to me like a manipulative address—when one of my students begins with "good teacher," I am relatively confident that a request to change a grade from a D to a C is forthcoming.

The question about inheriting eternal life is odd, since eternal life is not gained by checking off how many mitzvot, commandments or good deeds, one performs. Resurrection is a gift freely given. Why, therefore, did the rich young ruler and the lawyer ask their question? The answer that makes the most sense to me is that both men had heard Jesus speak about the kingdom of God; they knew of his healings and exorcisms and of his proclaiming forgiveness of sin. They think he knows something about preparation for the messianic age, and they want details. They both also want a short and easy answer: neither appears to be interested in a lifetime commitment.

> "The commandments you know: do not murder, do not commit
> adultery, do not steal, do not bear false witness, do not defraud;
> honor your father and mother."

For the lawyer in Luke 10 who asked about inheriting eternal life, Jesus agrees with his summary of Torah as "love God" (Deut. 6:5) and "love neighbor" (Lev. 19:18). For our rich young ruler, Jesus again turns to Torah, and he focuses now on the second part of the Decalogue, literally the "Ten Words" (the term appears in Deut. 4.3; 10:4), more popularly known by the nonscriptural term the "Ten Commandments." But Jesus adds a commandment not explicitly listed among the famous ten: "Do not defraud" (Greek: *apostereō*).

The term appears in the Gospels only here in Mark 10:19, so to find its connotation we turn to how it is used in earlier texts. In the Wisdom of Jesus ben Sirach (Ecclesiasticus), a book in the deutero-canonical collection/Old Testament Apocrypha, it occurs frequently in contexts of economic exploitation (e.g., Sir. 4:1; 29:7; 43:25). For example, Sirach 34:25 reads, "The bread of the needy is the life of the poor; whoever defrauds [*apostereō*] them of it is a murderer." Jesus may be insinuating that the man, or his family (much wealth is inherited), gained affluence through fraud, such as by withholding wages, overcharging, or failing to pay the agreed-upon amount for work.[14] In 1 Corinthians 6 Paul connects the term with internal problems in the assembly, and the Epistle of James 5:4, again sounding very much like material attributed to Jesus, insists, "Listen! The wages of the laborers who mowed your fields, which you kept back by fraud [*apostereō*], cry out, and the cries of the harvesters have reached the ears of the Lord of hosts" (NRSVUE).

Jesus's comment about defrauding relates to how people in the first century, and the twenty-first, might accumulate wealth.[15] His revised Decalogue prompts the questions: How did we come to our own economic situation? If by inheritance, what was the original source? Did we profit from the labor of the enslaved, the indentured, or the incarcerated; by underbidding competitors through cutting safety costs; by keeping unions out; by hiring workers overseas at lower rates than they would receive in our country? Alternatively, was our labor, or that of our families, exploited or alienated?

> And he said to him, "Teacher, all these I have guarded from my youth."

Our rich young ruler seems earnest, and he has done all the right things. He reminds me of the eager student who, on the second day of class, announces, "I've done all the readings you have assigned; what else should I read in order to get an A?" This, like the initial question of "What shall I do that I might inherit eternal life?" is not a good question. Rushing through assignments is not a good way to learn; seeking the grade rather than seeking knowledge is not a good way to live. The rich young ruler, like the student, is sincere; he is also immature. Life should not consist of checking off boxes; completing the to-do list is not a way of displaying love or even finding happiness, since the next day brings its own list of to-dos.

I am also taken by his notice that he has "guarded from my youth" the commandments. The same phrase shows up several times in the Septuagint. For example, Psalm 71:17 proclaims, "O God, from my youth you have taught me, and I still proclaim your wondrous deeds" (NRSVUE). Conversely, our young man is interested in proclaiming his own good deeds, not those of God; he is interested in his own salvation, not in loving neighbor or stranger. In his suffering, Job asserts, "from my youth I reared the orphan like a father, and from my mother's womb I guided the widow" (Job 31:18, NRSVUE). While not every newborn is a contender for the Nobel Peace Prize, at least Job has the right idea.

The rich young ruler's interaction with Jesus shows us that following the commandments *in order to be saved* is to begin with the wrong premise. Theologically, we respond to God's love by doing what God wants. Or, for nontheists, we follow the commandments because to do so makes for a better life. Adultery is not good for marriage; stealing, bearing false witness, and defrauding ruin communities. Coveting just makes us resentful and frustrated. We should honor our parents not to earn their love (ideally, we have that), but because such honoring keeps families together and enhances relationships. It also sets a good model for our children. Granted, not all parents act in honorable ways and thus do not deserve honor, but the general point holds nonetheless. At least my parents told me that we do what is right *because it is right*, and not to earn points or honor or reward.

> And Jesus, looking at him, loved him, and said to him, "One
> [thing] you lack; go, whatever you have, sell and give to the poor,
> and you will have treasure in heaven, and come, follow me."

The source of our money is only one of several issues this story raises. The next is what Jesus says to this fellow. For our rich young ruler, and just for him, one thing more is required. Jesus changes tone from the congenial questioning about Torah to the imperative: "Go . . . sell . . . give . . . come . . . follow." Yet he does so in love, for the rich young man is the only person Mark says "Jesus loved." The comment may well be Mark's notice to rich people: the love remains, even if you cannot, at present, do what you know in your heart to be right. It also indicts me, because I started off distrusting this fellow. If Jesus can find in him something to love, I could do the same, even for that grade-grubbing sophomore.

Luke's Gospel is not interested in everyone divesting, and neither is Jesus. Jesus relies on the hospitality of homeowners such as Martha (Luke 10:38–42) and the rich tax collector Zacchaeus (Luke 19:2), and he expects his disciples to find the same hospitality. He tells them, "Whenever you enter a house, stay there until you leave the place" (Mark 6:10 // Matt. 10:12–13 // Luke 9:4). He does not instruct the disciples to tell their hosts to put up For Sale signs. The inside circle of followers, such as Peter and Andrew, may have given up everything; the outer circle, including women such as Mary and Martha, keep their resources.

Jesus states, "You cannot serve God and wealth" (Matt. 6:24 // Luke 16:13), but he is also aware that one can serve *with* wealth. For a person whose self-definition is based in stock portfolios and not love or compassion, both Torah and Jesus shock, not soothe. Jesus was not exaggerating when he tells his disciples, "How difficult it is for those who have stuff to enter into the kingdom of God" (Mark 10:23). Then again, all things are possible.

We do not know what happened to this rich young ruler. I like to imagine that he came to be with Jesus in Gethsemane: when Jesus is arrested, the rich young ruler flees, and as he does, he leaves his linen cloth. We see him running away, naked (Mark 14:52). Following Jesus, he thus divests of everything.

This rich young ruler's story may well be our story. We can, for ourselves, determine how his story continues, and how our stories will continue as well.

THERE WAS A RICH MAN WHO . . .

The story of the rich young ruler is told by the Gospels about Jesus; parables about rich men are stories told by Jesus. The two genres reveal coherent themes: wealth may provide momentary satisfaction, but it can offer neither security nor salvation; people with resources should care for those who lack such resources; if you are known primarily for your wealth, you have a problem both in this world and in the world to come.

Luke's Gospel offers a number of parables beginning with the words *plousios anthrōpos tis*, "some rich fellow." Combined, these parables tell us that anyone who is known as "some rich fellow" is likely to do something unwise, or worse. The main character in the Parable of the Rich Fool (Luke 12:16–25), the master in the Parable of the Dishonest Manager (Luke 16:1–8), and the rich man (sometimes called "Dives") who overlooks the poor, diseased Lazarus (Luke 16:19–31) in the parable aptly titled the Rich Man and Lazarus, all find that wealth can neither be saved nor save.[16] In this chapter, we look at the first two parables, but first a few words on background.

More than a place-marker, the label "rich man" describes the character's most important characteristic. But not all wealthy characters receive this label. For example, Luke 15 introduces several high-income people in parables—a man who owned one hundred sheep (v. 4), the father of the prodigal son (v. 11)—but Luke identifies neither as "rich." In Luke's Gospel, the label "rich" belongs to those who show no concern to anyone save themselves. Conversely, Matthew 27:57 labels Joseph of Arimathea "rich" and identifies him as a "disciple" of Jesus (for Matthew, to be rich and to be a disciple are not mutually exclusive).

It is possible that Matthew presumes a wealthier audience than does Mark: only in Matthew do Magi give the baby Jesus gold, frank-

incense, and myrrh (Matt. 2:21); only in Matthew are the disciples instructed not to bring gold (Matt. 10:9). Nevertheless, Matthew insists
that those who have wealth donate their resources to those in need.
Joseph of Arimathea is not known primarily for his wealth; he is
known for going to the Roman governor, Pontius Pilate, asking for
permission to entomb the corpse of a man executed by the state on
the charge of sedition, wrapping Jesus's body in clean linen, and then
placing it in his own rock-hewn tomb.

A similar focus on the wealthy applies to Luke's Gospel, despite
Luke's reputation as addressed primarily to the poor. Parables beginning "there was a rich man who" appear only in the Third Gospel.
As Judith Lieu observes concerning the evangelist Luke, "despite all
his sympathies for the impoverished and excluded of society, it is the
attitudes and assumptions of the wealthy which form his starting
point, perhaps suggesting that they constituted a significant element
within his own community."[17] Her point receives support from Luke's
literary style: both the Gospel (Luke 1:3) and the Acts of the Apostles
(Acts 1:1), also written by Luke, take the form of a text dedicated to a
patron named Theophilus (whether to a real person or any "lover of
God," which is what "Theophilus" means). Wealthy people also lis-
tened to Jesus. They too sought his healings and exorcisms; they too
pondered his teachings concerning Torah and that final judgment;
and they too were among his followers. Jews knew that the well-off
had responsibilities toward people having need. Jesus, with his statements about the inbreaking of the kingdom of God, pushed them to
do more.

The Parable of the Rich Fool

The Parable of the Rich Fool (Luke 12:16–21) provides a portrait of
"superfluity, selfishness, and separation from the poor";[18] whether
we feel schadenfreude at the rich man's demise, or feel personally

indicted, may depend on the contents of our bank accounts. Then again, the reactions are not mutually exclusive.

> And he said a parable to them, saying,
>   Of some rich fellow the field well-produced good crops.
>   And he reasoned to himself, saying, "What shall I do, because not do I have [a place] where I can gather together my fruit?"
>   And he said, "This I shall do; I shall take down my storehouses and greater [ones] I shall build, and I shall gather together there all the grain and my goods. And I will say to my soul [*psyche*], 'Soul, you have many goods laid up for many years; rest, eat, drink, be euphoric.'"
>   But said to him God, "Fool! This night your soul they are asking back from you; and what you have prepared, to whom will it be?"
>   Likewise for the one storing up treasures for himself and not to God of riches.

Jesus begins the parable by describing how the rich man's land produced abundantly. The man did nothing. The point is rhetorical rather than descriptive: planting, irrigating, maintaining, and harvesting all require people to sow, water, weed, and reap. Both the rich man and Jesus overlook the workers, who may have been day laborers or enslaved (we return to overlooked workers in Chapter 2). In this parable, the focus on the rich man alone helps with characterization: there is no one else in his world. His ego, or his *psyche*, takes up all the space.

The rich man engages in interior monologue, which in biblical narrative often intimates conniving.[19] When he addresses his soul with, "Soul, you have many goods laid up for many years; rest, eat, drink, be euphoric" (v. 19), he creates his own dialogue partner. He has no one else with whom he can, or cares to, share either thoughts or goods. His words highlight his self-centeredness: *my* fruit, *my* storehouses, *my* goods, *my* soul. As one interpreter points out, "It is a classic problem of egoism that Jesus exposes in tedious redundancy, piling up eight first-person verbs (most in the future tense) and five first-person pronouns in three short verses (12:17–19)."[20]

Finally, the rich man decides to build bigger barns. The planning could be better. The wiser course would have been either to build bigger barns in the first place or to put extensions on the ones now standing. That his barns are initially inadequate suggests he has been acting foolishly for some time. Although Ecclesiastes 2:24a states, "There is nothing better for mortals than to eat and drink and find enjoyment in their toil," Ecclesiastes 5:10 states, "The lover of money will not be satisfied with money, nor the lover of wealth with gain. This also is vanity" (NRSVUE).

Suddenly, God appears, and this is the only time God speaks in a parable. God speaks directly to the rich man, with words of condemnation, not congratulations. Calling the man a fool, God tells him that he is about to drop dead. So much for full barns, self-satisfaction, and long-term planning. The term "fool" (*aphrōn*) together with the interior monologue recollects Psalm 13:1 (cf. 52:1), which notes that fools (the same Greek word) say in their hearts that there is no God. The connection makes our rich man a "functional atheist."[21]

Commentators typically see the ones demanding the man's soul as angels. That is a possible view, especially since in the Parable of the Rich Man and Lazarus, Luke states that when poor and diseased Lazarus died, he "was carried away by the angels to be in Abraham's bosom" (Luke 16:22; he then notes laconically that "the rich man died and was also buried"). Another reading is possible, although I've yet to hear it preached. It seems to me just as likely that thieves, aware of the rich man's wealth, solitude, and selfishness, broke in.

He may have been attacked, such as happened to the fellow rescued by the Samaritan on the road to Jericho. Jesus can come "like a thief in the night" (1 Thess. 5:2; cf. Matt. 24:43); so can real thieves. No reason to hoard money: it cannot remain safe.

Luke, who is given to moralizing, likely added the narrative frame. Right before our parable, Luke has Jesus state, "Look, and guard yourselves from all greed," because even if you have more than you need, your life is not determined by your possessions (Luke 12:15). The parable ends with another moral: "Likewise for the one storing up treasures for himself and not to God of riches" or more colloquially in the NRSVUE, "So it is with those who store up treasures for themselves but are not rich toward God" (Luke 12:21). The verses eliminate the threat of the parable and so make it easier for rich people to keep their money. Without the threat, whether of thieves or death or both, those barn builders can keep on building; they've got plenty of time to figure out how to distribute their property.

Nor does the frame, which focuses on greed, explain what one should do with what one has. I do not think it helpful, in present-day circumstances and especially for a person with dependents, not to have a bank account, or not to have insurance in case of a catastrophic accident. How, then, is one to be "rich toward God"?

Jesus, I think, would likely gloss the parable by speaking about storing up treasures in heaven, where these treasures are safe from natural forces such as insects and human scourges such as thieves (Matt. 6:20). One stores up treasures in heaven by being generous with one's goods and one's time. As Proverbs 11:4 (KJV) puts it, "Riches profit not in the day of wrath, but righteousness delivereth from death."

Reading this parable together with the story of the rich young ruler offers additional nuance. Our rich young man cannot escape the trap of wealth despite feeling that something is missing. The rich man of the parable, conversely, has no self-doubt; all he has is self. Jesus loved the young man; perhaps he saw in him the potential to redefine his life. Conversely, there's little love for the rich man of the parable; he is not "beloved child" but "fool." It is too late to change.

And yet, if Jesus can find love for the rich young ruler, perhaps we can muster any love for this rich fool. He was at one point someone's child; we do not know the circumstances that led him to have only his soul as his companion. If we simply say "poor fool," we have not let the parable fully work on us. A possible better step is to determine whether we know anyone like him and then work to interrupt that person's solitude. Another might be to see whether there is a part of us that is like him as well, and then move from internal monologue to external awareness of the people around us. According to the mishnaic text Pirke Avot, Rabbi Eliezer taught, "Let the respect owing to your fellow be as precious to you as the respect owing to you yourself, and do not anger easily, and repent one day before your death" (2.10). Long-term planning is all to the good, but in the meantime, we do well to assess our current state, our relationships, and our concern for others, and then we'll be better able to determine our worth.

The Parable of the Dishonest Manager

Our next *anthrōpos plousios tis*, "some rich person," is tricked by his estate manager in the story traditionally called the Parable of the Dishonest Steward (Luke 16:1–8a). It could easily be called the Parable of the Prudent Manager;[22] also in the running are the Parable of the Complicit Debtors, the Parable of Graft and Gratitude, and the Parable of the Dishonest CFO. Much depends on how we understand the estate manager. Is he a scoundrel? Is he Jesus? Do we shake our heads in admiration for his chutzpah and give him credit for being a rogue?

And [Jesus] was saying even to his disciples,

Some person who was rich, who had a manager, and this one was accused to him as having squandered his possessions. And calling him, he said to him, "What is this I hear about you? Give over the word [i.e., the account books] of your management, for not are you able still to manage."

And said to himself the manager, "What shall I do, because my lord seizes the management from me? To dig I am not strong; to beg I am ashamed.

"I know what I shall do, so that when I am put out from the management I might be received into their houses."

And calling one by one of those owing the lord, he said to the first, "How much are you indebted to my lord?" And he said, "One hundred containers of oil." And he said, "Take of you the letters [i.e., your bill] and sitting down, swiftly, write fifty."

Then to another he said, "You, how much do you owe?" And he said, "One hundred bushels of grain." He says to him, "Take you the letters [i.e., your bill] and write eighty."

And praised the lord the unrighteous manager because shrewdly he acted.

I suspect that the parable ends here at Luke 16:8a. The next several lines either come not from Jesus but from Luke or were spoken by Jesus on different occasions and placed here by Luke. The Gospel continues:

Because the sons of this age are more shrewd than the sons of the light to their own generation.

And I to you say, for yourselves make friends out of the

mammon of unrighteousness, in order that whenever it fails, they
may receive you into the eternal tents.

The one faithful in the least even in the greater is faithful, and
the one in the least who is wicked even in the greater is wicked.

If therefore in the unrighteous mammon you are not faithful,
[concerning] the true [thing], who will have faith in you? And if with
[the things of] others you are not faithful, what is yours who will
give to you?

No household worker is able to two masters to be enslaved, for
the one he will hate and the other he will love, or the one he will
cling to and the other he will despise, because you are not able to
God to be enslaved and to mammon.

Luke, it seems to me, is trying to get a moral message out of a story
riddled with what might politely be called "shenanigans."

Early church commentators, who wanted a moral message and
who had no qualms about allegorical reading, interpreted the parable
as being about giving alms.[23] I agree that the manager was generous;
the first problem is that he is generous with someone else's money;
the second that the debtors do not appear to need charity.

A few early church fathers, such as the North African writer
Tertullian, took the anti-Jewish route in attempting to make sense of
the parable. Tertullian "grounded an allegorical meaning upon the
address of the parable to the Jewish people who were facing removal
of their stewardship in the service of God, wherein they were to help
deliver people from their debt of sin. Instead of becoming friends
with the Gentiles, as the dishonest manager did, the Jews had treated
them harshly, which caused them not to be welcomed into 'eternal
habitations when they lost this grace of stewardship.'"[24] The debtors
were gentiles? Who knew? The Jews did not welcome gentiles? So

much for the Court of the Gentiles in the Jerusalem temple and the gentile "Godfearers" who worshiped with Jews in synagogues (see Chapter 3). I find allegorical explanations that require an answer key to make sense of the parable unconvincing. I doubt that upon hearing the parable, Peter turned to Andrew and asked, "Do you think debtors worship Zeus or Mithra?"

A more recent example of this approach is the claim that Luke "describes a carefully nuanced transition from the old 'economy' (16:2 [i.e., the way the rich man does things]) to the new one, the one we now call Christian. The real meaning of the Law is no longer the one offered by the Pharisees but rather the one attributed to Jesus. The Parable of the Dishonest Steward in the Lukan discussion wants to bring the faithful to the realization that radical inclusion of the outcast, whether religious or social, although a hard pill to swallow, is the will of God."[25] "Radical inclusivity" is a lovely idea, but there are no Pharisees or "outcasts" in the parable. Nor are the Pharisees, who teach among the people, making "outcasts" of others. Even the manager doesn't think of himself as an "outcast"; he's not yet cast out of his job, and he's planning on being "received" into people's homes. When we hear about Jesus doing something "radical" or as ministering to the "outcast," an anti-Jewish backdrop is often either implied or made explicit. We can do better.

We return to discussion of specific lines from the parable to figure out—as best as we can—what to do with it.

Parables that begin "there was a rich person who . . ." set up snap moral judgments and then prompt us to recognize that we may well be condemning ourselves. For example, we may want to see the man in the Parable of the Rich Fool as getting his just desserts (continuing the food metaphor): to be called "fool" by God, to drop dead and land in hell, or, at least to go broke. We are trapped in taking pleasure when someone else "learns his lesson." We thus become as uncharitable as the rich fellow even as we fail to engage in self-reflection.

When I see "there was a rich person who . . . ," part of me wants the rich person to fail, or at least to repent. And I am already indicted for being at best uncharitable. The first three Gospels all record Jesus as saying, "The measure you give will be the measure you get" (Matt. 7:2 // Mark 4:24 // Luke 6:38). Judging, especially without all the facts, is dangerous and often nasty.

> . . . who had a manager, and this one was accused to him as having squandered his possessions. And calling him, he said to him, "What is this I hear about you? Give over the word of your management, for not are you able still to manage."

The "manager" (*oikonomos*) is a free rather than an enslaved individual;[26] he is comparable to the "faithful and prudent manager" (*oikonomos*) of Luke 12:42, "whom his master will put in charge of the ones he enslaved, to give them their allowance of food at the proper time." Josephus uses *oikonomos* to describe Joseph, whom Pentepheres his master placed in charge of the other enslaved people in the household (*Antiquities* 2.57; see Gen. 39). The same term appears frequently in the New Testament to describe faithful followers with household responsibilities (Rom. 16:23; 1 Cor. 4:2; Titus 1:7; 1 Pet. 4:10).

So far, the title gives us no means of assessing this man's character. We know only, at the outset, that he likely has some financial acumen, and that to this point, the rich man trusted him. Were we rich citizens, we may look down on the manager as the hired help; were we agricultural workers, free or enslaved, working in the hot sun, we may resent him. The connection to Joseph of Genesis— pampered by his father, egocentric, and so manipulative that during the seven-year famine, he confiscates for Pharaoh the lands belong-ing to the Egyptians (see Gen. 47:19)—is not necessarily positive.

The rich man asks, "What is this I hear about you?" and then demands the ledgers. The information is gossip. What one "hears" is not necessarily what happened. The term I have translated "accused" (*diaballō*), which sounds like "diabolic," could suggest that the accu-sation was false. Again, our own situation skews our reading: Does management trust hourly workers? Are people in middle manage-ment positions, the people who mediate between the workers and the owners or stockholders, to be trusted by either those above or those below? Where the gossip originates may determine how we assess it. Where we are in the chain of command may determine how much credibility we accord what we have heard.

Here the parable increasingly entraps both characters and listen-ers. There are seven immediate problems; each decision we make will influence how we assess the characters and their actions. The parable thereby becomes an ancient version of "choose your own adventure."

First, although the rich man asks for both an explanation and the books, he receives neither. Does the silence suggest the manager's guilt?[27] Or, does the silence indicate the manager's knowledge of the rich man's temperament: he wouldn't listen anyway. Do the books show cheating, or not? Given the lack of literacy at the time, can the rich man even read the books? Not every investor can read a spreadsheet.

Second, since the rich man has already determined the manager's guilt,[28] what could the manager say that would change his mind?[29] Some people, once they have made up their minds, will listen to no argument and accept no counterevidence. What then do we do? And what do we do when these people are rich and so can generally act with impunity upon their false accusation?

Third, do we read the parable through the context of US law and presume innocence until proven guilty (I know of very few preachers who start here), or do we presume the manager is guilty, just as some of us may presume a person arrested and charged is also guilty? Our answer may well depend on our social class, our racial or ethnic identification, how we view the police and the courts, and the social location of the person arrested and charged.

Fourth, at this point in the parable, the rich man is in a bind. Should he keep the manager on the payroll, despite the charges of squandering, which may cause the rich man to look, or to be, foolish? Or, retaining the manager could be seen as disrespecting the people who brought the charges. But were the rich man to fire the manager, he would still look foolish for having not only hired him, but also allowed him freedom with his funds. Admitting his mistake can be dishonorable; failing to admit it can lead to greater financial loss. What is more important—maintaining public honor or personal property? What is wiser—taking the advice of unnamed and unknown gossipers, or ignoring it?

Fifth, whether the rich man regarded the manager as inept or venal, we can only guess (I have similar thoughts about certain politicians and people who run Fortune 500 companies). The first case, ineptitude, recalls the prodigal son, who "squandered" (the same term; Luke 15:13) his inheritance. Squandering one's own possessions is foolish, but it is not necessarily either sinful or illegal; squandering someone else's possessions (without their permission) is both. Our second option, that the manager is a conniver who played fast and loose with funds not his own, recalls another middle manager: the enslaved man in Luke 12:45, who "says in his heart [i.e., to himself], 'My lord [*kyrios*] is delayed in coming,' and he begins to beat others enslaved, men and women, and to eat and to drink and to get drunk." We'll meet him in the next chapter.

Sixth, we cannot determine when the manager became dishonest. He may have been dishonest from the start of the parable, and so the

charges were correct. But if the gossip and the accusations that follow
were false, then the charge of criminal activity coupled with the threat
of job loss become the proximate causes for why the manager took to
crime. Some individuals accused of criminal action because of their
social location (e.g., neighborhood, dress, race, age, gender, friends)
react to the charges by concluding, "If this is who society thinks I
am, I might as well be that person." Perhaps the manager originally
was innocent of the charges but then turned to crime: Should he be
judged less harshly than if he were engaged in criminal activity before the charge? Do we assess long-term bad behavior the same way
we judge a novice at wrongdoing?

Finally, the manager's initial silence takes on additional meaning
when read in its broader narrative context. Just as the manager offers
no response to the charges lodged against him, so the Gospels offer
another example of an individual silent in the face of charges. When
Jesus's accusers offer false and conflicting testimony (Mark 14:56)
about him, Jesus "was silent and did not answer" (Mark 14:61). Since
the high priest had already determined Jesus to be a political liability,
no response would have been effective. If we compare the manager
to Jesus, on whose side are we now?

> And said to himself the manager, "What shall I do, because my
> lord seizes the management from me? To dig I am not strong; to
> beg I am ashamed."

Rather than explain or excuse, the manager plots. In interior
monologue, again signaling conniving, he says to himself that he's
not strong enough to do manual labor and is too ashamed to beg. At
this point, I find it difficult to sympathize with him. The manager
starts well: he is aware of his physical limitations. But his reaction of
shame as regards begging is an offense to those who *do beg*.

Leaving a position of prestige and good pay for one of dishonor marked by poverty is easier said than done. For some of us, such humiliation would be worse than death. I have heard from rabbis, priests, and pastors across the country stories of people starving and freezing in upper-class and upper-middle-class homes because they lost their jobs and are too proud to ask for help. The next time we see a BMW pull up to the food pantry, instead of convicting the driver of greed, we might wonder: Does the driver lack shame, or does the driver lack sustenance?

As for the designation, "my lord" (*kyrios*), this is the same term used to identify Jesus (already in Luke 2:11; see also, e.g., 5:8, 12; 7:6, 13, 19; 9:54, 59). It can mean "lord" in the sense of God, since *kyrios* is the standard Greek translation of the Hebrew YHWH, the ineffable name of God in the scriptures of Israel. It can also mean "lord" in the sense of "sir" or "respected man." The use of the same title for "some rich fellow" and for the divine provides a moment to think about both theology and economics. Once society equates rich people with divinity, bad things will happen. Once rich people think they are gods, in that they can do anything they want, or buy anyone they want, bad things will happen.

> "I know what I shall do, so that when I am put out from the management I might be received into their houses."
> And calling one by one of those owing the lord, he said to the first, "How much are you indebted to my lord?" And he said, "One hundred containers of oil." And he said, "Take of you the letters [i.e., your bill] and sitting down, swiftly, write fifty."
> Then to another he said, "You, how much do you owe?" And he said, "One hundred bushels of grain." He says to him, "Take you the letters [i.e., your bill] and write eighty."

Seeking to retain a position as CFO, the manager summons the rich man's debtors. Meeting with them one by one, he asks them how much they owe. It's an odd question: the manager has the ledgers. By asking them the amount of their debt, he may be testing them to see whether they would lie. In that case, he would have leverage over them. He may even be inviting them to cheat since the question can signal that he is ready to deal. For a modern analogy, the new banker—perhaps one with a reputation for making risky loans—calls certain clients to tell them that because of a computer hack, their mortgage records have been lost. "How much do you owe?" the banker asks. A few people, seeing an invitation, a hint, a deal, may play along by dropping the cost of the debt. Perhaps the debtors might think that the rich man would not miss a few talents. Perhaps they viewed the original contract as unfair, so by decreasing the debt they will pay only what they think to be the fair amount. Are they opportunistic? Rationalizing? Cheating? Or, perhaps, they are clueless.

The debtors should have wondered why the manager posed the question. Do they know that charges have been brought against him? Do they trust him? Would we? Were I there, I might have asked the manager, "What's in it for you?" Then again, I like procedurals. It seems to me that the manager could hold a story arc on *Law & Order: Criminal Intent*.

Receiving the answers—"one hundred containers of oil . . . one hundred bushels of grain"—the manager instructs the debtors to inscribe a substantially reduced amount in their own handwriting. The fellow who owes the oil gets a 50 percent reduction; the one owing the grain owes 20 percent less. Klyne Snodgrass estimates that one hundred *kor* of wheat would likely feed 150 people. For the oil, "The yield of possibly 150 olive trees and equivalent to the wages of about three years for the average worker."[30] The debtors are also "rich men" although not explicitly identified as such.

The debtors may have lied; if they did, the parable becomes a story of some rich people getting richer while the creditor takes a loss. Alternatively, these debtors could pass along the lower costs to their clients, poorer people who need the oil and grain. This was not the first thought that occurred to me, but I am trying to find some sympathy for these debtors. If the bank, or a grocery store cashier, or the college financial aid office makes an error in our favor, do we report the error or remain silent? Do we use the money to buy something luxurious for ourselves, or do we pay it forward by giving it to the food bank? Or, does the amount matter? Do we pocket the dollar and report the $5K error, or vice versa?

The manager and the debtors do their work "swiftly" or "quickly," as crooked deals are done. The debtors have no time to reconsider their initial answers, or the new, better deal they have. I think the debtors are complicit in an illegal scheme. But as we've seen, there are other options.

Commentators, eager both to redeem the manager and to get a moral lesson from the parable, rush to provide explanations for the debt reduction. Some suggest that the manager has removed his own "well-padded" earnings on original trade.[31] Yet the manager's question was "How much are you indebted to *my lord*," not "How much is my commission?" Had the manager wished to reduce his commission, he did not need the debtors' permission. Another typical reading is that the manager reduced the "usurious interest," although nothing in the parable moves in that direction.[32] The parable says nothing about interest.

Dieter H. Reinstorf creatively proposes that the original charges are illegitimate and that the manager is a stand-in for Jesus, who lavishly scatters divine grace and forgiveness.[33] I see the parable as having possible connections to Jesus regarding the manager's silence in the face of (potentially) false charges. I can also see Jesus using the image of a scoundrel to make a point about forgiveness of sin and divine generosity. Anyone who can use the shocking image of a "thief in the night" to describe the coming of the Messiah can use a person guilty of a crime to represent divine action. However, I'm not happy with this allegory in that it connects the "rich man," a negative description, to God, and it portrays God and Jesus initially working at opposing ends.[34] Before we jump to theology, eschatology, and other "-ologies," we might begin where the parable begins, and it begins with economics and morality.

The manager is now, officially, "dishonest." The debtors are as well. The rich man is still rich, only less so. Part of me, the part who wants my finances protected by those who manage my pension, is disturbed by such deceitful practice. Yet I can easily imagine people in Jesus's original audience, presuming that the "rich man" gained his wealth by fraud as perhaps did our "rich young ruler," as finding satisfaction in these results. The manager has managed to get even with the "rich man."[35] One Lectionary Sermon website summarizes: "The shrewd manager realized he was about to get sacked. Naturally he felt he was entitled to a lump sum payment in lieu of severance pay and so he fixed himself up with a nice little retirement package at his employer's expense."[36] Are we on his side, or not, and why?

Whether the debtors would then employ the manager, or welcome him into their houses, is another matter. They might, given that the manager is aware of their complicity in the debt-reduction scheme. Better to hire him and keep him happy than to have him tell the "rich man" that his debtors cheated. And yet, to hire a known crook is to be vulnerable. What the manager did to the rich man need not be a one-off; he could do it again, and again.

And praised the lord the unrighteous manager because shrewdly
he acted.

The final shock of the parable occurs when the rich man, again
called "lord" (*kyrios*), praises that "unrighteous manager" for acting
shrewdly (*phronimos*). There is little else the rich man could do. The
ledgers have been fixed; what the debtors have written, they have
written. Nor would the scenario of the reduction of debts have been
socially anomalous. Creditors sometimes did reduce debts in periods of financial instability: the smaller amount could more easily be
paid, and such reduction would also serve to keep the debtors loyal.[37]
Meanwhile, what the rich man loses financially he gains in social
capital. The debtors would be expected to offer public praise for his
generosity. This concern for social gain at the price of financial loss
fits the conceptions of "honor" and "shame" presumed to character-
ize early Mediterranean society; it also provides what looks like a nice
resolution to the parable. Or, it's a nice resolution until we realize
that no one behaved well.

Perhaps the rich man saw in the manager his own practices: cheat
or defraud if it puts you ahead and you won't get caught; recognize
some gain, which is better than no gain; enjoy the game. The rich
man remains rich; the creditors will still pay enormous amounts; the
manager has made everyone complicit; everyone comes out okay if
not better.

Jesus again prompts the right questions. These include: Is
cheating the rich less of a problem than cheating the poor, and if so,
what's the income cutoff? Is it permissible to take advantage of an
accounting error?—and if so, does the amount matter? How much
do we know where our assets are invested, and who manages them?
Are the debtors as guilty as the manager, or are they mere dupes?
Is the rich man to be condemned, laughed at, or held responsible

for his own loss? Is honor more important than wealth, or even honesty? If everyone cheats, but everyone wins, do the ends justify the means?

Looking for a platitude, or a moral, or even a moral exemplar may not be the best approach to many of the parables. To find the point of discomfort is often the better prompt for a helpful interpretation.

I think the parable originally ended here at Luke 16:8a, with the rich man's commendation. This particular rich man is not dead, like the rich man who ignored poor Lazarus in the parable in Luke 16:19–31 (just a few verses after our text) or the rich fool who wanted to build more barns, but he's stuck, and he knows it.[38] At this point, mid-verse, the parable leaves the world of Jesus—the narrative of the parable itself, where the manager calls the rich man "lord"—and moves into the world of Luke. The rest of the section, extending to verse 13, strikes me as Luke's attempt to domesticate this parable. We sample a few of these disparate verses.

> Because the sons of this age are more shrewd than the sons of the light to their own generation.

The parable is certainly about acting shrewdly, which is something Jesus elsewhere commends: "I am sending you out like sheep into the midst of wolves, so be shrewd [*phronimos*; the NRSVUE reads 'wise'] as serpents and innocent as doves" (Matt. 10:16). To be savvy and to be faithful are not mutually exclusive. On the other hand, the first time the term *phronimos* appears in the Bible is in the Greek translation of Genesis 3:1, "Now the serpent was more shrewd [*phronimōtatos*] than all the other wild animals upon the earth that the LORD God had made." Being shrewd can cut both ways: we can read the manager as engaging in the work of discipleship, or we can read him as a snake. While Genesis imputes no motive to the snake, by the first century the snake had come to be understood as Satan (see 2 Cor. 11:3).

> And I to you say, for yourselves make friends out of the *mamōnas* of unrighteousness, in order that whenever it fails, they may receive you into the eternal tents.

Mamōnas, or in the KJV "mammon," derives from an Aramaic and Hebrew term meaning "wealth." It shows up in m. Pirke Avot 2.12, where Rabbi Yose advises, "Let your companion's *mamon* be as favored to you as your own." Otherwise put: don't risk someone else's account. Targum Pseudo-Jonathan to Exodus 18:21, concerning the people Moses should appoint to help govern the Israelites in the wilderness, adds that these candidates should despise receiving *mamon shikra*, the *mamon* of a lie or the *mamon* of unrighteousness. There's something about the word *mamon* that conveys a sense of distaste, comparable to the term "lucre."

It is worth discussing whether all mammon (stuff, money) is unrighteous or whether mammon is a neutral substance that takes on negative or positive characteristics depending on how it is used. The previously cited 1 Timothy 6:10 indicates that it is the "love of money," not money itself, that causes problems. Are we better off with a barter than with a monetized economy? Are we better off in a communal system rather than one promoting private property? For our "rich young ruler," all stuff is a problem; for the rich fool, stuff does him no good and may have enticed thieves rather than angels. But stuff can be put to good use.

Comments about "eternal tents" and "friends" do little to clear up the parable. One conventional reading is that the friends, "who are also the ones who do the welcoming, are the poor who should be recipients of charity."[39] This takeaway has nothing to do with the parable, where the "friends" are businesspeople with high-stakes investments.

If we recognize the irony of this saying, we can get back on track. Although English translations of Luke 16:9 typically speak of "eternal homes" or "eternal habitations" (I don't know anyone who lives in a "habitation"), the text says "eternal *tents* [*skēnai*]." "Tents" are not eternal. The only permanent tent in the biblical tradition is the tabernacle that the Epistle to the Hebrews envisions in heaven. The other "tents" in the Gospels are the temporary shelters that Peter wants to build for Moses, Elijah, and Jesus (Matt. 17:4 // Mark 9:5 // Luke 9:33). Acts, written by the author of the Third Gospel, uses the same term to describe the "tent of Moloch" (Acts 7:43), which God dismantles, and the "tent of David" (Acts 15:16), which had fallen. An "eternal tent" is about as logical as "righteous mammon." Contradiction can now lead to clarity. If we're stuck with what we've got, what now do we do?

. . . You are not able God to be enslaved and to *mamōnas* [the KJV reads, "You cannot serve God and mammon"; the NRSVUE reads, "You cannot serve God and wealth"].

By juxtaposing God and wealth, the phrasing suggests that they are both objects of worship, and they are both figures that can be seen as demanding total loyalty. The same saying appears in Matthew 6:24, in the context of the Sermon on the Mount. There it is followed by Jesus's instructions to his disciples on not worrying about what they are to wear or to eat. The point works better for rich people, who might debate what sauce to put on the chicken or what color cloak to wear. For people with food instability or lack of a winter coat, the call to avoid worry can sound cruel.

We may not be able to serve God *and* wealth, in the sense of two masters, but we can serve God *with* wealth. Money and property can lead to isolation (the rich man and his barns), to manipulation (the manager) and concern for honor (a possible reading of the rich man in this parable; the manager's own reluctance to slide down the social ladder), and to the temptation to squander (the prodigal son, our manager). But it can form the basis of benefaction and so of generosity. The parable shows us how money can be criminally manipulated, and how it can be used to create friends and generate honor. It tells us, as Jesus notes consistently, that money is not safe, and it cannot save. It raises questions of debt and debt-forgiveness, of middle management, patrons, and clients. It leaves us with no satisfactory answer, but a lot of good questions. That's what parables should do.

THE WIDOW'S OFFERING

In the temple, Jesus is instructing his disciples. He notices a poor widow, and so another story about economics—a story that should leave us uneasy—begins (Mark 12:41–44; cf. Luke 21:2–4):[40]

> And sitting down opposite the treasury, he was watching how
> the crowd cast money into the contribution box. And many rich
> people cast in much. And one poor widow, coming, cast in two
> lepta, which is a quadrans. And calling his disciples, he said to
> them, "Amen, I say to you, the poor widow herself cast in more
> than all of those casting into the contribution box. For all [of them]
> cast in from their abundance [or surplus], but she from her need
> [or want] cast in all of whatever she had, her whole life.

There are two competing interpretations of this short passage. The traditional view is that the widow both foreshadows the cross and provides a moral exemplar for the disciples: she gives her "whole life" to divine service, and thereby she anticipates Jesus's sacrificial offering. She thus represents the "poor and afflicted who find their joy in God alone."[41] She also finds an antecedent in Jesus's instruction to our rich young ruler; she is able to give away all that she has (Mark 10:21).

The second interpretation is that the widow is a victim of exploitation by rapacious scribes, whom Mark had just described as devouring widows' houses (Mark 12:40). No moral exemplar, she is at best an object of pity. Thus, Jesus's "teaching about the scribes and the widow provides a critique of two of the temple's most egregious offenses: religious hypocrisy and economic exploitation of the poor."[42] Mark does not locate these scribes in the temple, but the juxtaposition of the warning against them and the widow's poverty can suggest a cause-and-effect situation.

Both readings are good starts, but if we stop with either, we fail to see the complexities, and the challenges, of what Jesus points out to his disciples, then and now.

Cleansing the Temple Stereotypes

The first reading requires setting up a negative, and unsupported, image of the temple in order to make Jesus the social justice warrior. Numerous commentators describe the temple as epitomizing discrimination, whether against the poor, gentiles, women, children, or the impaired. They regard it as a "den of thieves" (Matt. 21:13 // Mark 11:17 // Luke 19:46, KJV) where rich priests rob poor peasants. To the contrary, the temple welcomed all people, rich and poor, men and women, Jew and gentile, enslaved and free, able-bodied and people with disabilities, even sinner and saint (so the Parable of the Pharisee and the Tax Collector [Luke 18:10–13]).[43]

The temple was not exploiting worshipers. Rather, it worked on a sliding scale for sacrifices; it charged no entry free; and the so-called temple tax, which Jesus paid (if we can believe Matt. 17:24–28, an odd story about Peter finding the coin, to pay the tax for both himself and Jesus, in the mouth of a fish; we should all be so lucky), was only a half shekel. Luke 2:24 tells us that Joseph and Mary "offered a sacrifice according to what is stated in the law of the Lord, 'a yoke [i.e., a pair] of turtledoves or two young pigeons'" (the citation, concerning Mary's purification after childbirth, is to Lev. 12:8).

The problem in the four verses concerning the widow is not the temple, but poverty. The focus is not her exploitation, but on her dedication.

Do You See This Woman?

Jesus tells us to "see" this woman, and that is the first step. We tend to focus on the donors for whom hospitals and civic centers are named and not on those who give a single dollar bill. His instruction anticipates a rabbinic midrash from Leviticus Rabbah: "A woman once brought a handful of meal as an offering. The priest despised it. He said, 'What sort of offering is that? What is there in it for eating or for a sacrifice?' But in a dream it was said to the priest, 'Despise her not; but reckon it as if she had offered herself as a sacrifice'" (3.5).[44] If our focus is less on the total amount and more on the percentage of income the amount represents, standards for naming buildings would need to be revised.

We also see our poor widow in the context of Jesus's other comments regarding economics. Had the "rich young ruler" sold "all he had and given to the poor," this widow might have had more coins. Had he or his family defrauded her, or her husband? What would she think of the Parable of the Dishonest Manager? What is a debt reduction of 50 percent to a person who has only two coins?

Not only do we see the widow, we "hear" in Jesus's description, "in *all* of whatever she had, her *whole* life," an emphasis on entirety, wholeheartedness. In describing the greatest commandment, Jesus begins with the mitzvah, the commandment, to "love the Lord your God with *all* your heart, and with *all* your soul, and with *all* your mind, and with *all* your strength" (Mark 12:30, citing Deut. 6:5 and adding "mind"; emphasis added). The scribe with whom he was speaking not only agrees, but also repeats the emphasis on fullness: "'to love him with *all* the heart and with *all* the understanding and with *all* the strength' and 'to love one's neighbor as oneself'—this is much more important than *all* whole burnt offerings [Greek: *holocauston*] and sacrifices" (Mark 12:33; emphasis added).

At this point, we should resist succumbing to the temptation to romanticize either the widow or poverty. Statements promoting her faith and confidence in divine providence in contrast to the "wealthy, who give only from their surplus (after their own needs are satisfied) and thus never feel the joyful pinch of self-denial in the cause of love" make me nervous.[45] Fasting for twenty-five hours on Yom Kippur, giving up sweets for Lent, or giving up lunch on Tuesdays in solidarity with the poor is not the same thing as having an empty pantry or a stomach swollen from malnourishment. Telling someone on extremely limited income to continue to "give" and to "sacrifice" to feel that "joyful pinch of self-denial" is not the best way of showing how the poor are blessed. The starving are not feeling a "joyful pinch."

The Widow as Victim

In 1982, Addison G. Wright wrote a profound article for the *Catholic Biblical Quarterly* that finally addressed the widow's poverty. Wright asks readers to "see" this woman's contribution in their own contexts: "Would we not judge the act to be repulsive and to be based on misguided piety because she would be neglecting her own needs?"[46]

This is the right question; the answer is complicated. Wright suggests that the widow's poverty is the result of temple teachings: "She had been taught and encouraged by religious leaders to donate as she does." This conclusion then leads to the standard critique: "Jesus condemns the value system that motivates her action."[47]

Such paths are not without warrant. Before noticing the widow, Jesus teaches: "Watch out [literally, 'see'—another 'seeing' verb] for the scribes, the ones who want in long robes to walk around, and greetings in the markets, and the first seats in the synagogues and the first couches at the banquets! They devour the houses of widows and for pretext pray a long time. These ones will receive a greater judgment" (Mark 12:38–40). The traditional reading sees the widow as the antithesis of the scribes: they show "counterfeit piety" whereas she shows "true piety."[48]

In this reading, as one commentator writes, the widow's story indicts the temple: "Jesus was there to take down the Temple and its corruption, a corruption that stooped so low that it would take advantage of widows in their poverty. . . . Seeing this widow abuse, I believe, strengthened Jesus' already strong resolve to give his life to take this corrupt religious system down."[49] Well, no. Jesus did not "give his life" to "take down" the temple. To the contrary. Jesus refers to the temple as "my father's house" (Luke 2:49), and the book of Acts on numerous occasions notes that his followers continued to worship there, with Paul offering a sacrifice (Acts 21:26). In Romans 9:4, Paul refers to temple worship (*latreia*) as one of the gifts God gave to the Jewish people.

Another commentator proposes, "Jesus' healings and exorcisms and his pronouncement of forgiveness of sins demonstrated that God's grace was now available outside the walls of the Temple," especially to those prevented from receiving divine compassion "because of the vigorous purity ethic enforced by some of the temple authorities."

The conclusion based on these premises is inevitable: Jesus views the widow with "a sense of sadness and a tinge of exasperation . . . he was grieved at the way the temple and its functionaries manipulated her to part with what little she had."[50]

Problems here are manifold. Nothing in the Gospels speaks to the temple as keeping people out because of purity regulations. Jesus commanded the man he healed from a skin disease to offer his gift at the temple, not to take down the system. Divine grace and compassion never were restricted to the Jerusalem temple, any more than they are restricted to a local church today. Nor does Jesus appear grieved with the widow's offering. Had he wanted to speak truth to power, he could have shouted, "Hey, lady, save your money." It wouldn't be the first time he disrupted temple activities.

One source for these popular associations of the temple with exploitation and corruption is the famous "cleansing of the temple" scene. Mark 11:17 reports Jesus saying, "Is it not written that 'My house a house of prayer will be called for all the nations'? But you have made it a cave of robbers." The "house of prayer" quotes Isaiah 56:7c, "My house shall be called a house of prayer"; the location, the Court of the Gentiles, already was a house of prayer for all nations.

The "cave of robbers" or "den of thieves" is a quote from Jeremiah 7:11, "You are making it [that is, the first temple destroyed by the Babylonians] a cave of robbers." Jeremiah is not talking about exploitation or corruption. The prophet is warning that too many people were failing to fulfill the mitzvot, the commandments. Jeremiah 7:9–11 asks, "Will you steal, murder, commit adultery, swear falsely, make offerings to Baal, and go after other gods . . . and then come and stand before me in this house, which is called by my name, and say, 'We are safe!'—only to go on doing all these abominations? Has this house, which is called by my name, become a den of robbers in your sight?" (NRSVUE). Nothing here about a corrupt system or economic exploitation. Lots here about individuals failing to live morally and then entering God's house in order to suggest to others, and perhaps to convince themselves, that they really are good people.

The stress on priestly corruption, peasant exploitation, and a rapacious religious system threatens to leave the people in the pews feeling self-righteous. Jesus, however, does not make matters so easy, and complacency is not an attitude he commends. Nor is he condemning the temple. When I read such commentary, I tend to think of collection plates, church bazaars, raffles, and various fundraisers. I do not see such offerings as mechanisms by which the "corrupt church" encourages the poor to part with what little they have. Similarly, given Jeremiah's point about worshipers who are not behaving morally and who are taking the temple for granted, I wonder whether clergy know what their congregants are doing outside of the worship service. Is what goes into the collection plate on Sunday morning from a robbery Saturday night, or from the foreclosure of a widow's house on Friday afternoon?

Our widow does not speak. Commentators who see her as exploited take away even more of her voice by casting her as victim of the temple system, while the temple may be where she feels both valued and noticed.[51]

Historical Notes

History can help us gain perspective on our interpretations. Here are two additional factors to consider when trying to understand the widow.

First, giving "all that one has" makes sense in a context where celibacy and martyrdom are also promoted. Both celibacy and martyrdom found a place in Second Temple Jewish thought and practice: Philo and the Dead Sea Scrolls speak to the matter of celibacy (see Chapter 5); 2 and 4 Maccabees give examples of Jewish men and women willing to be put to death rather than to transgress the commandments. But as the early followers of Jesus emphasized both celibacy and martyrdom, the rabbinic tradition, focusing more on the familial and the communal, resisted both ideas. While the rabbis insisted on the importance of supporting the poor (as we've seen, the term for charity, *tzedakah*, comes from the Hebrew meaning "righteousness"), they rejected divestiture, for that would endanger both family and community. Instead of martyrdom, they told stories of escape and so life.[52]

Mishnah Peah (*peah* refers to leaving the corners of the fields for the economically vulnerable, per Lev. 19:9; 23:22) begins: "These are the things for which no measure is prescribed: Peah, first fruits, the festal offering, deeds of loving kindness and the study of the Torah" (1.1). According to the Jerusalem Talmud, *limitless* charity "concerns actions done with one's body (such as visiting the sick or burying the dead)."[53] It does not extend to selling all one has on behalf of the poor.

Second, after the widow's offering in Mark 12, Jesus and his disciples leave the temple. The disciples marvel at the magnificence of the building, and Jesus responds, "See [again, Jesus helps us to focus— What do we see? How do we assess what we are seeing?] these great buildings? Not will be left here a stone upon a stone, which not will be destroyed" (Mark 13:2). The prediction is not entirely accurate; the Kotel (Hebrew: "wall") or Western Wall remains to this day. But he was close; in 70 CE, about forty years after he and the disciples look at the buildings, Rome would destroy them.

So we wonder: Do we contribute to the building fund (is the new steeple needed?) or to the food pantry, or to both? Whose names will be celebrated for the major donations? Who sees those who give proportionally more, even to the point of going without so that the institution can have more?

Seeing the Widow, Again

We return to this woman: Do we *see* her? Do we hear her own story? Is it our business, and should it be our business, to tell her how to spend her money? Do we attend to the smallest of contributions, particularly given the proportional amount she spends, or do we dismiss the drop in the bucket? Once again, Jesus helps us ask the right questions.

Jesus expected the imminent inbreaking of the kingdom of God. This eschatological focus provides us with another way of assessing economics, then and now. Do we save for our children, or do we donate to a cause we consider worthy, whether cancer research or evangelistic programs or putting books in the hands of children? Or, might we spend something on ourselves, just as Jesus approved the woman who poured expensive perfume on his head in anticipation of his burial?

Yet another approach is to take stock (literally, in some cases) of how we want to be known: as a "rich person"? and, if so, rich in what? Stock options or bonds? Indoor plumbing? A close family or friendship circle?

Finally, as I am writing this chapter, I am thinking about financial outlays in relation to Jesus. The 2023 Super Bowl featured several advertisements with the tagline "he gets us." In these clips, we learn that Jesus "gets us" because he knows what it's like to be poor, or lonely.[54] In reflecting on Jesus's comments about economics, I could not help but think that this ad campaign, with its $100 million budget, does not get Jesus. Jesus commissions his disciples to take no money on the road, and in visiting people, personally, to "cure the sick" and "cast out demons" (Mark 10:8). I wonder: Would not a better way of promoting the message of Jesus be less to say that "he gets us" and more to say that "we get him" and therefore invest in providing affordable health care, expanding psychiatric services, and visiting the lonely, rather than spending more than the budget of many counties, and countries, by presenting an ad during the Super Bowl?

A better question might be not "Does he get us?" but "Do we see this widow?" A better question might be not "How much was the donation in dollar amounts?" but "What is the best use of my funding?" Finally, a better question might be not "How much do I have?" but "How did I gain these resources?" and "Whom are my investments supporting?" Given that while all things are possible with God, and that Jesus loved that rich man who could not divest, and given that it is not money but the love of it that's a problem, we do well to sit with that line about the camel through the eye of the needle. Laying up treasure in heaven would be a good investment.

CHAPTER 2
ENSLAVEMENT

THE TOPIC OF the Bible and slavery is one that a number of congregations avoid. For some, it's too depressing. For others, it moves into uncomfortable questions about race, privilege, and reparations.

It's also a topic for which, I've found, lots of people presume a single positive biblical message: since the Torah's signature moment is the freedom of the Israelites from slavery in Egypt, *clearly* the Bible is all about freedom. Indeed, since Matthew portrays Jesus as a new Moses, from his rescue from slaughter as a baby to his giving the Sermon on the Mount, an evocation of Moses's receiving the Torah on Mount Sinai, clearly Jesus is all about freedom as well.[1]

Isaiah 57:14–58:14, which is the haftarah (the reading from the Nevi'im, prophetic books) on Yom Kippur, the Day of Atonement, proclaims:

> This is the fast I desire:
> To unlock the fetters of wickedness,
> And untie the cords of the yoke.
> To let the oppressed go free. . . .

> It is to share your bread with the hungry,
> And to take the wretched poor into your home. (Isa. 58:6–7, NJPS)

The Hebrew can, and perhaps should, be translated as commending the releasing of anyone enslaved, since slavery oppresses.

Similarly, many Christians affirm Jesus condemned slavery. Claiming the role of Isaiah's "anointed" as he spoke at his hometown synagogue, Jesus defines his mission as bringing "good news to the poor . . . release to the captives . . . recovery of sight to the blind, to let the oppressed go free, to proclaim the year of the Lord's favor" (Luke 4:18–19, paraphrasing Isa. 58:6; 61:1–2). Release to the captives, in this view, means freedom from slavery—and it could mean that, although Isaiah was speaking primarily of the release of the Jews taken by the Babylonians into exile in the sixth century BCE.

Ironically, this synagogue sermon follows the account of the imprisonment of John the Baptizer (Luke 3:19–20), a captive who is to be beheaded rather than liberated. Thus, the liberation is not of the incarcerated. Nevertheless, Jesus's job description in Luke 4 evokes the Jubilee year, when all debts are forgiven and enslaved Israelites are freed. Leviticus 25:41–42 mandates that at the Jubilee, which occurs every fifty years, the enslaved, and their children, are to be released from servitude. They are the servants, or "the enslaved" of God, redeemed from slavery in Egypt, who "will not be sold as those who are enslaved are sold." The language of Jubilee provides the wording for Philadelphia's Liberty Bell: "And ye shall hallow the fiftieth year, and proclaim liberty throughout all the land unto all the inhabitants thereof" (Lev. 25:10, KJV).

Alternatively, many Christians would state that Jesus frees humanity from slavery to sin, and hence he dies "as a ransom for many" (Matt. 20:28; Mark 10:45; cf. 1 Tim. 2:6).

The problem: neither Isaiah nor Leviticus nor Jesus nor the people who produced the Liberty Bell spoke of eliminating slavery.

The concern in this chapter is not freedom from exile, prison, or sin. It concerns slavery, which Orlando Patterson defines as "the permanent, violent domination of natally alienated and generally dishonored persons," a phenomenon that has existed throughout antiquity among pagans, Jews, and Christians and that exists today across the globe.[2] More, even after emancipation, the effects of slavery remain through the generations. Jesus's statements help us to confront slavery and its legacies; his instructions and his parables, like the story of the exodus, remain meaningful, provocative, and both comforting and indicting.

Both in Jesus's world and in the worlds he creates through his parables and instructions on discipleship slavery is normative. Jesus heals enslaved individuals and so returns them to servitude; Jesus uses the language of slavery to talk about humanity's relationship to divinity, which offers the (to me very problematic) image of God as a "master" who enslaves. Jesus encourages disciples to act not just as servants, but as enslaved—as people owned by others—and so to cede control of their bodies and their wills. He models enslavement by washing the feet of his disciples (John 13). Paul confirms this picture by describing Jesus as having emptied himself of divinity, immortality, and freedom and taken "the form of a slave [Greek: doulos]" (Phil. 2:7) to save humanity from sin and death. Would enslaved people hearing Philippians think "he gets us," as per the Super Bowl ad campaign, or would they wonder why, if Jesus promotes love, the Christian kyrios (the title refers here to both the address his followers gave Jesus and to "masters" or "lords" who enslaved others) thought it appropriate to own human beings?

We start by reviewing how slavery operated in ancient Israel,

Egypt, the Roman Empire, and Jesus's direct context. Then we turn to select Gospel examples: the boy enslaved by the centurion in Capernaum (a topic that also introduces the question of same-sex relations), the enslaved man who loses an ear in Gethsemane, and a few parables that prominently feature enslaved characters.

Some readers find ultimate freedom in regarding themselves as enslaved by God, their only, and benevolent, master. Others find casting God as a "master" who enslaves and worshipers as enslaved to be abusive, even blasphemous. The conversation about the Bible and slavery, including how Jesus's words about enslaved men and women have served both to liberate and to horrify, is difficult, but it is essential.[3]

ANCIENT ISRAEL AND EARLY JUDAISM

The following comments about ancient Israel, Hellenistic Jewish sources, the broader New Testament context, and rabbinic commentary on slavery, are selective. They are also horrifying.

Ancient Israel should never have legalized slavery, and its Jewish and Christian heirs should never have perpetuated the system. Genesis recounts, repeatedly, the abuses that occur when one person owns another. Sarah the matriarch abuses her "enslaved girl" (Gen. 16:6; Hebrew: *shifchah*; Greek: *paidiskē* [NJPS: "maid"; NRSVUE: "slave"]), the Egyptian Hagar, pregnant with her husband's child. Joseph's brothers sell him into slavery; then, instead of doing away with the institution when he becomes Egypt's second-in-command, Joseph "enslaved [the people] from one end of Egypt to the other" (Gen. 47:21). The book of Exodus reverses these roles: Hagar's people, the Egyptians, enslave Sarah's descendants. Abuse continues.

Conversely, Jewish and then Christian ethics are premised on liberation from slavery. A new Pharaoh, who "knew not Joseph" (Exod. 1:8, KJV) and who mistrusted a foreign group within Egypt's borders, enslaved the Israelites. "Their cry for help rose up to God from the slavery" (Exod. 2:23c). God commands Moses to tell his people, "I am the LORD, and I will take you out from under the burdens of Egypt and deliver you from their slavery" (Exod. 6:6).

The defining marks of Israelite identity are the exodus from Egypt and the revelation of the Torah (Hebrew for "instruction") at Mount Sinai. The two are inextricably linked, for the Decalogue begins, "I am the LORD your God, who brought you out from the land of Egypt, from the house of slavery" (Exod. 20:2). God liberates. People, in the divine image and likeness, should do the same.

The next chapter, Exodus 21 sets up laws designed not to free the enslaved, but to protect them. Ancient Israelite slavery primarily concerned indentured or bonded labor designed to pay off debts. It forbade slavery related to kidnapping; for example, Exodus 21:16 states, "Whoever kidnaps [literally 'steals'] a person, whether he has sold him or is holding him, should be put to death" (NJPS). Deuteronomy 24:7a restricts the command to enslaved Israelites: "If a person is found to have kidnapped [literally 'stolen'] the soul [Hebrew: *nefesh*] of his brother from the children of Israel, and his mistreats [i.e., enslaves] him and sells him, that kidnapper shall die."

Exodus 21:20–21 reveals how abusive the system could be: "When a man strikes an enslaved male or female with a rod and the enslaved person dies beneath his hand [i.e., immediately], that one [the enslaved] shall surely be avenged. But if the enslaved person survives a day or two days he stands, there is no avenging, because he [the enslaved one] is his owner's [the enslaver's] silver [property]." The same point holds for a parent striking a child. Should the owner permanently damage the body of the enslaved, manumission is required: "If a man [i.e., an enslaver] strikes the eye of his enslaved male or the eye of his enslaved female and destroys it, he must surely free that one to compensate for his [or her] eye. And if the tooth of his enslaved male or the tooth of his enslaved female, he causes to fall out, he must free and send out to compensate for his [or her] tooth" (Exod. 21:26–27). Violence, an ever-present threat for the enslaved of Jesus's time, was likely widespread in ancient Israel as well.

EXODUS AND ETHICS

Torah grounds morality on the Egyptian experience: "As a native [NJPS: 'one of your citizens'; NRSVUE: 'native-born'] among you shall be to you the ger [stranger/alien/migrant/immigrant]; the ger among you, you shall love him as yourself, for you were gerim in the land of Egypt" (Lev. 19:34; cf. Deut. 10:19). The problem is that the experience in Egypt was not simply that of an immigrant: under Joseph's government, Israel lived as immigrants; but in the later generation, they were enslaved. While ger is often translated "stranger" (NJPS) or "alien" (NRSVUE), the issue is primarily the distinction between being born into a community and someone who is an immigrant (ger). "Alien" can convey a sense of incompatibility, such and "alien environment"; "stranger" can convey the sense of being weird, or dangerous. Therefore, I prefer to use a translation suggesting immigration or migration.[4]

Three times Deuteronomy commands Israel to remember its former enslaved status, and each time the commandment undergirds ethical exhortation. For example, Deuteronomy 24:22 mandates, "Remember that you were enslaved in the land of Egypt" to ground social programs: "When you gather [the grapes of] your vineyard, do not glean what after you [i.e., left]; for the ger, the orphan, and the widow it shall be" (Deut. 24:21). When Israel was enslaved, the people were not treated fairly; therefore, they should not perpetuate unfair systems.

Deuteronomy 5:15 connects the keeping of the Sabbath to remembering being enslaved in Egypt. Yet the previous verse, Deuteronomy 5:14, also evoking Egyptian slavery, undercuts the ideal of freedom:

"the seventh day is a Sabbath to the LORD your God; you shall not do any work—you, and your son and your daughter, *and your enslaved man or your enslaved woman*, and your ox and your donkey, and any of your beasts, and your *ger* who is at your gates, *so that your enslaved man and enslaved woman may rest as well as you*" (emphasis added).

Deuteronomy 15 begins by announcing that every seventh year, debts shall be remitted, and it includes in this sabbatical the liberation of indentured slaves: "If your brother, whether a Hebrew man or a Hebrew woman, is sold to you and works [the same root is used for 'slavery'] for you six years, in the seventh year you shall send him [or her] out, free, from you" (Deut. 15:12).

This law expands Exodus 21, which mandates that enslaved males, but not females, are to be freed in the sabbatical year. The conceit is that these daughters would marry the purchaser or his son and in that way shift their status from enslaved to free. In 2 Kings 4:1, the wife of one of Elisha's "company of prophets" pleads with Elisha, "Your enslaved [Hebrew: *eved*; Greek: *doulos*, i.e., 'slave'] my husband is dead, and you know that your enslaved [*eved, doulos*] feared the LORD, but a creditor has come to take my two children as enslaved [Hebrew: *avadim*; Greek: *douloi*, the same words in the plural]." Today, parents who "sell" children for debt remission would be called, in most parts of the world, human-traffickers.[5] In antiquity, they would be pitied, not condemned. Perhaps their desperation, seen here with the dead prophet's wife, could help readers understand the desperation some of these parents today face.

Leviticus 25:39–40 (cf. Deut. 15:7–18) states that Israelites who become so impoverished that they sell themselves shall not be treated as if they were enslaved. Instead, they are to be regarded as "hired or bound laborers" (NJPS).[6] They are then released at the Jubilee, if they have not already worked out their debt. Thus, no Israelite can hold another in perpetual slavery.

However, if an enslaved man or woman insists, "I do not want to leave you" because "he loves you and your household, and is happy with you" (NJPS) then the householder shall pierce the person's earlobe with an awl into the door, indicating permanent enslaved status (Deut. 15:16–17).

Next, Deuteronomy 23:16–17 forbids returning any enslaved person to "his lord," whether or not the enslaved person is an Israelite, who seeks refuge; instead, they "shall live with you, among you, in the place that they choose, in one of your gates [i.e., towns], where it seems good to them; you shall not oppress them." This injunction is distinct among Near Eastern law codes.

Given the impending Babylonian attack on Jerusalem, the Judean king Zedekiah appears to have issued the first emancipation proclamation. According to Jeremiah 34:10, the king ordered all the population of Jerusalem, both the chiefs and the people as a whole, to proclaim liberty to enslaved men and enslaved women. The people complied. But when the threat passed, they reclaimed those they had enslaved. Jeremiah condemns this breach of covenantal responsibilities; because the people did not keep the promise of liberation, Jeremiah predicts military and ecological devastation.

Queen Esther tells her husband, the Persian king who signed a death warrant for the empire's Jews, "we have been sold, I and my people, to be destroyed, to be killed, and to be annihilated." For Esther, slavery, as dreadful as it is, is preferable to genocide: "If as enslaved men and enslaved women we had been sold, I would be silent" (Esther 7:4). Esther, who was trafficked (yes, I know that some will find this description a harsh judgment) by being taken by Persian authorities, marinated in myrrh for half a year, and then placed in the king's bed in the competition for a new queen, may well have understood the horrors of slavery. Yet Esther may also be saying whatever she thinks will persuade her drunken lout of a husband to stop the genocide. For others, to die free is preferable than to live enslaved.

The best that can be said is that "although the [Hebrew] Bible takes slavery as a given, it makes attempts to humanize the institution and even sporadically expresses how the world might be a better place without it."[7]

Hellenistic Jewish texts vary in their attitudes toward slavery. The Wisdom of Jesus ben Sirach, ca. 200 BCE, advises, "If you have one enslaved [Greek: *oiketēs*], let him be to you like yourself, because with blood you have bought him." Indeed, the enslaver is to treat him "like a brother, for you will need him as you need your soul" (Sir. 33:31–32). The motive is less compassion than self-interest. The verse does not consider the enslaver with hundreds or thousands of enslaved workers in the fields or mines. Sirach also commends torture for enslaved individuals who prove insolent or indolent: "Yoke and thong will bow the neck, and for a wicked one who is enslaved there are racks and tortures. Put him to work, so that he may not be idle" (Sir. 33:27–28).

The heroine Judith, whose story dates to ca. 150–100 BCE, frees her enslaved woman who had accompanied her (willingly?) into the enemy camp (so Jth. 16:23). The freedom is part of Judith's will. Judith, by the way, dies at age 105.

Despite apologetics to the contrary, Jewish households at the time of Jesus participated in the wider Roman imperial practices regarding slavery.[8] Later biblical texts, Philo, Josephus, and rabbinic literature regard it as normative.[9]

THE EXODUS BEYOND ISRAEL

The original exodus was more about God's promises to Abraham, Isaac, and Jacob than about abolition. The last plague, the death of the firstborn sons, encompassed "the firstborn of Pharaoh who sits on his throne to the firstborn of the enslaved [non-Israelite] woman who is behind the millstones" (Exod. 11:5). In celebrating the exodus, we do well to remember non-Israelites enslaved in Egypt, people who suffered the same fate as those who owned them.

Jewish communities have extended the exodus narrative to contemporary issues. For example, the Religious Action Center of Reform Judaism makes available "Invisible: The Story of Modern Day Slavery. A Passover Seder Supplement."[10] Although the exodus from Egypt is an Israelite and then a Jewish story, other groups also see themselves in the narrative. Instead of arguing that such readings are forms of cultural appropriation, I see them as indicating the power of the story. The non-Jewish followers of Jesus regarded themselves as "grafted" into Israel's story (Rom. 11:19) and as "adopted" by Israel's God (Rom. 8:15), and thereby they could also claim identity with enslaved and liberated Israel.[11] Recognizing this common history can help not only in Jewish-Christian relations today, but also in fostering collaborative programs in which all people should have an investment.[12]

THE ROMAN IMPERIAL CONTEXT

In the first century, at least one-third of the population of the Roman Empire was enslaved.[13] Human beings bought and sold and bred other human beings. The enslaved could enslave others; they could also, under auspicious circumstances, buy their own freedom. For some, slavery was preferable to being free but homeless and hungry. For others, such as the gladiator Spartacus, who led a revolt known as the Third Servile War, in 73–71 BCE—a war Voltaire called "the only just war in history"—it was not.

The New Testament enshrines slavery, both literal and metaphorical. Paul advises members of his assemblies to remain in the state in which they were called. To those enslaved, Paul advises that they not be concerned with their status: "For whoever was called in the Lord when enslaved is a freed person of the Lord, just as whoever was a freed person when called is enslaved of the Christ" (1 Cor. 7:22). Addressing enslaved members as "freed" in and by the Christ, Paul classifies himself—a freed person—as enslaved;[14] as with the scriptures of Israel, only people who are free self-identify as slaves of God. Perhaps the verse even hints at the possibility that Paul himself was from a family that had been enslaved.

The Epistle to the Ephesians (Eph. 6:5–6; cf. 1 Tim. 6:1–3), written in Paul's name, mandates in its household code (a literary form instructing masters/husbands/parents and enslaved/wives/children to maintain hierarchical relations), "Enslaved, obey the lords [from *kyrios*] according to the flesh [i.e., human enslavers] with fear and trembling . . . as [you obey] the Christ," and not only because you are being watched, but "as enslaved of Christ" (*hos douloi Christou*). The First Epistle of Peter (1 Pet. 2:18–21), directly addressing the enslaved, grants them divine approval for suffering unjustly, since the Christ did the same.

The book of Acts, likely dating to the early second century and thus one of the New Testament's latest books, three times relies on stories told at the expense of enslaved individuals. According to Acts 12, the followers of Jesus have gathered at the home of Mary, the mother of John Mark, after the Judean king Herod Agrippa I arrested Peter. An angel arranges Peter's prison break (it could happen) and delivers Peter to Mary's house. Peter knocks at the outer gate, and an "enslaved girl [*paidiskē*; NRSVUE: 'maid'] named Rhoda came to answer" (Acts 12:13). Overcome with joy at hearing Peter's voice, she rushes to tell the assembled worshipers that Peter is outside. She does not, however, open the gate. Mary and her friends, likely praying for Peter's release, accuse her of being insane (Acts 12:15) for making the unbelievable, to them, claim of the apostle's freedom. (We can see here one possible reason why Mark [16:8] depicts the women at the tomb fleeing silently and saying nothing to anyone: the claim of a resurrected, crucified man would have sounded insane.) Peter remains outside, still knocking. Finally, the gate is opened. Peter, likely frustrated, announces his release and leaves. Luke does not report anything more on Rhoda. She was right; the free worshipers were wrong; and yet for early readers, she reinforces the convention of the "running slave," foolish and scattered.[15]

Second, according to Acts 16:16, the narrator and Paul meet an enslaved girl, another *paidiskē* (NRSV: "slave girl," the same term that identifies Rhoda; NRSVUE, "female slave") who "had a spirit of divination" and therefore brought her owners (Greek: *kyrioi*, "lords") a great deal of money. The girl, possessed by the god Apollo (it could happen), announces to the narrator and Paul, "These are enslaved [*douloi*] of the Most High God, who proclaim to you a way of salvation" (Acts 16:17). The *paidiskē* is enslaved both to her earthly masters and to the god who possesses her (bad); Paul and the narrator are enslaved to (the one) God (good). Acts then triples the girl's enslavement when Paul, annoyed at her involuntary gift of free advertising, commands the spirit possessing her, "in the name of Jesus Christ" to "come out of her" (Acts 16:18). Her owners' consequent loss of income prompts them to get Paul arrested. F. Scott Spencer summarizes, "He shuts her up, puts her out of work, and then the story drops her completely."[16]

Third, Acts 20:9 mentions a young man named Eutychus: the name, meaning "good fortune" or "lucky," could be that of an enslaved person. Sitting in an upper-story window, Eutychus listens to Paul speak, and speak, and speak. Unable to keep from sleeping, the unlucky Eutychus falls three stories down and dies. Paul, ever helpful, raises the boy back to life.[17] The assembly returns to the room, eats, and then Paul speaks on until morning. The warning against preaching too long comes at the expense of Eutychus.

These stories take their place among the countless others that make humiliation or torture matters of amusement (I was never a fan of the Three Stooges, Tom and Jerry, or the Road Runner).

Now that we have the context in which slavery is normative, we turn to how Jesus interacted with enslaved individuals and their owners, and how we might want to interact with those stories.

JESUS ON SLAVERY

Jesus encounters enslaved individuals, presents the enslaved as figures in parables, and exhorts his followers to act as enslaved to each other. Yet the subject of Jesus and slavery has not until recently been a subject of much scholarly discussion.[18]

There are at least five reasons for this silence. The first reason why we have, until recently, heard so little about biblical slavery is that translations frequently mask the presence of the enslaved. For example, as the brief discussion above of Acts shows, the New Revised Standard Version of the Bible (NRSV) characterizes Rhoda as a "maid" and Paul's advertiser as a "slave girl," but the same Greek term (*paidiskē*) is employed in both instances. The updated edition of the New Revised Standard Version of the Bible (NRSVUE) reads, "female slave" for the character with the spirit of divinization; Rhoda remains a "maid."

Instead of translating the Greek *doulos* and the Hebrew *eved* consistently as "slave," numerous versions offer "servant."[19] *Doulos* and related terms appear 118 times in the New Testament, far more than my students suppose. Mary the mother of Jesus famously describes herself, in the King James Version, as the "handmaid [Greek: *doulē*] of the Lord" (Luke 1:38), a designation that continues to appear in modern translations. Today, with the popularity of the novel and then television series *The Handmaid's Tale*, one might have thought that "handmaid" in relation to Mary would be canceled.[20] The NRSVUE uses "servant." In case we missed the image at the beginning of Mary's Magnificat in Luke (Luke 1:46–55), it reappears again when Mary exults, "he has looked with favor on the lowliness of his slave" (*doulē*; Luke 1:48). Again the NRSVUE offers "servant." "Servant" suggests to me someone on the payroll, not a member of the household, and not one to carry the child of the employer. The enslaved image is, for Luke, one of total dedication, since Mary willingly gives her body to serve divine purposes. I do wonder what enslaved women in Roman households, impregnated with their enslaver's child, might think upon hearing Luke's Gospel.[21]

Mary is not the only faithful figure who self-identifies as enslaved. In the Jerusalem temple, she meets Simeon, a "righteous and devout" man (Luke 2:25) upon whom, according to Luke, the "Holy Spirit" rested. Simeon takes the infant Jesus in his arms and begins his psalm, "Master [*despotēs*, whence the English 'despot'], now you are dismissing your enslaved man [*doulos*] in peace, according to your word" (Luke 2:29). Most English translations again offer "servant." The image is of God as the enslaver and Simeon as enslaved. Hence, "dismiss" is not to a life of freedom, but to death.

Paul calls himself the enslaved (*doulos*) of Jesus Christ (e.g., Rom. 1:1; Gal. 1:10; Phil. 1:1), and Titus 1:1 identifies Paul as enslaved of God. Most translations read "servant," but "enslaved" is the better translation, since Paul sees himself as belonging to God. "Enslaved of God" also is applied, among others, to Moses and David, prophets and kings, and even Israel.[22] While we speak of the "suffering servant" described by Isaiah 53 and applied by several New Testament passages to Jesus,[23] Isaiah 53:11 reads, in the Hebrew, *eved*, "enslaved"; the Greek (Septuagint) offers a verbal form of *doulos*, "to serve as one enslaved."

In the run-up to the Emancipation Proclamation in 1863, some clergy argued, on the basis of the King James Version of the Bible, that "*If they*—that is, Moses, David, Paul, etc.—*were slaves, the translators* of our Bible *would have called them so*" (emphasis in the original).[24]

Some of Jesus's teachings lose their punch because of translators' hesitancy to see Jesus as approving of slavery. John 15:15a in most translations quotes Jesus telling his disciples, "I do not call you servants any longer, because the servant does not know what the master is doing, but I have called you friends" (NRSVUE). The Greek reads *douloi*; the NRSVUE notes that "slaves" is a legitimate translation. The association between discipleship and slavery makes sense in historical context: like people who are enslaved, Jesus's disciples are, to return to Patterson's definition, "natally alienated" in that they break with their biological families to join Jesus; Jesus reinforces this break when he creates, at the cross, a new parent-child relationship between his mother and his beloved disciple. The disciples are also "generally dishonored," as Jesus tells them, "Blessed are you when they reproach you and persecute and speak all kinds of evil against you [some manuscripts add 'falsely'] on my account" (Matt. 5:11).

A second reason the enslaved go missing in the Gospels is that we readers do not see them.[25] Although the analogy is not entirely accurate, this overlooking is comparable to how those in privileged positions fail to notice people in service industries: hotel housekeepers, custodians, restaurant servers, and so on. In the Parable of the Prodigal Son, we miss the enslaved individual who informs the older brother that the father has prepared a feast (Luke 15:26–27). In missing the enslaved one, we miss the irony when the older son says to his father, "For so many years I have been serving you like one enslaved, and I have never passed by your command" (Luke 15:29). The older son sounds clueless as to the social positions of the enslaved, given that "ancient law did not recognize slaves as having fathers" and that "a male slave, for example, had no legal connection to his own offspring, thus excluding him from the cultural status of fatherhood."[26] The older brother feels alienated; the enslaved *are* alienated.

The third reason we overlook the enslaved in the Gospels is the tendency, already begun by the evangelists if not by Jesus himself, to allegorize them into representatives of apostles, disciples, evangelists, and the faithful. For example, in the Parable of the Weeds and the Wheat (Matt. 13:24–30), enslaved agricultural workers ask the "lord" (*kyrios*), "Did you not sow good seed in your field? From where, then, has it weeds?" (Matt. 13:27). These enslaved characters become, in our imagination, apostles or church leaders; the weeds and the wheat are the apostates and the faithful.

A corollary to this approach, our fourth reason the presence of the enslaved gets overlooked, is the theologizing of the language of enslavement. For example, correctly reading Paul's language, one commentator explains, "Real slavery results from sin; therefore, believers, who have been 'purchased' by God, must avoid carnal enslavement to others."[27] Marianne Bjelland Kartzow notes that for Jesus's followers, "for a free person to be called 'Christ's slave' was considered an honor and normally did not affect his or her physical body, social status, or life conditions. . . . [Here] Paul is replacing social reality with metaphor in a way that did not necessarily work in real life for real people. Of course, real slavery could trouble the slave of the Lord."[28] Enslaved people in the Roman Empire did not have the opportunity to "avoid carnal enslavement to others."

Finally, some commentators who have looked at the Gospels' slave language tend to find "good news" and so mitigate the horrors of the institution. J. Albert Harrill summarizes approaches that conclude, "ancient slavery was relatively humane and so wholly unlike modern slavery in the New World."[29] "Wholly unlike" is not quite right; were it correct, Patterson's definition would not hold across the centuries.

Numerous articles that begin along the lines of "slavery in the first century was quite different from slavery in early American history"[30]—for example, ancient slavery was not based on race; enslaved individuals in antiquity, especially in households, had a greater chance at manumission than did the enslaved in the United States[31]—are historically correct. However, rhetorically they sometimes work to exculpate the biblical text. Keith Bradley summarizes: "Christian ideology, it must be said, did not lead as far as can be told to any radically progressive social change at all. One reason is that modern ideas of social leveling or egalitarianism were completely alien to ancient mentality."[32]

Some commentators conclude that Jesus's parables concerning slaves and comparisons of his and the disciples' roles to that of slaves show an improvement in the understanding of slaves: Jesus notices slaves and therefore does not ignore them. Speaking of Luke's Gospel, one commentator offers, "The parables reveal the same sensitivity to outsiders and the socially marginalized, whether it be slaves (e.g., Luke 12:35–38), women (Luke 15:8–10; 13:20–21; 18:1–7), or children (Luke 7:31–35; 11:11–13)."[33] Not all women or children are "outsiders" or "socially marginalized" as Herodias and her dancing daughter indicate. The citation is to Jesus's blessing of the enslaved (that is, the disciples) "waiting for their lord [*kyrios*] . . . so that they may open the door for him as soon as he comes and knocks" (Luke 12:36).

That Jesus sees enslaved individuals as having both initiative and a moral compass is nothing new.[34] Already the stories of Aesop, an enslaved man, challenged the idea that the enslaved were automatons.

From Greek and Roman antiquity, *including the Gospels*, come numerous accounts of enslaved individuals being beaten, tortured, branded, maimed, and killed. The Roman philosophers Seneca (*Di Ira* 3.24) and Martial (*Epigrams* 3.94) condemned excessive violence meted out to the enslaved; they had reason to do so. Tacitus notes that the Germans rarely beat those whom they enslaved (*Germania* 25), which implied that Romans had no such qualms. Juvenal satirizes a matron who mercilessly whips enslaved members of her household for failing to comb her hair correctly (*Satires* 6.474–501).[35]

Commentators continue to insist that Jesus challenges "the first-century norms and values of slavery in radical terms."[36] He did not. Jesus's depiction of enslaved people in his parables supports rather than undermines Roman imperial values,[37] which is why "antislavery and abolitionist crusaders" had to wrestle with the fact that Jesus did not condemn slavery.[38] In antiquity, "There was never any sustained opposition to slavery, and the new religion of Christianity probably reinforced rather than challenged its existence."[39]

Finally, the common assertion, "it is plain that the NT [New Testament] writers simply could not outright condemn slavery,"[40] is incorrect. Josephus states that the Essenes reject slavery (*Antiquities* 18.21) as unjust, and Philo describes the Therapeutae (masculine) and Therapeutrides (feminine), Jewish ascetics who lived in adjoining dormitories and met for communal meals, Bible study, and antiphonal prayer, as finding slavery to be contrary to nature (*On the Contemplative Life* 70–72). In *Special Laws* (2.67–68), Philo writes that both enslaved men and women do not work on the Sabbath in anticipation of both the freedom they will achieve by serving well and full freedom for everyone. Not everyone agreed with Aristotle that to be enslaved was "natural."[41] Moreover, Jesus's followers did manage to impose change on social structures; for example, Paul forbids gentile members of the assemblies from worshiping their local gods, suggests that eating meat offered to idols is not a good idea, and is seriously displeased with sexually engaging with prostitutes (who may well have been enslaved).

Some Christian readers have suggested to me that Jesus did not realize the evils of slavery because he knew no enslaved people. Rather, he was familiar with day laborers, such as those who appear in his Parable of the Laborers in the Vineyard in Matthew 20:1–16 or the "hired men" (*misthōtoi*; i.e., wage earners) who worked alongside the apostles James and John in their father's boat (Mark 1:20). Even if he did not come into contact with enslaved people in the smaller villages of lower Galilee, he would have seen them in his trips to Jerusalem and heard about them in the stories of his scriptures. Moreover, his parables reveal, all too clearly, the horrors of slavery.

Yet the stories about Jesus, and stories told by Jesus, are invitations for rereading the Gospels. Importing our own sensibilities into an ancient text is how we read; we should do the history, but we should not, especially if we read to find guidance for today, check our morality at the door of the church, synagogue, or classroom. We can attend to the enslaved in the Gospels. Noticing them is a first step; realizing that we have overlooked them is the next; and being open to what they might, after two millennia, teach us about issues such as freedom, torture, power, and options is the third.

THE CENTURION'S "BOY"

In Luke 7:2–10, we meet Jesus as he enters Capernaum:

> And of a centurion was one enslaved [*doulos*], doing badly and about to die, who was to him highly valued/esteemed. And hearing about Jesus, he sent to him elders of the Jews to ask him if, coming, he might save his enslaved one. And coming to Jesus, they urged him, earnestly, saying, "Worthy is this one that you would grant to him this, for he loves our nation [*ethnos*] and the synagogue this one built for us." And Jesus went with them.
>
> And when he was not far off from the house, sent friends, the centurion, saying to him, "Lord [*kyrios*] do not trouble, for not am I worthy that you would come under my roof. Therefore, neither did

I count myself worthy to you to come. But say a word, and cause
to be healed my boy [*pais*].

"For even I am a person under authority being placed, having
under me soldiers. And I say to this one, go, and he goes, and to
another come, and he comes. And to my enslaved, do this, and
he does."

And hearing these [words], Jesus marveled at him, and turning
to the ones following him, the crowd, he said, "I say to you, not
even in Israel this faith/trust have I found."

And returning to the house, the ones sent found the enslaved
one [*doulos*] healthy.

This story opens with a centurion, a Roman army officer, who
dispatches Jewish elders to Jesus to request that he heal his *doulos*,
who is "doing badly and about to die." The setup is a standard healing
narrative. The ailing person is not the daughter of a synagogue ruler
(Mark 5:22–23) or a Syrophoenician woman (Mark 7:26), but an enslaved individual. Luke 7:2 describes the enslaved individual as *enti-
mos*, which most versions translate as "highly valued" (e.g., NRSVUE:
"valued highly"). This rendering suggests to me an expensive piece of
furniture and so conveys the impression that the enslaved individual
is property. Luke uses the same term in 14:8, where Jesus instructs,
"When you are called by someone to a wedding banquet, do not sit
down at the place of honor, in case someone *entimoteros* than you has
been invited by the one who called you." The NRSVUE translates the
comparative form of the word as "more distinguished." Since *timē*
means "honor," the translation in Luke 14:8 is closer to the mark. I
sense a difference between calling a person "highly valued" or "precious" and calling a person "distinguished" or "honored."

The elders make their plea by foregrounding not the ailing one's
usefulness to the centurion, but the centurion's friendship to their

community. They tell Jesus, "Worthy is this one that you would grant to him, for he loves our nation [*ethnos*] and the synagogue this one built for us" (Luke 7:4–5). Given that the centurion is a Roman officer, these elders may see themselves, ironically, as enslaved to the centurion in that he has made them an offer they cannot refuse. The story now raises questions of patron-client relations. The centurion is the patron who donates the synagogue; in return, he expects clients, the elders, to do favors for him, from praising his generosity (here we recall the debtors in the Parable of the Dishonest Manager discussed in Chapter 2) to, in this case, approaching Jesus for a favor. In part, this system gives the clients some autonomy, in that they can choose whether or not to honor their patron; in part, it gives the patrons more control, in that they have bought loyalty. The account also raises questions about labor, since it is unlikely the centurion built the synagogue himself by hand; he works for Rome, not for Habitat for Humanity. Perhaps that treasured but ailing enslaved man was involved in the construction.

Jesus assents to the elders' request. As he approaches the centurion's home, the centurion sends another delegation, this time of "friends," to say to Jesus in his name, "not am I worthy that you would come under my roof" (Luke 7:6). The elders are clients, not "friends." Now the story invites us to consider our relationships with the people we regularly encounter: Is the barber or butcher a "friend," or is a friendly attitude a good business practice? Are students "friends" of the faculty? Are congregants "friends" of the clergy? Indeed, can unequals be friends?

Commentators sometimes argue that the centurion, by speaking of his lack of worth, is respecting Jewish practice, since "we need to remember that Jesus, a rabbi, would be rendered unclean if he were to go into the home of a gentile."[42] This argument is based on Peter's comment in Acts 10:28: "You yourselves know that it is unlawful for a Jew to associate with or to visit a Gentile; but God has shown me that

I should not call anyone profane or unclean." The problem here is that Peter was wrong. There is no law forbidding Jews from associating with gentiles or visiting them in their homes. Entering the door does not make one "unclean." If associating with gentiles were forbidden, it makes no sense to welcome them into synagogues or the Jerusalem temple. Nor did those elders who petitioned Jesus have a problem with purity laws. Nicholas Schaser correctly observes, "Peter's misunderstanding provides Luke with the theological rationale for Paul to take the missionary mantle from Peter as the apostle to the Gentiles."[43] Jews (broadly defined) could and did associate with gentiles.

The elders see the centurion as "worthy" because of what he did; the centurion dismisses his own self-worth because of who he is, that is, part of the Roman military system. The centurion's comment about his lack of worth, spoken through his friends, makes me wonder about how our assessment may change depending on need, on circumstances, on talents, and—as we saw with our rich friends in the previous chapter—on assets.

Asserting that Jesus needs only to proclaim the healing from a distance, the centurion now, through his friends, refers to "my boy" (Luke 7:7). Is "boy" a term of affection? Is it an indication of age, so that this highly valued enslaved individual is ten years old, or fourteen? Or is the enslaved one an adult, with the term "boy" used to infantilize him, or to express power over him?

Again through his proxies, the centurion describes his place in the military: he too is under authority, and others are under his authority. Thus, he can command soldiers to go or to come, and they will obey him. On the one hand, the centurion locates himself within a system that looks something like slavery: he is "placed under authority" and so knows how it feels to be ordered. The enslaved and the enlisted can choose to disobey commands, but always at their peril. Nor does the centurion suggest that the military system is unfair, so he would have no reason to see slavery as unfair either. On the other hand, although he is a master, with regard to his "esteemed boy," his commands will go unheeded. The enslaved individual, ill in body, is physically incapable of obeying them. At least the centurion does not hold him responsible for his illness or beat him for not following orders.

Jesus turns the discussion from suffering enslaved to ethnic observation: "not even in Israel this faith/trust have I found" (Luke 7:9). He finds that the centurion, unlike his fellow Jews, displays trust in his authority, since the Greek *pistis* means both "trust" and "faith."

Jesus never meets the centurion or sees the enslaved individual. The story ends with the messengers, the "friends," returning to the house and finding the enslaved one restored to health (Luke 7:10). The likely end of the story, one that Luke does not record, is that the household returns to the status quo. The centurion will say "do this," and the "boy" will obey. The centurion becomes the model of piety, not of liberation or egalitarianism. The takeaway from the story becomes, "gentile soldiers are better than the Jews," and not the relationship between slavery and colonialism.

Another common takeaway is that the story shows Jesus modeling the command to "love your enemies," since any Jew would find members of the Roman military to be enemies.[44] Again, I doubt it. The centurion who builds a synagogue is not an enemy but a patron. Were he an enemy, then it would be the Jewish elders who are modeling that love. In the New Testament, as in life, some soldiers are enemy combatants and some are peacekeepers; much depends on who is making the determination.

I do not read the centurion as an enemy, but I have a hard time regarding him as a role model. This resistance is a result of my own culture, for I doubt that Luke's readers had anything but admiration for him. I resist seeing the centurion as a model because he is an enslaver. Do we excuse the people who owned other people in the past because they were not as enlightened as we are or because they did not beat those they enslaved? Today we strip names of enslavers off buildings, and we remove from public squares statues of people who enslaved others. How, then, do we assess either the centurion, who enslaves, or Jesus, who praises him?

Matthew 8:5–13 offers a parallel to this story, but Matthew's version describes not first a *doulos* but a *pais*, the same term used in Luke 7:7, which could mean "child" or "boy"; it can indicate someone who is enslaved, but that is not a necessary reading. For Luke, the individual is clearly enslaved, because of the opening word of *doulos*. In John's iteration of the same story (John 4:46–54), the supplicant is a "royal" (Greek: *basilikos*) who asks about his "son" (*hious*). Perhaps John was uncomfortable with the notion that Jesus would perform a miracle for a member of the Roman military.

The various versions, with their language of "boy," raise yet one more social and political concern. In 2004, two faculty members at Chicago Theological Seminary published, in the well-regarded *Journal of Biblical Literature*, an article on Matthew 8 that sought "to demonstrate the plausibility of reading the centurion's *pais* as his 'boy-love' within a pederastic relationship."[45] Although their thesis has been questioned,[46] the suggestion that the slave's "paralysis" was related to a sexual encounter reminds us not only of the vulnerability of the bodies of the enslaved, but also of the trauma that results from sexual violence. The enslaved character in this story does not appear and does not speak. But the text invites us to give him words.

THE INJURED MAN ENSLAVED TO THE HIGH PRIEST

The only enslaved person Jesus explicitly encounters in the Gospels appears, once again, as injured or ailing. Mark 14:47 describes how, as Jesus is arrested in Gethsemane, one of "those who stood near" took a sword and severed the ear of the high priest's *doulos*.

The victim could have been Caiaphas's agent, a spectator, or a disciple (the descriptions are not mutually exclusive). The evangelists are much more interested in who wielded the sword, and in Jesus's healing, than in the enslaved man himself. Each Gospel then adds details. Matthew 26:51 adds that the perpetrator was "one of those with Jesus." Luke 22:51 has Jesus respond, "No more of this!" and then touch the ear to heal it. While Luke may be suggesting that Jesus wants to end violence, it is more likely that Jesus is seeking to prevent his disciples from fighting the arrest and so being obstacles to his fate.[47]

Finally, John 18:10 outs Simon Peter as the one with the sword; names the *doulos* Malchus, a name that ironically derives from the Hebrew word for "king"; and states that Peter lopped off his ear. At the end of the incident, while Malchus again has two good ears to hear, thanks to Jesus's ability to heal, he remains in the state in which he is called.

The name "king" anticipates the inscription on the cross, "King of the Jews," and reminds us that Jesus dies the humiliating and painful death meted out to those who were enslaved, and that his body will be restored. As M. Shawn Copeland points out, death by crucifixion was "the mark of the criminal and the slave."[48]

ENSLAVED CHARACTERS IN PARABLES

Already noted are the enslaved characters in the parables of the Weeds and the Wheat and the Prodigal Son. They also appear in the parables of the Unforgiving Enslaved Man (Matt. 18:23–35), the Wicked Tenants (Mark 12:1–12; Matt. 21:33–42; Luke 20:9–10), the Great Feast or Wedding Banquet (Luke 14:15–24 // Matt. 22:1–14), the Wise and Foolish Enslaved People (Matt. 24:45–51; Luke 12:35–48), the Enslaved Who Serves as Expected (Luke 17:7–10), and the Talents/Pounds (Matt. 25:14–31; cf. Luke 19:11–28). Each parable presents slavery as normative, and each has become so domesticated that we often miss its violence.

In these parables, enslaved people are shamed (Matt. 22:6), beaten (Matt. 21:35; 24:49), dismembered (Matt. 24:51), tortured (Matt. 18:34; 24:51; 25:30), killed (Matt. 21:35; 22:6), and stoned (Matt. 21:35). Most of my students never notice; few express discomfort. And when discomfort arises, readers rush to allegorize: the enslaved individual is a prophet or a disciple. Or, we conclude that the violence of these parables must be justifiable, because we identify the perpetrator as God, and God must be just.

Such enslaved characters function like the hapless ensigns in the original *Star Trek*: the poor schnook is going to be phasered, tasered, eaten, incinerated, or assimilated. We find such scenes conventional; we become indifferent to the fate of minor characters or we enjoy the variations on the scene. We've not much changed from "Greco-Roman audiences [who] regarded as hilarious the spectacle of a slave facing dire threats of extravagant tortures."[49]

We need not be enslaved to such images. By interrogating their appearances in parables, we can instead find new freedom. We cannot rescue Jesus from failing to condemn slavery, but when we approach the parables as speaking about real people who were enslaved and real people who enslaved them, real bodies broken and real lives destroyed, we engage/confront the ethics of the parables, and of our own lives. Our focus is not on the numerous interpretations of each parable, which speak variously to anti-Jewish interpretations, gender issues, and broader economic concerns; instead, we look at what we learn from their depictions of enslaved people.

The Wicked Tenants

This parable, which could just as easily be called the Parable of Victims and Victimizers, appears in multiple forms (Mark 12:1–12; see also Matt. 21:33–42; Luke 20:9–19; Gospel of Thomas 65–66). Here is Mark's version, likely the earliest account:

> A man planted a vineyard, and he placed around it a fence, and he dug a trench and built a (watch)tower, and he gave it over to farmers, and he went away. And at the appropriate time he sent to the farmers an enslaved person so that from the farmers he might receive the fruits of his vineyard. And taking him, they beat (him) [the Greek can also mean "skinned" or "flayed"] and sent him away empty. And again, he sent to them another enslaved person. And that one they beat on his head and dishonored. And another he sent, and that one they killed, and more others, some they are beating, and some they are killing. Yet one, he had, a son, beloved. He sent him last to them, saying, "They will respect my son." But those farmers said to themselves, "This one is the heir. Come, let us kill him, and to us will be the inheritance." And taking, they killed him, and they cast him out of the vineyard.
>
> What therefore will the lord [kyrios] of the vineyard do? He will come and he will destroy the farmers, and he will give the vineyard to others. [Luke here adds the crowds' response, "no way!"—the only use of the expression, usually translated "by no means!" or "heaven forbid!," outside Paul's letters.]

The scene concludes with Jesus's opponents (for Mark and Luke, the scribes and the chief priests; for Matthew, the odd combination of chief priests and Pharisees) recognizing that Jesus told the parable against them.[50]

Many if not most interpreters understand the "lord of the vineyard" to be God and connect the "beloved son" to Jesus (a connection difficult to miss); as the son is cast out of the vineyard, so Jesus is crucified outside Jerusalem. Yet when the lord displays anger, it is over the death of his son, not the deaths of the people he enslaved. Rarely do interpreters consider this lord's lack of concern about the enslaved characters who are beaten, flayed, dishonored, or killed. Most move straight to allegory: the enslaved characters represent Israel's prophets.[51] That most prophets were not killed is a minor glitch.

The same allegorical reading holds for the Parable of the Wedding Banquet in Matthew 22:1–14, which describes how guests who refuse the king's invitation seized, insulted, and killed the king's enslaved representative (Matt. 22:6). So the king "sent his troops, destroyed those murderers, and burned their city" (Matt. 22:7). More death, now with destruction. The allegorical takeaway for Matthew 22:1–14 is that the murderers represent Jerusalem's Jews, responsible for Jesus's death (see Matt. 27:25), and the destroyed city is Jerusalem—burned by the Romans in 70 CE. Or, commentators invent a context: "Matthew, stirred no doubt by synagogue persecution, adds to the parable of the Feast that they 'seized his slaves, humiliated them, and killed them.'"[52] "No doubt" is not an argument. Why members of a synagogue persecuted the followers of Jesus goes unaddressed (most likely, these followers were telling gentiles to stop worshiping their local gods, to stop eating meat offered to idols, and so to reject the gods of their families, their cities, and their empire; such proclamations would have endangered local Jewish communities). The comment takes away the focus on the brutality and transfers it to the persecuting synagogue.

The allegorical move to make the abused and the killed prophets and disciples also requires a jump in the characters' self-identification. Prophets and disciples know they are doing the right thing; they are aware that they may be persecuted or martyred. Yet the enslaved people in the parables are abused not for descrying social evils or for condemning exploitation; they are abused for performing their assigned tasks. Dying for God is not the same thing as dying for the man who inherited you or bought you in the agora.

A few commentators attempt to subvert the allegory by setting the Parable of the Wicked Tenants in the context of Galilean tenant farming. Proposing that the fields had been taken over by Jerusalem elites to whom the owners defaulted on debts, they see the tenants as landowners now reduced to sharecroppers. Their violence is thus a response to the violence inflicted on them.[53] I remain unconvinced that the parable "functions as a peasant's satire of political economy where the landowner is impotent and foolish, and the vineyard tenants are vindicated," especially given the deaths of the enslaved and the son (murder is difficult for me to set aside).[54] Then again, I've not been a homeowner forced to pay the banker who foreclosed on my mortgage.

The hypothetical model of the oppressed peasants, which has nothing to do with what the tenants say, fails because of slavery. Jennifer Glancy observes that "to argue that the tenants act as oppressed persons rising against a powerful and wealthy opponent, [commentators] must ignore the inconvenient description of the owner's agents as slaves."[55] Or, the allegory requires ignoring that these so-called oppressed peoples, rather than taking down their oppressors, instead assault/scapegoat the even-more oppressed enslaved messengers.

Outside of the allegory, I cannot find a satisfactory explanation for the "lord's" lack of concern for those he enslaved. I try to empathize with the tenants. I cannot. Had the tenants said to the enslaved messengers, "We need this food, because we are starving," I'd join Team Tenant. But refusing to turn over produce is not the same thing as beating, or killing, the messengers. In these cases, the end does not justify the means. In the end, no one wins: the enslaved messengers lose; the farmers lose; the lord loses, and few things are worse than losing a beloved child.

The increasing violence, and the increasing horror of the parable, removed from its various allegorical interpretations, again helps us to ask the right questions. For example, the parable asks why we expend resources when there's no chance of success. We send troops to fight hopeless battles. We send expendable agents (i.e., soldiers) rather than engage in face-to-face negotiations. We resist negotiation, because it is easier to demonize than to discuss. Can we imagine ourselves as one of the tenants or one of the enslaved, as the lord or his son? Can we imagine what we could have done differently, at each step? If we can, we are better prepared for situations that can escalate into violence.

Next, although I am not convinced that the landowner exploited the farmers, overcharged for their grain, and/or expropriated their land, the parable can critique the surety that wealth brings. At the parable's end, the owner—having lost his assets and his heir—now leases his vineyard to new tenants. He had no more guarantee as to whether this new group will fulfill their obligations. What has he learned—and what have we learned—from the death and destruction?

Finally, and to me of greatest import: Can we see the enslaved characters, tortured and killed, and ignored, as those whose lives today are considered of lesser import and then recognize that they too are in the image and likeness of God? Is it only when the *heir* is killed that action should be taken? The modern analogy: the poor Black or brown child disappears, and no one notices; but when the victim is white and rich, the country pays attention.

Wise and Foolish Enslaved People and the Enslaved Individual Who Serves as Expected

The most prominent use of "enslaved" as a metaphor for discipleship occurs in John's version of the Last Supper, where Jesus "takes [his] garment [off], wraps a cloth around himself, pours water into a washbasin, and begins to wash the feet of the disciples and to wipe [them] with the cloth that was wrapped around him" (John 13:4–5). Peter protests: the action is entirely inappropriate for his lord.

Jesus explains: "If I, your Lord and Teacher, have washed your feet, you also ought to wash one another's feet" (John 13:14). He then pronounces, "an enslaved person [doulos] is not greater than his lord [kyrios], nor is the one sent [apostolos; whence 'apostle'] greater than the one who sent him" (John 13:16). The statement appears to be John's rewording of Matthew 10:24, "A disciple is not above the teacher, nor an enslaved person [doulos] above the lord [kyrios]." Luke 6:40 offers another rewording, "Not is a disciple above the teacher, but every disciple who is fully qualified will be like the teacher." In the context of John's Gospel, the enslaved figure is Jesus; the lord is God (the Father), just as Jesus is the one sent and God (the Father) is the one who sent him. Jesus can act as one enslaved because he knows "that the Father had given all things into his hands and that he had come from God and was going to God" (John 13:3). His slavery is both voluntary and temporary. This connection to the lives of the enslaved may have been sustaining to those who were enslaved: Jesus gets them. It may have given them hope of freedom, if not in this life then in the next. For others, it might have been a sad joke.

This foot-washing scene does not appear in the Synoptic Gospels (Matthew, Mark, and Luke), but a parable presenting a similar scenario does. It seems likely to me that John, uninterested in parables (there are no parables in John's Gospel), turned the parable into an action, just as John turned the centurion of Matthew 8 // Luke 7 into a "royal official" and his doulos into his "son." Luke 12:35–48 (cf. Matt. 24:45–51), in a literal translation, has Jesus teach:

"Being with your waists wrapped around [i.e., having cloths wrapped around your waists] and [having your] lamps being lit.

And you are like people who are waiting for their lord [*kyrios*],
when he might return from the wedding feast, so that when he
comes, even knocking, immediately they may open [the door]
to him.

"Blessed are those enslaved to whom the lord, coming, will
find awake! Blessed are those enslaved whom the lord [*kyrios*]
finds on the alert when he comes. Amen, I say to you, that he will
dress himself and have them recline at table, and coming, will
serve [*diakoneō*] them.

"If in the second or even in the third watch he might come and
find them so, blessed are those [enslaved]." . . . And the lord said,
"Who then is the faithful and prudent [or 'shrewd' from *phronimos*]
manager [*oikonomos*] whom the lord will put in charge over his
house servants [*therapeioi*] to give at the proper time the food
allotment? Blessed is that enslaved one [*doulos*] for whom, when
his lord comes, he will find him doing thus. Truly I say to you, that
over all his possessions he will put him in charge.

"But if that enslaved one might have said in his heart, 'Is
delayed my lord in coming,' and if he begin to beat the other
enslaved males [*paidas*] and enslaved females [*paidiskas*], and to
eat and to drink and to get drunk, the lord of that enslaved one
will come on a day when he does not expect him, and at an hour
that he does not know, and he [the lord] will cut him in pieces, and
he will put his part with the unfaithful. That enslaved one, the one
knowing the will of the lord and neither preparing nor doing his
will, will be beaten much. But the one not knowing, doing what
was worthy of blows, will be beaten little. And from everyone to
whom has been given much, much will be sought from him; and
from the one to whom has been set before [i.e., entrusted] much,
even more they will ask of him."

The parable relies on several images from the Roman cultural repertoire. First is what could be called "when the master's away," known in Roman comedy as *absente ero*.[56] Second is the debased, debauched enslaved. Both Greek and Roman texts offer the prevailing idea that enslaved people are venal.[57] A third image of the enslaved is the bully, known as the *villicus*, who does what bullies do: he "terrorizes everyone under his control, rural and urban alike."[58] Such behavior then shamed the enslavers, seen as unable to control those in their charge. Finally, "Aristocratic Roman households had on-staff professional torturers [*lorarii*], and torture facilities and at-home services were available for hourly hire."[59] The enslaved feared not only the enslaver, but each other.

A few readers have problems with such images. The 1952 Revised Standard Version resisted the idea of physical mutilation—"cut him in two" is not a metaphor—and so translated *dixotemēsei* (Matt. 24:51 // Luke 12:46) as "punish."[60] The NRSV's "cut him in pieces" is a bit better, but it still sounds metaphorical. It also offers "cut him off" as an alternative, which sounds more to me like what a rich daddy does to the child who has just failed a fifth stint in rehab.

The enslaved bully who takes advantage of his position, or who drinks what he wants and treats the bodies of other enslaved members of the household as he wants, finds himself cast out or beaten. The fate is the same as that of the enslaved messengers in the previous parable, yet a number of my students see the punishment of this *villicus* as appropriate. Is undeserved beating a problem but *deserved* beating less so? I have a problem with the idea that beating—from spanking to torturing—anyone is a good idea. Perhaps our thoughts on this question depend on how we were raised.

Luke tells us, "That enslaved one [*doulos*], the one knowing the will of the lord [*kyrios*] and neither preparing nor doing his will,

will be beaten much. But the one not knowing, doing what was worthy of blows, will be beaten little." Unhelpful is the notice that Luke 12:47–48 shows "gradations of punishment characteristic of Jewish piety,"[61] since Jewish piety is not about punishment meted out on a curve. Similarly unhelpful is the notice, from ethicists, that Luke 12:42–46 // Matthew 24:45–51 shows us "judgment on unjust domination."[62] If an enslaved person's beating of another enslaved person is unjust, so should anyone beating anyone be unjust.

Then there is the prudent enslaved person who anticipates what is required: "The good slave (*servus frugi*) completed and developed what the master had only suggested or even unconsciously desired—a task that in the practice of Roman slaveholding encourages the actual slave to develop moral intuition."[63] The point was not to earn a reward, as the rabbinic document Pirke Avot 1.3, here in reference to fidelity to God, also avers: "Do not be like the enslaved [*avadim*] who attend the great one [*rav*, 'master' or 'teacher'] for the sake of receiving a reward; rather be like the enslaved who attend their great one without that expectation" (Jesus was not the only one to invoke the language of slavery in a positive sense). Service should be joyous, with the satisfaction in the doing. This sounds like what I told my children regarding doing homework and practicing the violin. Being enslaved in any case should not, it seems to me, be joyous, since such metaphors reinforce the idea that slavery in some cases is justifiable.

In behaving as expected, enslaved members of a household face two possibilities. The first is the odd scene in which the master does the serving. This onetime event does nothing to alleviate the enslaved individual's condition. Slavery remains in place; the enslaver and the enslaved do not eat together as equals. Jesus speaks about the first being last and the last being first (Matt. 19:30; 20:16; Mark 10:31), but as long as there are firsts and lasts, inequity remains. The second possibility is even more problematic: competent enslaved individuals are given even more work.

And the disciples have lots of work. Jesus states, "whoever wishes to become great among you must be your servant [*diakonos*], and whoever wishes to be first among you must be enslaved [*doulos*] of all" (Mark 10:43b–44; cf. Matt. 20:27–28). Luke, not happy with this idea of enslaved-as-model, rephrases the statement in terms of patron-client relations: Jesus tells his disciples at the Last Supper, "the greatest among you must become like the youngest and the leader like one who serves [*diakoneō*]." And then he asks, "For who is greater, the one who is at the table or the one who serves?" While he answers his own question, "Is it not the one at the table?" he also counters, "But I am among you as one who serves" (Luke 22:26–27). Glancy observes, "Luke's modification implies that the Markan formulation is potentially offensive."[64]

Luke may have found Mark's metaphor offensive because Luke did not want to tell Theophilus, the patron to whom the Gospel and Acts are dedicated, that Jesus acted as one who was enslaved. On the other hand, our next passage, Luke 17:7–10, offers precisely that model for Theophilus:

And who among you, having an enslaved person plowing or shepherding sheep, who, having come in from the field, will say to him, "Immediately, passing by here, recline [at the table]"? But will you not say to him, "Prepare what I might eat, and wrapping around yourself [i.e., putting on your cloth], serve me while I eat and drink, and after these, you will eat and drink"? Not do you have grace to the enslaved [i.e., you do not thank the enslaved] because he did what was commanded. Likewise, even you, whenever you have done all that was commanded to you, say,

"We are worthless/useless/unprofitable enslaved people; what
we were obligated to do, we have done."

I dislike this passage.

The disciples in the narrative, and Luke's audience, first identify
with the enslavers (most people prefer the term "masters"): they own
individuals who worked in the fields and the household. The shock
comes less with the enslavers inviting the enslaved to recline at table
with them; the shock comes when Jesus tells the enslavers to think
of themselves as "worthless/useless/unprofitable [*achreioi*]."[65] Mary
Ann Beavis dryly notes that such an image "would have been dis-
tasteful to some listeners."[66] The only other New Testament use of
achreioi is in Matthew 25:30, the Parable of the Talents, where it refers to the "worthless" enslaved man thrown into the outer darkness
where there is weeping and teeth-gnashing.

The parable's rhetoric is known in Hebrew as *qal v'chomer*, from
the lesser to the greater; more familiar is the Latin term, an *a fortiori*
argument: if for *X*, how much more so for *Y*. If people expect loyal
service, *how much more* should God expect service?[67]

For A. Marcus Ward in 1970, the image of the Christian-as-enslaved,
although "less congenial in a world wherein the condition of a slave is
no longer a commonplace," is for those who acknowledge God's authority "a classic and timeless expression of their spiritual reality." He
bases this claim on the "Methodist Covenant," which confesses, "I am
no longer my own but Thine. Put me to what Thou wilt, rank me with
whom Thou wilt; put me to doing, put me to suffering. . . . I freely and
heartily yield all things to Thy pleasure and disposal."[68]

In 2014, Alec Hill, former chair of InterVarsity Christian Fellowship, published in the evangelical flagship magazine *Christianity Today*
an article titled "Inside My Slavery."[69] Focusing on Luke 17:7–10, Hill

observes, "To counter the notion that I am the center of the universe, for the past eight years I have started my quiet time every morning with the same four words, *I am your slave.*" After citing several other sayings in which Jesus uses "slave" language to refer to discipleship, he draws three benefits from this language. First, it encourages submission and thus allows us to cede control to God so that "our bondage is really our freedom." Second, it reinforces the concern that Christians have a duty to act, to care for others. Third, the language reminds us that we serve only one master.

Many of my students find this argument to exemplify white privilege. For them, the image of God as master/enslaver and disciple as enslaved is irredeemable and offensive. Others resonate with Hill's argument. For them, being enslaved to God (or Jesus) is the ultimate sign of freedom, for it means no earthly power controls them and that they are enslaved to nothing on earth, whether drugs or power or money. More, they take pride in being the treasured possessions of the benevolent, omnipotent master.

Our own sensibilities must interact with texts, but this is only the first step. The next is to hear the texts through someone else's ears and then, in conversation, to move the discussion forward. Luke 17:7–10 and related passages are opportunities not for cancel culture but for considered conversation.

The Talents

Our next example of a parable using enslavement language once again concerns competent enslaved individuals who are "rewarded" with more work and incompetent enslaved individuals who are cast into the outer darkness (Matt. 25:14–31; cf. Luke 19:11–28, the Parable of the Pounds). Below is Matthew's version, likely earlier and certainly more violent than Luke's.[70]

Therefore, remain awake, because not do you know the day or the hour. For just as a person, taking a journey, called his own enslaved people and handed over them his possessions. And to one, he gave five talents, and to one, two, and to one one, each according to his own ability. And he went on a journey. Immediately going, the one receiving the five talents was working with them, and he gained another five. Likewise, the one having two gained another two. But the one having received one, going out, dug earth, and hid his lord's [kyrios] silver.

After a long time, the lord of those enslaved comes, and he settles the matter with them. And coming forward, the one having received the five talents handed over an additional five talents, and he was saying, "Lord, five talents to me you handed over; see, an additional five talents I have gained." Said to him his lord, "Well [done], good enslaved one and faithful. With few [things] you were faithful, with many [things] I shall put you in charge. You go into the joy of your lord."

And coming, even the one with two talents, said, "Lord, two talents you gave to me. See, an additional two talents I have gained." Said to him his lord, "Well [done], enslaved one good and faithful. With few [things] you were faithful, with many [things] I shall put you in charge. You go into the joy of your lord."

And coming, even the one having received the one talent, said, "Lord, I knew that a harsh/cruel man you are, reaping where not did you sow, and gathering where you did not scatter. And fearing, going out, I hid your talent in the earth. See, you have what is yours."

And answering, his lord said to him, "Evil enslaved one and unready/timid. You knew that I reap where I did not sow and gather where not did I scatter. It was therefore necessary for you to

throw my silver to the tables [i.e., take it to the bank], and coming,
I will receive [what]ever is mine with interest.

"Therefore, take up from him the talent and give to the one
having the ten talents. For to the one having, all will be given, and
he will have abundance. But to the one not having, even what he
has will be taken from him. And that unworthy [*achrieos*] enslaved
one, cast [him] into the outer darkness, where there will be the
wailing and gnashing of the teeth."

The setting is not impossible: the enslaved served as business
managers, financial advisers, bankers, and investors.[71] Nor is giving
money to the enslaved for purposes of business transaction odd.
Roman economy institutionalized the *peculium*, "money given to
slaves to do business with."[72] A talent of silver was somewhere between sixty and ninety pounds of silver; one talent equals about six
thousand denarii, about what a laborer would earn in twenty years.[73]

The parable shows that competent people wind up with more responsibility and more work. The individual known by the "lord" to
have limited gifts finds his inadequacy confirmed when the "lord"
takes everything he has and dispatches him to the outer darkness.
For the enslaved, there is no good news here. One result is more
work; the second result is more pain.

Yet commentators do find good news here. Leaping into allegory,
many see Jesus as the king/lord who leaves the church in anticipation
of his return (the "second coming"), the enslaved as the disciples, and
the incompetent and fearful man as the one who fails to utilize his
ecclesial or theological resources, whether for evangelization, supporting the poor, or doing "good deeds." Questions of actual slavery, actual
money, and actual torture are safely tucked away.

Another popular reading proposes that the third man, by with-
drawing the money from circulation, is engaging in social justice

work, since the money "cannot be used to dispossess more peasants from their lands through its dispersion in the form of usurious
loans."[74] Therefore the third figure is the faithful one. I am not convinced. Had he been interested in helping the poor, that man could
have given the talent to them or invested it on their behalf. He could
have acted as Rabbi Akiva did regarding Rabbi Tarfon's money, as we
saw in Chapter 1. If the third fellow is the hero, no one wins. Further,
the money he buries will find its way into the market in any case, so
he has simply delayed the inevitable.

We could read the third man as an ancient version of the clever
and subversive so-called lazy slave whose "foot dragging" prevents
the master from getting what he expects.[75] Keith Bradley describes
how the enslaved could both protest their position and gain limited
autonomy by stealing, shirking duties, running away, even committing suicide.[76] Despite my sympathy for this view, and my acknowl-
edgment that the approach could be seen as a form of protest, I have
a hard time working up sympathy for the third man. He does not
steal or shirk; he rather shrinks from fear. I understand him not to
be protesting, but to be petrified.

A few commentators take an alternative allegorical reading and
see the talents as analogous to Torah study: "the one who learns
the most from Torah receives more, while the one who neglects the
study of the ways of the Lord will lose what he or she has acquired."[77]
It's a nice thought, but the allegory requires an answer key to make
sense, even as it avoids the concerns for either slavery or economics.
I'm also not thrilled with the notion that someone would avoid Torah
study for fear that a divine master would punish in response, or that
one person's refusal to study and so act would require others to study
harder.

Before moving to comforting allegories, we do well to allow the
parable to challenge. For example, in what sense are the first two

enslaved individuals rewarded, in that they now have more work to do, and the threat of the enslaver's temper remains? Those who excel at their jobs know that the more they do, the more they will be asked to do; to refuse, to step off the treadmill, can be dangerous (I am thinking here especially of contingent faculty, clergy, and health-care professionals). How do we cease being "good and faithful enslaved" and start becoming "good and faithful free people"?

Second, Glancy observes, "By concluding with examples of wicked slaves enduring corporal punishment, the parables allude to what is probably the strongest incentive slaves had for loyalty to their owners, that is, the fear of disciplinary retribution," and, "To a large extent, the faithful slave is a by-product of the fear of corporal punishment."[78] Whatever is done under threat of physical harm is not done for its own sake, and it is not done with any sense of joy or pride. Such images turn God into a bully, or a sadist. How can we read the parable with resistance? Can alternatives be found for incentivizing and for trusting? How do we move from enslaver-enslaved or even patron-client relationships to friendship or to family?

Third, although it is possible that "the audience would have sympathized with the third enslaved figure and understood the reasons for his behavior," I doubt the other enslaved individuals, who now have more work, would have been among the sympathizers.[79] If we take the master as God, this reading becomes impossible, at least to me. Why would we see God as a "harsh/cruel man" rather than as "a God merciful and gracious, slow to anger, and abounding in steadfast love and faithfulness" (Exod. 34:6; cf. Num. 14:18; Neh. 9:17; Pss. 86:15; 103:8; 145:8; Joel 2:13; Jon. 4:2; Sir. 5:4, and elsewhere)? If the lord of the parable is our image of the divine, then our image needs reconfiguration.

On the nonallegorical level, the third man raises more questions. He is the "weakest link" in the household system. While enslaved household members had little reason for solidarity, today this figure provides the opportunity for aiding the weaker members of our team. This parable appears after the Parable of the Wise and Foolish Virgins (Matt. 25:1–13), which depicts "foolish" virgins who do not bring enough oil to keep their lamps lit as they await the delayed bridegroom. They ask the wise, who brought extra oil, to share, but the wise refuse. When the bridegroom finally arrives at midnight, the foolish virgins are at the local twenty-four-hour oil shop: the groom invites the wise virgins to the wedding feast, and he bars the door to the foolish. Where is the solidarity?

Parables are supposed to make us think. To ignore the slavery, the brutality, the lack of solidarity, the cancellation of individuals—this is hardly good news. To set people against each other is not a form of peace-building, let alone enemy-loving. These parables provide splendid opportunities to challenge our theologies and our relationships, to remember our pasts and see their effects in the present, to think of alternatives to violence and coercion, and to reflect on how slavery continues to this day, perhaps in our own neighborhoods.

AND NOW?

The Bible begins the movement toward ending slavery with its teaching that all humanity is created in the divine image and with its mandates to love the neighbor and the stranger.

Hillel's so-called silver rule summarizing Torah, "What is hateful to you, do not do to another" (b. Shabbat 31a), and Jesus's Golden Rule, "In everything do to others as you would have them to do you, for this is the Law and the Prophets" (Matt. 7:12; cf. Luke 6:31), should have eliminated slavery.[80] Similarly Hierocles, a second-century CE Stoic, proclaimed, "A slave will be well treated by one who considers how he would like to be treated by him if he were the master, and himself the slave."[81] In none of these sayings was abolition part of the package.

Some followers of Jesus understand these parables as comparing God to an enslaver, waiting for his enslaved workers to disobey and then responding to that disobedience with death and damnation. Others see their slavery to God as a form of freedom from whatever "enslaves" today—drugs, alcohol, gambling, money, fame, and so on. The first approach threatens to create a congregation of servile, paranoid, and/or infantilized members. The second strips the evils of actual slavery away by cleaning up the metaphor or by transferring it to cases where individuals can choose, difficult though it may be, to end the addiction. We need not be enslaved—if I can use this word—to either image.

Nor should we seek to rescue Jesus from failing to condemn slavery. He is a person of his time, and metaphor that worked for him and for his early followers such as Paul may no longer work today.

Warren Carter writes, "The Gospel readily reinscribes and thereby sanctions violence against slaves by not offering any critique."[82] That is our job.

CHAPTER 3
ETHNICITY AND RACE

IN THIS CHAPTER we take a closer look at what today would be called "ethnicity and race"; otherwise put, we shall assess Gospel teachings on the relationship between insiders and outsiders, between Jews and gentiles, and then between Jews and Samaritans. When we clear away the false constructions of Jewish-gentile and Jewish-Samaritan relations, we are better positioned to listen to stories by and about Jesus, and so better prepared to ask the questions that can help us live in a diverse world. Such questions include: How do we define ourselves without projecting negative images onto people outside our families or tribes or nations? What do we do with texts that today sound prejudicial or intolerant? What do we owe to people who are not members of our group? What might we expect from them? Finally, how do we relate to outsiders without sacrificing the particulars of our own identity on the altars of interreligious or multicultural appreciation?

We begin with defining terms: Who belongs to which group? Jews at the time of Jesus (and to this day) claimed a common ancestry from Abraham and Sarah, to Isaac and Rebekah, to Jacob, whose name was changed to Israel, and then through his sons and grandsons. So too, as a people or nation, they regarded themselves as having a common homeland (the land of Israel), language (Hebrew), and set of practices.

The term in the Bible usually translated "gentiles" or sometimes "nations" (Hebrew: *goyyim*; Greek: *ethnikoi*) primarily connotes non-Jewish and non-Samaritan people. For Jews, the "gentiles" are the "not us." The term has both ethnic and what we might call "religious" connotations, and separating religion (ritual, theology, etc.) from ethnicity is both difficult and messy. We could also, in many cases, translate the term not as "gentiles" but as "pagans," but this translation has problems. For many readers today and indeed since fourth-century Christian use, "pagan" has negative connotations in that it suggests at best a false religion if not a socially degenerate one. In other contexts it connotes a modern phenomenon connected to nature and/or goddess worship, which is not the same thing as ancient non-Jewish and non-Samaritan practice and belief. When Paula Fredriksen describes the non-Jewish and non-Samaritan followers of Jesus as "ex-pagan pagans," that is, people who abandoned their traditional gods for the God of Israel as revealed in Jesus, her use helpfully removes the negative connotations of the term while simultaneously emphasizing the religious dimension that the word "gentile" may lack.[1]

Whether in terms of ethnicity or in terms of what comes to be called "religion," Samaritans are not "gentiles." Ethnically, they are connected to Jews because of claims of common ancestry, from the Northern Kingdom of Israel, conquered by Assyria in 722 BCE, and before that from the Israelite tribes Ephraim and Manasseh. Jews and Samaritans also share a more-or-less common ancestral homeland. Religiously, Samaritans worship the God of Israel and share with Jews the Pentateuch as a sacred text, although there are differences between both the Hebrew and Samaritan Pentateuchs and Hebrew and Samaritan practices. For example, the Samaritans claim, following Deuteronomy 12:5, that the place "that YHWH your God will choose" for the temple is Mount Gerizim in Samaria, not Mount Zion in Jerusalem.[2]

Whether Jews got along with gentiles and Samaritans depended on both the individuals involved and local circumstances. The same point holds today for Protestants and Catholics, members of the Church of Christ and members of the Disciples of Christ, or, for that matter, Methodists and Methodists, or Baptists and Baptists.

Because Jews never settled down to be a "religion," in the narrowly defined sense of a group sharing common theological beliefs, some Christian commentators suggest that they were "tribal," with the connotation of not only ethnocentrism but also xenophobia. They consequently see any contact Jesus has with gentiles as "breaking down barriers" or "transgressing" Jewish practice. Other commentators presume that Jews, seeing themselves as a "chosen people," were soteriologically exclusive, a fancy way of saying, "I'm saved and you're not," or "God loves me but not you." Then, they conclude, Jesus invents universalism. These claims fail the historical tests. As we'll see, Jews welcomed gentiles into synagogues and the Jerusalem temple. Not only were there gentile proselytes to Judaism (one, Nicolaus the proselyte from Antioch, appears in Acts 6:5), but also Jewish prophecy anticipated the conversion of the gentiles to the God of Israel in the messianic age.

Also common in Christian preaching and teaching is that Jews regarded Samaritans as enemies and oppressed them as an ethnic and religious minority, while Jesus invents the Samaritan Anti-Defamation League. Yet the Gospels suggest that, at least as far as Samaritans go, he found their tradition in error. Nor were Samaritans the oppressed minority.

This chapter begins with general biblical and postbiblical Jewish views of gentiles/pagans and Samaritans with a focus on proselytism. Jews do not proselytize; we do not knock on people's doors and ask if they've met Moses, since Jews, as a people or nation, for the most part did and do not think it was necessary to be Jewish to be in a right relationship with God. Christians, as members of a "faith community" or "religion" in the sense of a group held together not by geography, ethnicity, language, or ancestry but by creed and confession, did proselytize, and some still do. A look at conversion can help us see the benefits, and dangers, of theological truth claims and the insistence on uniformity of belief.

We then turn to three soundings from the Gospel tradition. First is Jesus's exorcizing the demon(s) in Gerasa, where he also destroys the local economy (Mark 5:1–20). Here we look not only at Jesus's initial interaction with gentiles (it doesn't go well), but also at how the Gospel views the Roman Empire. We also look at Jesus encountering a Syrophoenician woman in Tyre in Mark 7 and the replay of this story in Matthew 15:23–28, where the woman is called a Canaanite. The story shows him both restricting his mission to fellow Jews and then broadening it to include gentiles. Issues here include what today would be called "intersectionality" (the relationship among gender, ethnicity, and class) and resource allocation, as well as how the same story can convey different impressions.

Finally, we come to one of my favorite Gospel narratives, Jesus's conversation with a woman in Samaria (John 4). This account raises questions about Jewish-Samaritan relations and about missionary efforts. For example, does one show love to *gerim*, "strangers," or "immigrants" or "migrants" or "resident aliens" (cf. Lev. 19:34 on loving the *ger* because "you were *gerim* in the land of Egypt") by insisting that they give up the practices and beliefs of their own culture and tradition and convert to Christianity so that they can be "saved," or does love mean allowing the *gerim* to be who they are, apart from Christian practices and beliefs?

PROSELYTISM

The biblical text and postbiblical Jewish tradition include numerous gentiles, from the Egyptian midwives who rescue Israelite babies consigned by Pharaoh to drown in the Nile, to Moses's Midianite father-in-law, to Rahab the Canaanite brothel owner who protects the Israelite spies when all they can do, on getting leave after forty years in the wilderness, is visit Rahab's house. Joshua 6:25 reports that Rahab's family "lived in Israel until this day."

Text and tradition also insist that gentiles be treated with compassion. As noted in Chapter 1, immigrants or migrants (*gerim*, i.e., not Jews) are entitled to the same social services as the vulnerable within Israelite society. Gentiles were also to be welcomed in places where Jews assembled. The outer court of the Jerusalem temple was called the Court of the Gentiles because gentiles worshiped there and, on occasion, offered sacrifices to Israel's God. Honoring local gods was both good politics and good theology. I do something similar when I visit a Christian church and contribute to the collection. Gentiles also affiliated with Jews in local synagogues; called "Godfearers," these gentiles were interested in Jewish teaching, ethics, and history but not interested in converting to Judaism, which would have included circumcision for men and likely created problems with their families and their civic duties.

It is possible that the centurion whom we met in Chapter 2, who according to the Jewish elders "loves our people and built our synagogue for us" (Luke 7:5), was a Godfearer. He may also have been a friendly patron. But he was not the only one. For example, a synagogue inscription in Greek from mid-first-century CE Acmonia in Phrygia indicates the patronage of a gentile woman.

Occasionally, commentators claim Jews were both xenophobic and engaged in conversionary efforts. An excellent example of such inconsistency appears in the notes to the *New American Bible Revised Edition* featured on the home page of the United States Conference of Catholic Bishops. For Matthew 18:17, where Jesus advises that an unrepentant member of the assembly (*ekkelsia*, usually translated "church"; the term in the Septuagint refers to the Jewish community) is to be treated "as a gentile and a tax collector," the notes read: "just as the observant Jew avoided the company of Gentiles and tax collectors, so must the congregation of Christian disciples separate itself from the arrogantly sinful member who refuses to repent even when convicted of his sin by the whole church."[3] Yet it is precisely to the sinners that Jesus targets his mission (Matt. 9:13), and the "Great Commission" of Matthew 28:19 is to "make disciples of all the Gentiles." Thus, for Matthew 18:17, the point is to remove from the assembly, and then to re-evangelize.

However, concerning Matthew 23:15, Jesus's woe against the scribes and Pharisees for crossing "sea and land to make one proselyte, and when that happens you make him a child of Gehenna twice as much as yourselves," the notes read, "In the first century AD until the First Jewish Revolt against Rome (AD 66–70), many Pharisees conducted a vigorous missionary campaign among Gentiles."[4] "Observant Jews," such as Pharisees, cannot both attempt to convert gentiles and avoid those same gentiles. The note is also incorrect: Pharisees were interested in teaching *fellow Jews*, not in converting gentiles.[5] "Observant Jews," and probably those more lax in their practices, likely avoided tax collectors because they were in league with the Roman occupation. But there is no evidence that the vast majority of Jews, observant or not, avoided gentiles. I suspect the focus on "observant" Jews is designed to suggest that Jesus was somehow less observant. That too would be an incorrect conclusion.

Because Jews were, and are, a "people"—defined not only by practices such as male circumcision, Sabbath observance, synagogue

affiliation, a relationship to the Jerusalem temple and the paying
of the temple tax (until the temple was destroyed; Rome converted
the payment into the *fiscus Judaicus*, the "Jewish tax," paid by men,
women, and children, for the upkeep of the temple of Jupiter Cap-
itoline in Rome; payments ceased by the third century), but also by
a sense of common ancestry and attachment to the homeland—
they did not seek converts.[6] Nor did their tradition encourage conversion, since the scriptures already attested to righteous gentiles.
Some Jews at the time of Jesus thought conversion impossible, since
one could not change one's essential (or ethnic) identity. For others,
conversion—beginning in the Hellenistic period—was possible, as is
the case with the Ammonite Achior in the book of Judith and "Nicolaus, the proselyte of Antioch" (Acts 6:5), a fellow who had been born
a gentile, converted to Judaism, and joined the Jesus movement.[7]

Jewish tradition spoke of gentiles following not the 613 commandments of Torah, as traditionally numbered, but the seven commandments given to Noah. These developed during the Hellenistic
period and then into rabbinic texts. Since God made a covenant with
Noah, including the promise never again to wipe out the world by
flood (it's the fire next time, as 2 Pet. 3:7 and, later, James Baldwin,
affirmed), it stands to reason that humanity would have promises
to keep as well. The Noachian commandments forbid idolatry, blas-
pheming the God of Israel, murder, sexual sin, stealing, and eating
the limb from a living animal; they also mandate establishing courts
of justice (b. Sanhedrin 56a; cf. Tosefta Avodah Zarah 8.4, Genesis
Rabbah 34.8).

One dominant Jewish view was that in the world to come, or the
messianic age, gentiles would turn from idolatry to worship the God
of Israel. They do not convert to Judaism; rather, they give up pagan
practices. The concern was anticipated as early as 1 Kings 8:41–42,

where, at the dedication of his temple in Jerusalem, Solomon affirms that foreigners, "not of your people Israel" (v. 41), will come there to worship. Zechariah 8:22–23 (cf. Zech. 14:16–17) predicts the day when "many peoples and strong nations [*goyyim/ethnē*] shall come to seek the LORD of hosts in Jerusalem. . . . In those days ten men from nations of every language shall take hold of a Jew, grasping his garment and saying, 'Let us go with you, for we have heard that God is with you.'" Consequently, there was no need to attempt to convert gentiles: their recognition of Israel's God would be by divine fiat. Jewish lack of missionary outreach is thus not based in xenophobia; it is based in recognition of ethnic diversity.

The followers of Jesus "evangelized"—the term comes from the Greek *eu* (good) and *angelos* (messenger, whence "angel"); initially a secular term meaning "good news," such as a tax holiday, it becomes a technical term for proclaiming the good news, or gospel (*euangelion*, whence "evangelical") of Jesus. They evangelized because they believed that only through Jesus could one be in a right relationship with God and so be saved in the sense of gaining eternal bliss. For these missionaries, evangelization was motivated primarily by love—the desire to save people from damnation and show them the good news of following Jesus. The targets of this evangelization may have had different impressions.

Although we have little evidence of overt proselytizing by Jews, a type of passive invitation may have existed given extensive socializing. Jews associated with gentiles in synagogues and in the Jerusalem temple, in the streets and in the marketplaces.

This socializing indicates that Jesus's relations with gentiles—such as the fellow in Gerasa, or Gedara, possessed by demons; and the Syrophoenician, or Canaanite, woman—are not transgressive or even surprising. But they are instructive.

THE DEMON-POSSESSED MAN IN GERASA

Mark 5:1–20, the account of the "Gerasene demoniac," is most frequently approached via the topics of healing/exorcism and, more recently, of politics/empire.[8] Building on these approaches, we add the focus on Jewish-gentile relations. Although Mark never explicitly states that either the demon-possessed man or the population of Gerasa was gentile, and although Josephus tells us that the rebel leader Simon bar Giora was "by birth of Gerasa" (*War* 4.503; Josephus also notes in *War* 2.480 that unlike many cities that attacked their minority Jewish populations, Gerasa did not), the location across the Jordan, the name Legion, the presence of the pigs, and Jesus's refusal to allow the healed man to follow him all indicate that the area and the characters living there were gentile.

The story is one of healing, but it is also about politics, sexuality, economics, and Jewish-gentile relations. It poses difficult questions about property destruction, the nonhuman animal, how we understand and attempt to control aberrant behavior, self-harm, and even antipagan polemic. Again, Jesus helps us ask the right questions. Here is a literal translation:

> And they came to the other side of the sea, to the region of the
> Gerasenes. And when he went out of the boat, immediately met
> him out of the tombs a person [*anthrōpos*] in an unclean spirit,
> who the dwelling he had in the tombs; and not even by a chain
> was able any one ever him to restrain. Because he often, with
> shackles and chains, was restrained, and were torn apart by him
> the chains, and the shackles to be broken; and no one was strong
> him to subdue/tame. And through every night and day in the
> tombs and in the mountains he was crying out and cutting himself
> with stones. And seeing Jesus from afar, he ran and bowed down

to him. And crying out with a great voice, he says, "What to me and to you, Jesus, Son of God the Most High? I implore you by God, do not torture me." For he had been saying to him, "You come out, unclean spirit, out of the person!"

And he was asking him, "What is your name?" And he says to him, "Legion [is] my name; because many are we." He was pleading with him much not them to send out of the region.

And was there at the hill a great herd of pigs grazing. And they exhorted him, saying, "Send us to the pigs so that we might into them enter." And he permitted them. And came out, the unclean spirits, and went into the pigs; and rushed, the herd, down the steep bank, into the sea, as two thousand, and they drowned in the sea.

And the ones grazing them [i.e., swineherds] fled, and they announced in the city and in the fields. And they came to see what it is that had happened. And coming to Jesus and seeing the one having been demon-possessed sitting, clothed, and in his right mind, the one having had the legion; and they were afraid. And they reported to them, the ones having seen what had happened to the demon-possessed and about the pigs.

And they began to exhort him [Jesus] to go away from their borders. And when he was getting into the boat, urged him, the one having been demon-possessed, that he with him might be. And not did he [Jesus] permit him, but he says to him, "Go to your house, to those who are yours, and announce to them how much the Lord [kyrios] for you has done and has shown mercy to you." And he went out and he became to proclaim in the Decapolis how much had done to him/for him Jesus, and all were marveling.

Anti-Roman, Sexually Coded Satire

Dawn Ottoni-Wilhelm offers the traditional interpretation of Mark's story: "With compassion, tenderness, and purposeful attention to outsiders, Jesus crosses geographic, ethnic, social, and economic boundaries for the sake of God's love for all people." She continues, "A land that was considered 'out of bounds' for Jews is now blessed to receive God's word," and Jesus "opens God's way to a region and people considered 'out of bounds' by Jews."[9] The "good news" of Mark 5 is, therefore, that by going to Gerasa, Jesus breaks ethnic borders. This sentiment, which presumes boundaries for Jesus to transgress, works only if we ignore both the Jews living in Gerasa and the narrative's symbolism.

The location, Gerasa, is the first indication that the account has references ready for decoding.[10] In Hebrew, *gerash* means "to expel" or "to drive out"; Adam and Eve were expelled (*gerash*) from Eden (Gen. 3:24); Sarah demanded that Hagar and her son Ishmael be expelled (*gerash*) from Abraham's camp (Gen. 21:10); Pharaoh expels (*gerash*) the Israelites from Egypt following the plagues (Exod. 12:39); Jonah complains of being driven (*gerash*) from God's sight (Jon. 2:4), despite the fact that he was attempting to run away from his prophetic commission; and Proverbs 22:10a exhorts, "Drive out [*gerash*] a scoffer, and strife departs." The city of Gerasa is thus "Expulsion Junction."

The narrative also echoes scripture. Isaiah 65:4 speaks of people who "sit inside graves and in secret places lodge overnight; who eat the flesh of pigs." Biblically informed listeners could not miss the connection. Gerasa is not the best site for a destination wedding.

Yet Gerasa is also a real city, a Roman colony about forty miles inland from the Sea of Galilee in what is presently northwestern Jordan (Matt. 8:28 shifts the location to Gedara, which is on the shore and which has cliffs; Matthew's version makes more geographical sense but it loses the pun). Josephus reports that during the first Jewish revolt, Rome's general, Vespasian, sent his troops to Gerasa where the army killed thousands of young men, took their families captive, and

plundered the city (*War* 4.9.1).[11] The demons in Mark 5 call themselves "Legion," a Latin term for a cohort of six thousand soldiers.
In modern terms, Legion would be the "Sixth Fleet" or the "101st
Airborne." The name equates Roman occupation with demonic possession. Securing this connection between empire and demon is the
fact that the siglum of the Tenth Fretensis, the legion that captured
Jerusalem in 70 CE and remained stationed there following the destruction of the temple, was the boar.[12]

The satire continues by deploying sexual imagery. Men in antiquity,
"manly men," act the part: they are self-controlled, are rational, display
courage and wisdom, promote truth and justice.[13] "Legion" thus codes
as effeminate. The verb phrase "enter into"—as in "entering into" the
pigs—refers not only to military incursions; it is also slang for having
sexual relations. That Legion's body is naked makes the innuendo
stronger. The demons have, in effect, sexually penetrated (you can fill
in the shorter profanity) the man they possess. Pigs too are sexually
coded; in Roman slang, pigs and "piggy" suggest hairless or depil-
ated, pink, penetrable organs.[14] Thus Legion sexually takes the pigs,
an image of bestiality. I have never heard this approach to the story
preached. Just as well.

Regarding the death of the pigs: While sometimes seen as "a
concrete illustration of God's preferential love and compassion for
humanity, as possessing value far above any other creature: 'You are
worth more than many sparrows' (Luke 12:7; see Matt. 12:12),"[15] I find
this reading disturbing. First, not only do pigs not stampede, but also
they are good swimmers (I did look this up), so the death need not
have been expected. The scene makes little sense historically, but it
is a brilliant anthropological narrative. For example, people at the
time generally thought that demons abhor water. They are found
usually in "dry places" such as Egypt, which is where the lovesick but
murderous demon in the book of Tobit flees after being exorcised

(see Tob. 8:3). This avoidance of water is, by the way, another reason people in antiquity found baptism appealing: the water could
be understood as a means of exorcising demons. Thus, the pigs are
attempting to perform their own exorcism. While Jesus may have
been attempting to avoid having the demons possess anyone else, he
simply could have banished them rather than granted permission for
them to find another host. Second, I suspect we would read the story
differently if the two thousand dead animals were kittens or puppies
or if they were named Babe, Wilbur, Piglet, Pumbaa, Porky, Peppa,
Olivia, and Miss Piggy.

More Healthy Soundings

If we read the narrative for sensitivity rather than for satire or slander, then we might see in the symptoms described for the demon-
possessed man the phenomenon today known as self-injury. Mark
speaks of how the possessed man was "in the tombs and in the
mountains . . . crying out and cutting himself with stones." I had
initially thought the cutting was accidental, as rocks have crags that
can easily cut naked flesh. But one of my students pointed out that
the man might be engaging in deliberate harm. The Mayo Clinic
describes cutting as a way of coping with "emotional pain, sadness,
anger and stress."[16] For a first-century context, the proximate cause of
this harm could be the presence of Roman troops.

The cause could also be a familial or personal concern. Politics is
not the only lens through which the story can be read. Given the sexual
codings of the story, we could see the possessed man as engaging in
self-harm because he saw himself as different, in terms of gender or
sexuality, from the norms of the Decapolis.[17] In this reading, it is not
what today would be called a queer identity that needs to be exorcised,
but the mental injury that prejudice against queer people causes.[18]

At the end of the account, the locals want Jesus to leave. I have my doubts that, as one commentator asserts, "it is easier to accept the presence of a crazy person outside the boundaries of town than a healed man who will walk among them, confronting them with the reality of God's transforming power in their midst."[19] The townspeople may well be delighted that their compatriot is cured. Or, their concern may be less with "God's transforming power" than that the man will have a relapse and be more aggressive, or dangerous, to himself and others. The idea that demons can return is not unknown: Matthew 12:43–45 // Luke 11:24–26 describe an unclean spirit who, after being expelled and wandering in waterless regions, returns the original host, and brings his friends. And just as likely, the residents of Gerasa are concerned that Jesus has just ruined the local economy.

Hisako Kinukawa proposes that the destruction of the herd "possibly affected religious rites and rituals (Mark 5:11–17)."[20] This is possible, although Mark makes no mention of local sacrificial practices. If Kinukawa is correct, the story is not only a political and sexual satire, but also an antipagan polemic. Such a reading is the opposite of the claim that Jesus is "transgressing" boundaries in order to promote a multicultural agenda.

The healed man seeks to remain with Jesus, but Jesus refuses his request. Instead, he instructs, "Go to your house, to those who are yours" and proclaim to them how the "Lord . . . has shown mercy to you." The statement can suggest that the man has a home, and a family. Alternatively, Jesus gives him the means by which he can find a home and family: proclamation provides purpose. Religion can be, as Marx described, the "opiate of the masses," a drug that makes people quiescent. It can also be a type of possession, but of the good sort, a dream that opens utopian possibilities.[21] The possessed man is now someone else; with the good news of Jesus, he has a new basis for determining his identity.

Whereas Jesus tells the man to return home—that is, to the cities of the Decapolis—to proclaim God's mercy, the man proclaims Jesus. This is Mark's increasingly less subtle way of telling the audience that Jesus, despite his suffering and death, really is divine. Mark hints that the formerly possessed man was successful, because when Jesus returns to the Decapolis in Mark 7:31, the locals bring to him a man suffering hearing loss and a speech impediment. There is no fear here of God's transforming power; to the contrary, they know Jesus has the ability to heal, and he does so (Mark 7:32–36). Jesus orders those aware of the healing to remain silent, but they do not. The fact that Jesus next, in the Decapolis, feeds four thousand people (Mark 8:1–9) suggests that the man possessed by Legion as well as those aware of the healing miracle got the news out.

The exorcism of the man in Gerasa raises more difficult questions regarding interpretation. First, the story equates Roman troops with demons. To demonize anyone or any group—an army, a political party, a politician, or a religious leader—is to give them more power than they have. We can counter the work of human beings, but to counter a demon requires supernatural abilities. More, to demonize is to dehumanize, and those whom we dehumanize we can more easily kill. Once we say "they're like animals," then of course "we" who are not animals want to pen those animals, or hunt them, or slaughter them.

Yes, the story is a satire, and yes, it mocks Roman troops and celebrates their symbolic death. Many of my students, especially those now in the military or law enforcement or who are veterans, do not find these images amusing. "Pig" (taken as a negative) has become synonymous with police, and "kill the pig" (sometimes abbreviated KTP) is slang for doing something violent and/or disgusting. To celebrate the end of war is one thing; to celebrate the death of soldiers is another. To celebrate the deaths of civilians is worse still. Further, to celebrate the suicide of soldiers, for that is in effect what the story of the dead pigs does, is to overlook the increasing rise in military suicides. Yes, I am overreading the story: neither Mark nor Jesus was thinking about military suicide. But in today's context, the text opens up this conversation too.

For an intertext, along with Isaiah 65, I like to read Mark 5:1–20 in light of the midrash on Exodus 15, Moses's "Song of the Sea," which celebrates the drowning of the Egyptian troops in pursuit of the Israelite slaves. According to the Babylonian Talmud, God silences the angels who began to sing in celebration of the exodus: "My handiwork [i.e., the Egyptians, also created in the image and likeness of God] are drowning in the sea, and you are reciting a song before me?" (b. Sanhedrin 39b). To rejoice over the death of anyone is to deny that we are all in the image and likeness of God.

Such observations should not undercut the value of satire, for satire then and today is an excellent survival mechanism and a form of resistance. Charlie Chaplin's 1940 film *The Great Dictator*, in which he played Adenoid Hynkel, is a splendid example. At the end of the film Chaplin, dressed as Hynkel but speaking as Chaplin, addresses his audience—both pictured within the film and those viewing the film—and encourages them to maintain the freedom of their minds. Produced outside of the Reich and prohibited from being screened in the Reich, the film aimed at mobilizing opposition to Nazis. But satire that draws on negative cultural views of particular forms of sexual expression—such as sissifying the troops—risks reinforcing negative views of nonheterosexual, non-cis-gendered men. Satire at the expense of marginalized groups is funny only for the majority.

Continuing the thoughts this story raises about the military: The image of Legion as raping the man acknowledges that rape occurs when the powerful—the army, the guard, the clergy, the paterfamilias—see those in their charge to be sexually available; we have already seen this process in Chapter 2. Victims may well find the drowning of Legion a satisfactory, even welcome conclusion. I therefore wonder where the women of Gerasa are: Were they raped? Did they welcome the Roman soldiers? Did they own the pigs? Were they Jews? They are probably already a minority in the city and now in danger because of Jesus's actions, because for minoritized people, if one member of the group presents a problem, all may be attacked.

Next, Mark 5:1–20 can be taken as a critique of colonialism. To self-injure, to "act out," can be seen as a reaction to occupation. As the invader attacks the land, so the inhabitant inscribes that attack on the body. Self-injury becomes, ironically, a manifestation of control because the self-injury is controlled by the individual, not by external forces.[22] Conversely, Mark can be read as reinscribing the power of empire, only in this case it is Jesus, not Caesar, who reigns. Tat-Siong Benny Liew observes, "Presenting an all-authoritative Jesus who will eventually annihilate all opponents and all other authorities, Mark's utopian, or dystopian vision, in effect, duplicates the colonial (non) choice of 'serve-or-be-destroyed.'"[23]

Mark 5:1–20 is also an opening for clergy and religious educators to speak about and provide guidance related to neurodiversity and mental illness. As discussed in Chapter 4, equating physical impairment with negative judgments can stigmatize and so exacerbate the problem. On the other hand, stories of possession offer an opportunity for those experiencing mental illness to read themselves into the story. Christine Guth reports from her subjects in a study of how people who identify as mentally ill see the possessed man: "I relate to the demoniac because he causes fear and has to deal with others' fear, even though he is a completely different person on the inside. They don't see him; they see the demon," said one respondent. Another "identified with the man's subjection to forceful mistreatment and with his hostile suspicion of approaching visitors (5:8). He commented, 'It's like the man says, "So, Jesus, are you going to torture me too?" That's my general attitude when I go into mental health facilities. I am tired of being tortured.'"[24]

And Now?

I am not convinced that Mark 5:1–20 records history: the name "Gerasa" and its association with expulsion; its inland location; the symbolism of the pig, especially in relation to the Roman troops involved in the conquest of Jerusalem; the connection of tombs with death and impurity, which so neatly establishes Jesus as the counterforce of life and purity; the unlikelihood that Jesus undertook any sort of gentile mission since if he thought of the salvation of the gentiles, he would have seen them turn to the worship of Israel's God by divine fiat—these factors and others suggest to me more Marcan literary creativity than historical reporting. The account may function better as parable than as history, but this shift in genre does not make it any less valuable.

Any story that can prompt discussions of the military, gender and sexual identity, the benefits and debits of satire, mental illness, colonialism, economics, the nonhuman animal, and so much more is already good news.

THE SYROPHOENICIAN WOMAN IN TYRE/THE CANAANITE WOMAN ON THE BORDER

Mark 7:24–30 recounts how Jesus, after another dispute with Pharisees, attempts to escape from the crowds by taking refuge in a home in Tyre. A woman, "a Greek, a Syrophoenician by birth," finds him and implores him to perform an exorcism for her daughter. He refuses. Worse, he calls her a "little bitch" (*kynarion*, a diminutive form indicating a "little dog"). Rather than return the insult, she tells him that even the dogs are entitled to food. For her clever response, Jesus performs the healing.

In Matthew 15:21–28, one of the few narratives where Matthew's account is longer than Mark's original, the scene takes place outside, on the border of Upper Galilee and Tyre; the woman is a "Canaanite"; the disciples are involved; and Jesus tells the woman that he was sent "only to the lost sheep of the house of Israel" (v. 24). Only when she begs him does he relent, and he does so not because of her cleverness, but because of her "faith." Luke and John do not mention this account, possibly because neither imagines Jesus as having begun the gentile mission, or possibly because neither imagines someone persuaded Jesus to change his mind. John may have avoided the story because of an uninterest in exorcisms; Luke may have avoided it because of an uninterest in presenting a woman as telling Jesus what to do.[25] Determining why a text does not appear is necessarily speculative. Because I take Matthew's story as a heavily edited version of Mark's original, I concentrate here on Mark's account.[26] The concerns are again Jewish-gentile relations, and they are complicated by the issues of class and gender.

They are also complicated by numerous commentators who conclude that the account is *really* about Jesus transgressing borders by speaking with women and by speaking with gentiles.

Mark 7:24–30 reads:

From there, rising up, he went out into the region of Tyre. And entering into a house, no one he was wanting to know. And not was he able to hide. But immediately, hearing, a woman, about him, of whom had her daughter a spirit unclean, and coming, she fell by his feet. And the woman was Greek, Syrophoenician according to race [Greek: *genos*, as in "genealogy"], and she was asking him in order that the demon he might cast out of her daughter.

But he was saying to her, "Permit first to be fed the children, for not is it good to take the bread of the children and to the little dogs cast."

But answering, even she says to him, "Lord [Greek: *kyrios*; also, 'Sir'], even the little dogs under the table are eating from the crumbs of the children."

And he said to her, "On account of this word, go; has gone out from your daughter the demon."

And going into her house, she found the child lying upon the bed, and the demon having gone out.

In the first century, Tyre was a wealthy port whose influence extended into northern Galilee. Josephus (*War* 3.3.1) reports that Mount Carmel at one time "belonged to the Galileans" but was now under Tyrian control. This setting locates Jesus, the Galilean Jew, rebuffing the request of an upper-class woman whose people encroached on his homeland.

The city also functions in the Gospels as a negative foil for Jewish areas. In Matthew 11:21–22 (cf. Luke 10:13–14), Jesus issues woes against Chorazin and Bethsaida, "for if in Tyre and Sidon had been done the mighty works that were done among you, long ago in sackcloth and ashes they would have repented. But to you I say, for Tyre and Sidon more tolerable it will be on the day of judgment than for you." The comparison works only if Tyre and Sidon are seen as sinful. Isaiah 23, a relatively late chapter in the prophetic corpus, speaks of the destruction of Tyre, "whose merchants were princes, whose traders were the honored of the earth" (v. 8). Similarly, Ezekiel 27–28 spends much energy predicting the destruction of Tyre by the Babylonians. The prophecy missed; the city accepted Babylonian control, but Nebuchadnezzar, the king who sacked Jerusalem, left Tyre intact.

Acts 21:3–6 records that Paul docked in Tyre for a short time, and there he met with disciples, including their "wives and children." Thus, the story of the Syrophoenician woman could have functioned, had Luke included it, as the origin story of these Tyrian disciples.

Mark's narrative begins with the notice that Jesus attempted to hide. The motif is consistent with Mark's "messianic secret," in which Jesus as a general rule (the Gerasene episode in Mark 5:1–20 is an outlier) commands that his miracles be kept secret; however, no one obeys. The suggestion that in Tyre, "perhaps Jesus was an illegal immigrant who did not have the proper documentation to be in Phoenician [sic] and was afraid to be stopped and questioned by authorities" is "anachronistic."[27] Anachronism should not, however, stop an interpretation from consideration, any more than contemporary studies of trauma and colonialism should not be employed in understanding the possessed man in Gerasa.

I mention this reading of Mark 7 because it shows how stories can take on new meanings when people read from their social locations. At the same time, sometimes applying our present situations to ancient contexts can lead to mischaracterizations about how those ancient contexts functioned. For historically minded readers, Mark's *lack* of concern about Jesus's travels provides a corrective to the common claims that Jesus, by going to Gerasa or Tyre, "transgresses" boundaries or extends his mission to the "marginal." It is *not* the case that "the Jews avoided contact with Gentiles because they represented immorality, idolatry, and ritual impurity."[28] People generally were free to travel, and travel they did, be it Jesus in the Decapolis and Tyre, Josephus in Rome, or Paul, wherever. Jews also traveled from the diaspora to Jerusalem. Crossing a county line is not the same thing as crossing a barrier. But Mark's text, placed into conversation with present contexts, can help us navigate questions of location: Where are we comfortable and where are we wary? Where are we welcomed, and where are we distrusted, or feared, or seen as the enemy? Where are we in the majority, or the minority? For diaspora communities, where is "home"? The text also helps us interrogate our own reactions: When we meet someone from "outside," who is "not us," what is our first reaction—fear or curiosity, hospitality or the desire to call 911?

The major concern regarding Jewish-gentile relations in Mark 7 is Jesus's calling the woman a little dog. To explain this slur—"little bitch" is not a compliment—commentators then offer a litter of speculations. First is the assertion that "dog" was a "pejorative term *often used* by Jews to refer to Gentiles" (emphasis added).[29] "Dog" is an insult, but we have no evidence of this frequent Jewish use. When the psalmist cries, "For dogs are all around me; a company of evildoers encircles me" (Ps. 22:16, the same psalm that underlies Mark's crucifixion narrative and that begins, "My God, my God, why have you forsaken me?"), the point is enemies, not gentiles. Biblical scholar Mark Nanos writes, regarding Philippians 3:2, in which Paul warns, "Watch out for the dogs, watch out for the evil workers, watch out for the cutting off [i.e., circumcising]," that "there is *no* evidence predating Paul that Jews called Gentiles cum Gentiles dogs. And it is also *not* merely *uncommon* in the later rabbinic tradition to describe Gentiles, or Christians, or Christianity, where it would perhaps be understandable (though still not commendable) for a suffering minority community enduring such name calling and concomitant destructive policies—even that anachronistic evidence does not exist."[30]

The irony is that patristic writers, the church fathers whose writings are contemporary with the texts of rabbinic Judaism, the Mishnah and the Talmud, called Jews "dogs." John Chrysostom, writing in Antioch ca. 387, affirms in his *Homilies Against the Jews* that "although those Jews had been called to the adoption as sons, they fell to kinship with dogs. . . . Once the Jews were the children and the Gentiles dogs. But see how thereafter the order was changed about: they became dogs, and we became the children."[31] This motif of Christians calling Jews "dogs" continued into the Middle Ages.[32]

Mark's account sets up a two-stage mission. Jesus first engages Jews and only after that the gentiles. In Mark 7:27 Jesus states, "Permit first to be fed the children." The little dogs/gentiles then have their turn. The verse helps explain why Jesus did not initiate a full-scale gentile mission. The historical explanation would have been his following the common Jewish belief that the gentiles are brought into the kingdom through divine fiat in the messianic age. The model fits Paul's refrain that "God's saving power" is "for the Jew first and also for the Greek" (Rom. 1:16; 2:9, etc.). But gentiles, perhaps unfamiliar with this Jewish view, may well have asked why Jesus did not visit Antioch or Damascus, Greece or Rome. The idea of a two-stage mission provides the answer.

Matthew 15:26 initially eliminates the two-step process. In Matthew's edited version of the same story, Jesus states, "It is not good to take the bread of the children and cast it to the little dogs." Nothing here about letting the children "first" be fed. Matthew then explains how gentiles enter the system. First, the Canaanite woman does not speak of bread from the "children" but from "the tables of the lords/masters" (*kyrioi*). She thereby acknowledges the privileged position not only of Jesus but also of the tradition he represents. Second, Jesus says to her, "Woman, great is your faith" (Matt. 15:28). He grants her request not because of her cleverness, her "word" as Mark puts it, but because of her faith.

In both the Jesus tradition and Paul's letters, the Jews are the first to receive the covenant, which is then extended to the gentiles. Similarly, they were first to encounter Jesus, with the gentile mission substantially beginning after the proclamation of his resurrection. This sense of Jewish priority bothers some of my students: it smacks of ethnic privilege. Underlying this concern is their discomfort with the notion of a "chosen people."

As one commentator stated in regard to Matthew 15:21–28, Jesus comes from "a people that has emerged and grown as a nation with an ideology of chosenness, a common ideology among the imperialist nations [that] reduces the concept of Basileia [the Greek word for 'kingdom'] by filtering it through that oppressive ideology."[33] Ancient Israel, frequently conquered, hardly epitomized imperialism. Nor is a concern for national autonomy necessarily an oppressive ideology. In such cases, filtering ancient texts through contemporary contexts can be at best misleading.

The concept of chosenness can prove helpful, depending on how chosenness is defined. In Jewish thought, to be chosen means to follow Torah and so to be a light to the gentiles (Isa. 42:6; 49:6; cf. 60:3). The prayer said before the reading of the Torah in the synagogue is "blessed are you, Lord our God, sovereign of the universe, who has chosen us from among the nations, and who has given us the Torah." The point is responsibility, not meritocracy. In 1 Peter 2:9, the designation of chosenness applies to the followers of Jesus: "But you are an elect race [genos eklecton], a royal priesthood, a holy nation [ethnos hagion]" called out of darkness into light.

The idea of being chosen can create a sense of elitism, but instead it should prompt a sense of personal and national responsibility. According to the Jewish tradition, chosenness is not based on internal worth; it is based on God's external love (Deut. 7:7). Paul picks up this idea in 2 Thessalonians 2:13, where he tells his gentile friends, "God chose you as the first fruits for salvation." For minoritized groups, chosenness can function as an affirmation of their identity and difference and so as a resistance to coerced or demanded assimilation.

When Jesus tells the Syrophoenician woman to wait her turn, she refuses. This pattern of refusal-response-redress is a literary convention known in both Roman and Jewish literature. The person with power, Augustus Caesar or Hadrian, the prophet Elisha (2 Kings 4:28–31) or Rabbi Judah the Prince, receives a petition from someone with less social capital. The authority, busy or preoccupied, assigns a delegate or ignores the request. The petitioner, with a clever word, keeps the conversation going, refuses to exacerbate the insult, and achieves the desired goal.[34]

Mark's story instructs the privileged and the needy. For the privileged, the message is to attend to outsiders as well as insiders, to show concern and compassion not only to those who have the ability to reciprocate, but to those who do not. Given the mother's high status, "a Greek, a Syrophoenician by birth," and so also privileged position, the story shows that money and social position cannot buy miracles. More, it shows that illness and impairment afflict the wealthy as well as the poor. Here the story finds connections to the healing of the centurion's "boy" in Matthew 8:5–13 and Luke 7:1–10 (Chapter 2). The centurion and the Syrophoenician mother are both in elite positions, and they both show that they need help not only from people with more power, but also from outsiders. The centurion acknowledges his own position as being under authority as part of the chain of command; the Greek mother acknowledges Jesus's insult and then uses it to claim what she believes is her due: "even the little dogs under the table" eat the "crumbs of the children."

For those in need, regardless of ethnicity or class, Mark's narrative reveals the benefits of maintaining relationships with those who have power, of not ramping up insult but deflecting it, of tenacity and of cleverness. The woman's response of taking Jesus's insult, accepting it rather than verbally striking back, and then insisting on her right and dignity, is an enacted version of Jesus's own instruction in the Sermon on the Mount of turning the other cheek, giving the shirt, and going the extra mile.

And Now?

The questions the narrative poses remain relevant, and difficult. Do we accept an insult for the sake of a goal (does the end justify the means)? When do we subordinate ourselves, and when do we rely on privilege? When do we show beneficence to outsiders in need—someone not of our church or synagogue, ethnic group or nation? In the age of limited resources, who should receive what we have to offer? How does one say no to a desperate mother? And what, finally, should the response of this Syrophoenician mother be? She returns home to find her daughter exorcised of her demon: now what?

THE SAMARITAN WOMAN AT THE WELL

John 4:4–42 is a long text, so the following translation offers only a selection. I encourage you to read the entire narrative: the literary construction is brilliant.

> It was necessary that he pass through Samaria. He comes, therefore, into a city of Samaria called Sychar, a neighbor of the region that gave Jacob to Joseph his son. And was there the water-spring of Jacob; Jesus, therefore, being tired from the road trip, was sitting near the well. It was about the sixth hour [i.e., midday].

Came a woman from Samaria to draw water. Says to her Jesus, "Give me to drink." For his disciples had gone into the city in order that they might buy food.

Says there to him, the Samaritan woman, "How it is that you, being a Jew, from me, are asking something to drink, being that I am a Samaritan woman?" For not are sharing Jews with Samaritans. Answering, Jesus even said to her, "If you had known the gift of God, and who it is that is saying to you, 'Give me to drink,' you would have asked him, and he would have given to you living water."

Says to him the woman, "Lord/Sir [kyrios], not a bucket do you have, and the well is deep. Where, therefore, have you living water? You couldn't be greater than our father Jacob, who gave to us the well, and he himself from it drank, and his sons and his flocks?"

Answered Jesus and said to her, "Everyone who drinks from this water will thirst again. But the one who might drink from the water that I myself will give, will not be thirsty into the ages, but the water that I will give to him will become in him a spring of water leaping up into eternal life."

Says to him the woman, "Give to me this water, so that I shall not thirst nor have to keep coming here to draw."

He says to her, "Go, call your husband [andros; literally, 'man'] and come here." Answered the woman and said to him, "Not do I have a husband." Jesus says to her, "Well you have said that 'Not do I have a husband.' For five men you have had, and now the one you have is not your husband. This, true, you have said."

Says to him the woman, "Lord/Sir [kyrios], I see that you are a prophet. Our fathers on this mountain worshiped, and you [plural] say that in Jerusalem is the place where it is necessary to worship."

Says to her Jesus, "Believe me/trust me, woman, that is coming an hour when neither on this mountain nor in Jerusalem will you [plural] worship the Father. You worship what you do not know; we worship what we know, because the salvation is from the Jews. But is coming an hour, and now is, that the true worshipers will worship the Father in spirit and truth, for the Father, these he seeks, the ones worshiping him. The God is spirit, and the ones worshiping him must worship in spirit and truth . . ."

And upon this, came his disciples, and they were marveling that with a woman he was speaking; no one said either "What do you seek?" or "Why are you speaking with her?" [Here, the woman returns to the city and tells the people that perhaps she has met the Messiah. They go to Jesus and welcome him in their town, where he stays two days. Many come to believe in him.]

. . . To the woman they [the people in Sychar] were saying, "No longer on account of your speech it is that we believe; for we ourselves have heard and we know that this one is truly the savior of the world."

Jesus's encounter with the Samaritan woman in John 4 is among the longest narratives in the Gospels, and among the most mangled when it comes to interpretation. Commentators frequently take the most negative rabbinic commentary about Samaritans, determine that the opinion is normative for all Jews, and then read Jesus as conquering anti-Samaritan prejudice.[35] The flagship Jesuit magazine *America* reports: "The Samaritan woman, socially marginalized by her impurity according to the Law, becomes a model for all Christians" since "even though both groups followed the Law of Moses, differences in the interpretation of purity laws led to a strict separation between" Jews and Samaritans.[36] Commonly cited is the Mishnah Niddah 4.1, "Samaritan women are deemed menstruants from their cradle." Commonly *not* cited is a comment in the same Mishnah, "their uncleanness is a matter of doubt" and, in the next

Mishnah, "When Sadducean women are accustomed to follow in the way of their fathers, look, they are like Samaritan women." Since the rabbinic tradition writes out the Sadducees, it cannot be speaking for all Jews. Ignored are comments, also from the Mishnah, such as Berakhot 7.1, concerning the inclusion of Samaritans in saying the common grace after the meal.

Some commentators, taking this rabbinic comment as an exception, conclude, "Although some Jews could imagine eating with Samaritans (Mishnah Berakoth 7.1), doubtless many Jews would not eat with a Samaritan on the latter's home turf for fear of incurring ritual defilement."[37] "Doubtless," like the expression "no doubt," is presumption, not fact. Historian Alan D. Crown correctly writes: "It was only in the generation after Judah ha-Nasi [post-200 CE], following the Bar Kokhba revolt, that we see the development of anti-Samaritanism in a series of negative statements by the rabbinical teachers, culminating in the ruling that the Samaritans are unquestionably to be considered as Gentiles. Likewise there is evidence from the church fathers that in the first and second centuries the Samaritans were regarded as Jews."[38]

Against negative Jewish stereotypes, Jesus becomes the boundary breaker who consorts with the marginal and outcast, which in this configuration includes Samaritans and gentiles. Given that the gentiles ruled the empire and John 4 is set in Sychar, a Samaritan village, neither "marginal" nor "outcast" is the correct term. Comments such as "if Jesus can be this gracious to Samaritans, whom his fellow Jews treat not as a people but as dogs," he must be "the Savior of the world" are unhelpful.[39] Arguing that he transcends "the stigmas of racism and sexism" are similarly apologetic.[40] The need to find a negative foil over and against which Jesus looks good is historically inaccurate, theologically false, and ethically wrong. Meanwhile, occasional negative comments and actions by Samaritans about Jews, such as the Samaritans' refusal to offer Jesus hospitality in Luke 9:51–56, go unmentioned. Similarly ignored in such studies is how the Samaritan in the famous parable in Luke 10 found himself on the Jerusalem-to-Jericho road and how he was able to find an open inn in the Judean city of Jericho. Samaritans traveled to Judea in the Gospel accounts; no one is calling them dogs.

It is also common for commentators to view the woman as an "outcast" because of her multiple marriages, explaining that she goes to the well at noon because she has been ostracized by the other women who go early in the morning, and then regard Jesus as the sensitive male who disregards the woman's sexual history. For example, "Possibly the woman's public shame (4.16ff.) contributed to her isolation."[41] It is, once again, the commentators and not John who portray the woman as sexually immoral.[42] There is no indication of any isolation or ostracism; if there were, the townspeople would have ignored her notice that Jesus might be the Messiah. Rebekah is alone at a well when she encounters Abraham's enslaved man (Gen. 24:15–27) or, at least, no other figure is there to help her with the task of caring for the servant's animals.[43] The better takeaway from these impositions on the woman is to put our own tendency to judge others as shamed or guilty when, in fact, they are neither.

The Samaritan woman comes to the well at noon because she is the opposite of the Pharisee Nicodemus, who meets Jesus at midnight in the previous chapter. For John's Gospel, with its dualistic thinking, some people are in the dark and so cannot believe in Jesus; others walk in the light and can. The Samaritan woman also comes at noon because the setting is "Jacob's well," and the afternoon is when Jacob met his cousin, later wife, Rachel at that same well: in Genesis 29:7, Jacob says to Rachel, "Look, it is still broad daylight" (literally, "the big day"). The Samaritan comes at noon because the motifs of thirst, drinking, and noon repeat in John's Gospel. The only other time John mentions noon (literally, "the sixth hour") is in 19:14, when Pontius Pilate places Jesus in front of the "the Jews" and states, "Here is your king." At noon the Samaritan woman, a non-Jew, acknowledges Jesus to be the Messiah; at noon the Roman governor, a non-Jew, acknowledges Jesus to be king of the Jews. Finally, in John 19:28, the narrator reports that the crucified Jesus, as he dies, states, "I thirst." We return to the well in Samaria to realize that his thirst is not simply from a parched mouth, but for his relation to humanity.

Now that we've cleaned out the misleading stereotypes, we can return to John 4 to see how the interaction between Jesus and the Samaritan woman again helps us focus on the questions that need to be asked in encountering people outside of our communities. The text also provides various responses, each worth weighing.

Arriving in Samaria

In John's Gospel, *and only in John's Gospel*, Jesus travels through Samaria, meets a woman, and because of her proclamation that he might be the Messiah, gains followers from the Samaritan village of Sychar. John likely knows that Mark's Gospel never mentions Samaritans and that Luke 52–53 depicts residents of a Samaritan village as refusing Jesus hospitality because he was on his way to Jerusalem, where Jews worshiped at the temple on Mount Zion, not at the site of the former Samaritan temple on Mount Gerizim. Matthew 10:5 even has Jesus instructing his disciples, "Enter no town of the Samaritans." To avoid contradicting the Synoptic tradition, which knows of no Samaritan mission, John depicts Jesus alone when he engages with the woman; his disciples have gone to buy lunch, quite likely in another Samaritan village.

Like the accounts of the man possessed by Legion and the Syrophoenician mother, much in the story of the Samaritan woman is historically questionable.[44] I am not arguing that this conversation or something like it never happened; I am suggesting that since there is so much literary and theological overlay in John's account, getting back to a historical core is difficult. The story draws upon the motif from Israel's scriptures of men and women meeting at wells, with marriage as the result. Rebekah and Abraham's enslaved man meet at a well, and the result is the marriage of Rebekah and Isaac. Rachel and Jacob meet at a well, and after some conniving by Rachel's father, she and Jacob marry. Moses meets his future wife Zipporah at a well (Exod. 2:16–21); however, when the future king Saul encounters women at a well, instead of finding a bride, he asks for help in finding his father's lost donkeys (1 Sam. 9). This failure to fulfill the convention anticipates the premature end of Saul's reign.

Evoking such conventions only to take them in new directions is a hallmark of John's Gospel. Another example is John 20, where Mary Magdalene becomes frantic when she finds Jesus's tomb empty. The scene draws on Hellenistic romances, with their depictions of separated lovers, the view of one that the other has died, and cases of mistaken identity. But unlike young lovers in the romances, Jesus and Mary Magdalene do not marry; instead, he commissions her to proclaim his resurrection to his (male) disciples.[45] Although there may be a historical core to John 4, the location, timing, setting, characters, and dialogue rather suggest to me a brilliant theological midrash based on earlier scripture combined with John's distinct christological view.

Our narrative begins, "It was necessary that he pass through Samaria." Jesus did not have to pass through Samaria to travel between Judea and Galilee; there were alternative routes. This route is therefore a theological, not a geographical, necessity.

John enhances the import of the location by specifying, "a city of Samaria called Sychar, a neighbor of the region that gave Jacob to Joseph his son. And was there the water-spring of Jacob." Sychar is otherwise unknown, although it may suggest the name "Shechem," the location that became the capital city of the Northern Kingdom of Israel, Samaria. Following the Assyrian conquest, the name of the city becomes the name of the country. Joshua 24:32, for example, connects Joseph's inheritance from Jacob with a setting at Shechem. John's reference to Joseph is also appropriate to the narrative, since the Samaritans considered themselves the descendants of Joseph's children, Ephraim and Manasseh. Finally, the double reference to Jacob reinforces the connection between Jews and Samaritans, since Jacob was their common ancestor.

This detailed introduction, "a city of Samaria called Sychar, a neighbor of the region that gave Jacob to Joseph his son," reminds me of the increasingly common practice of programs that begin by acknowledging the land's original custodians. Living in the Roman Empire, John insists that this land was originally owned by Jacob and then given to Joseph, and so to his descendants, the Samaritans.

The line also fits into John's genealogical interests. In one of the Gospel's most tense passages, the "Jews" accuse Jesus both of being a Samaritan and of being possessed by a demon (John 8:48). The line comes after Jesus accuses the "Jews" of being "of your father the devil" (John 8:44). For John, Jesus is the Son of God and the "Jews" are children of the devil.[46] Ultimately, ancestry and so genealogy take subordinate positions to the new community that the Johannine Jesus brings into being. As Jesus told the Pharisee Nicodemus in the previous chapter, "Amen, amen, I say to you, unless one is born from water and spirit, one is not able to go into the Kingdom of God" (John 3:5). For the Johannine Jesus, one must be born "anew" or "from above" or "again" (the Greek term *anōthen* in John 3:3, 7 can be translated all three ways). The maternal womb is replaced, and with it so are genealogy and ethnicity. In turn, for John all of Israel's history—the history of both Jews and Samaritans—finds its culmination in Jesus. We can call this approach "universalism" in that it crosses ethnic borders. We can also call it colonialism, in that it replaces or reconfigures all indigenous traditions with a new identity.

Asking for a Drink

Jesus brusquely orders the Samaritan woman, "Give me to drink." This opening line reminds me of his response to his mother's notice that the hosts at the wedding at Cana had run out of wine: "What to me and to you, woman?" (John 2:4; the NRSVUE tones this down to "Woman, what concern is that to me and to you?" and offers as a secondary translation, "What have you to do with me, woman?"). The scenes at Cana and Sychar are connected: quenching thirst, water that is more than it seems, women making demands on Jesus, Jesus calling a woman "woman" and uttering enigmatic comments, wedding and bridegroom imagery, references to time, signs that lead to faith. Since we know that Jesus will respond to his mother's notice by turning water into wine, we can be assured that he will also provide the Samaritan woman with what she needs. The problem: we readers do not yet know what this need is. Nor, fully, does she.

Jesus's request for water is not a sign that he "invites impurity."[47] Also wrong is the claim, "Surely no right-minded Jew would do that even if he were dying of thirst!"[48] Samaritans and Jews follow the same dietary regulations and forms of ritual purity. The issue for John 4 is not purity; it is sectarian difference. John's comment in 4:8 that the disciples had gone into the city to buy lunch would make no sense if consuming food or water touched by Samaritans generated impurity. Jesus asks the woman for water because he is thirsty, both for water and for being in relation to humanity. The oxymoron, that the one who provides "living water" also "thirsts," contributes to the power of the imagery.

The woman holds Jesus in conversation ironically by suggesting that they have nothing to talk about: "How it is that you, being a Jew, from me, are asking something to drink, being that I am a Samaritan woman?" Whether the next line about Jews and Samaritans not sharing is part of her dialogue or John's editorial aside is not clear, but in either case, it is overstated. Josephus tells us that Herod Antipas (the one who kills John the Baptizer) and Herod Archelaus (the deposed ruler of Judea) are sons of Herod the Great and Malthace, his *Samaritan* wife (*Antiquities* 17.20; *War* 1.562). We also have that famous parable depicting a Samaritan going down the Jerusalem-to-Jericho road; at the start of the journey and at its end, he would have been engaged with Jews. That he stopped to help may have been a surprise to an audience who had just heard how Samaritans refused Jesus hospitality; that Jews and Samaritans talked with each other, and sometimes made common cause, usually against Rome, would not have been.

I am struck that the Samaritan woman identifies Jesus as a "Jew." John may be engaging in more irony here. The term "Jew" (Greek: *Ioudaios*) can also be translated "Judean," a translation a number of commentators prefer, whether because it focuses more on geographical origin than on the "religious" identity that the term "Jew" today conveys, or because it can serve to exculpate the "Jews" from killing Jesus: instead, it was the Judeans.[49] If we translate "Judean" here, then the woman is incorrect, since John emphasizes that Jesus is from Nazareth in Galilee, not Judea (John 1:45, 46; 18:5, 7; 19:19). Yet if we translate "Jew," the woman may still be in error, at least for John's take. For John, the Jews are the "children of the devil" (John 8:44), which Jesus clearly is not. She may, for John's purposes, be just as wrong about Jesus's identity as she is about Jews and Samaritans not sharing.

Misguided also are typical comments that "she begins by questioning Jesus' breaking with Jewish tradition, first by speaking in public to a woman."[50] While society, both Jewish and gentile, was homosocial in that men socialized predominantly with men and women predominantly with women, there was no law against speaking with a woman in public—if there were, one wonders how Jesus's mother instructed the wine steward to listen to her son in Cana (John 2), or why Martha challenges Jesus at her brother's tomb (John 11), or how a woman could challenge Peter at the high priest's court (John 18), or how Mary Magdalene could tell Peter and the Beloved Disciple about the empty tomb (John 20), and so on. Nor, by the way, is there anyone other than Jesus and the woman in this "public" place.

Nothing—*nothing*—in rabbinic literature forbids men and women from speaking with each other. In Pirke Avot 1.5 (cf. Avot deRabbi Natan 7.3), Rabbi Yose ben Yochanan of Jerusalem states, "Let your house be wide open, and make the poor members of your household," which means give the poor a seat at your table and take care of their needs, "and don't talk too much with women." Strangely, the first two of his sayings rarely find their way into Jesus's discussions and parables concerning table fellowship. The final line, which admonishes against *excessive* speech, is not unexpected in a homosocial society.

Theological Discussion Begins

Jesus asks the woman for water. She demurs. He then moves into theological discourse: "If you had known the gift of God, and who it is that is saying to you, 'Give me to drink,' you would have asked him, and he would have given to you living water." If this happened to me at the water cooler, I'd be calling security. But the woman hangs in there. We readers do as well, because by chapter 4 of John's Gospel, we know that the Johannine Jesus is inclined to pun (as with Nicodemus, on being born *anōthen*, although Nicodemus never quite catches on). In speaking to the woman of "living water/running water," Jesus encourages her to move from the mundane to the transcendent.

Commentators frequently see the woman as showing "no sign of understanding what Jesus is talking about,"[51] but because it is midday and not midnight (when Jesus and Nicodemus have their conversation), John's symbolism indicates that the woman will gain understanding. Jesus's language is cryptic, but she's going to play along. She first observes that he lacks a bucket and the well is deep, and so she asks where he's going to get this "living water," which is in Greek the same expression as "running water."

But she is not stuck on the mundane, since she then asks Jesus whether he could be greater than "our father Jacob." She already knows he is intimating something more than running water. Moreover, by mentioning Jacob, she suggests a connection between Jesus the Jew and she the Samaritan. In speaking to "others," finding something, or someone, shared can be a good overture.

Jesus responds, again enigmatically, about how the "water I myself will give" will become in others "a spring of water leaping up into eternal life." He is not taking her bait about discussing the connections and divisions between Jews and Samaritans. He is, however, moving into another literary convention, one already intimated by the woman's comment about the deep well and the bucket. Talk of springs and wells, dipping buckets and even living water, is the language of flirting, which, given the convention of meeting a spouse at a well, nicely follows.

A number of my students do not like this idea. They want to see Jesus as fully human (although without sin—how that works, given that part of being human is to understand guilt, repentance, and forgiveness, is above my pay grade; I'm a historian, not a theologian), but they do not want to see him as flirting, let alone having a sense of humor.

The Husbands

Jesus next orders the woman to call her husband. What might *she* be thinking of this request: Does he want to determine whether she is married? If she will lie about her present relationship? With all that talk of deep wells and spouting springs, and with the courtship of Jacob and Rachel in the background, is she wondering if he is available?

Perhaps sensing a threat, she dissembles: "Not do I have a husband."

Jesus then reveals what he knows about her: that she has been married five times and is currently cohabiting with a man who is not her husband. Jesus is not turning to "the woman's sin . . . [the] morally messy past" in order to bring her to confession and then absolution;[52] the woman is not acting "like this were the first time she realized the seriousness of [her life] or finally arrived at self-knowledge or a sense of sin."[53] Aside from a tendency to associate women and sexual sin, commentators rush to this view since it then puts Jesus in the position of redeeming her from sin. That he *says nothing* about how her past has been morally messy they take to be an indication of his pastoral care. The only people who determine she has a bad reputation are the critics, since the Samaritans, who take her word that she might have met the Messiah, have no problem trusting her. Their argument about Jesus, which follows from this sexualized conclusion, is based on the silence of the text. We do better when we pay attention to what he does say, and we do better when we do not project shame or guilt onto others.

The dialogue may be another indication of John's rewriting material in the Synoptic Gospels. For example, John may have turned Luke 16:19–31—the Parable of the Rich Man and Lazarus, which contains the name "Lazarus" (the only named person in a parable) and is partially about the inability of people to repent even when someone returns from the dead—into the story of the raising of Lazarus. Underlying John 4 may be the question raised by the Sadducees—who are sometimes confused in rabbinic literature with Samaritans—about marital status in the resurrection of a woman who had been married to seven brothers (Matt. 22:25–28; Mark 12:20; Luke 20:29–33).

At the very least, the question about the husbands becomes another play on the convention of meeting a wife at the well. Not only is this woman from the wrong group, but she's also not the expected virgin. Clearly, something other than matchmaking is going on.

The woman, recognizing that Jesus knows her marital history, turns the conversation from marriage to Jewish-Samaritan relations by asking Jesus about the correct place to worship. Jesus answers with a somewhat convoluted discourse that boils down to two points. First is the prediction of the time when worship will take place on neither Mount Gerizim in Samaria nor Mount Zion in Jerusalem. Instead, the time is coming, and for John's readers "now" is given that John is writing after the destruction of the Jerusalem temple, when worship is focused on "spirit and truth" and so, by implication, is not connected to a place. Samaritans, who still worship on Mount Gerizim, would disagree, as would Jews who, although legally not permitted to worship on the Temple Mount, where the Dome of the Rock and the Al-Aqsa Mosque now sit, still hold the site as sacred. Second is the assertion that Samaritan worship is wrong. Jesus was not a pluralist. He was not a "we are all climbing up the same mountain" universalist. He regards Samaritan tradition as a deviation.

Nor does Jesus invent the "radical concept of atopic worship: humans do not have to travel to a particular place to worship because God meets them wherever they worship in spirit."[54] Jews, and Samaritans, could worship God anywhere. The Hasmonean king John Hyrcanus I burned down the Samaritan temple around 112/111 BCE;[55] the Romans burned down the Jerusalem temple in 70 CE. Neither event made it impossible for Samaritans and Jews to worship. For John, no temple is needed because, first, Rome had already burned down the Jerusalem temple, and second, Jesus replaces the temple as the (locus of) sacrifice. Given that Jesus, for John, replaces the temple, the issue is less atopic ("not at a specific place") worship than a franchise where worship takes place among the followers of Jesus. The ethnic/geographical focus is removed, which is appropriate for a group, later to be called Christians, that is based in a belief system rather than on a connection to a particular ethnic group.

Again, the tradition helps us think. People have connections to land, and to buildings. This is why many congregants find the consolidation of houses of worship, whether Roman Catholic or Methodist or Jewish, so difficult. Location represents a home, a history, just as did Jacob's well to the Samaritan woman. Telling someone that "place" is unimportant or that one place can be re-placed is usually not a good move. John is looking forward to those "many mansions" (John 14:2, KJV) that Jesus is preparing for his followers. Knowing why some groups feel an attachment to place and others do not, and how politics informs both positions, can help with understanding across borders.

The Results

While Jesus is making this pronouncement to the Samaritan woman, the disciples return with lunch. They marvel that Jesus is speaking with this woman, but *not* because rabbis were not permitted to speak with women. It is just as likely that they rarely saw him engage women in conversation.[56] They are marveling because she is a Samaritan woman and that she is alone with Jesus at a well. The sexual innuendos cannot be avoided. No wonder they did not ask him any questions.

The woman leaves her bucket behind, symbolizing that she now has living water and no longer needs the earthly kind, and announces to the people in Sychar that she may have found the Messiah. The people go out to see for themselves. Another Johannine motif is in play in which one person brings another to Jesus: Andrew brings Peter, Martha brings her sister Mary, and so on. The Samaritans welcome Jesus to their town, where a symbolic wedding of sorts occurs as he stays with them two days, and they believe in him.

John 4 accomplishes several goals: It depicts Jesus as fulfilling and then surpassing conventions found in the scriptures. It also anticipates the cross, where Jesus again thirsts and where his body becomes the new temple and site of sacrifice. It contrasts the Samaritan welcome with his reception in his native land, for as he says at the end of the scene, "A prophet in his own fatherland honor he does not have" (John 4:44).

John's Gospel is retelling the stories from the Synoptics and so it reveals that stories can be and even should be told in multiple ways. This ability to see different nuances, even different details, in our own history should make us more sympathetic to the stories people outside our group tell. Rather than look for consistency, we can look for conventions, or reactions, or pronouncements that have their own political and sociological rationales.

For John, both Samaritan and Jewish identities become subsumed into the group around Jesus. Spiritual descent, being born by water and spirit (John 3:5), replaces family, genealogy, and ethnicity. For Jesus himself, Jews remained Jews, Samaritans remained Samaritans, and gentiles remained gentiles. Even when Paul states in Galatians 3:28 that in the Christ there is neither Jew nor Greek, slave nor free, male nor female, he is not erasing these identities. His point is that in the eyes of God, such identifiers are not important. As the medieval Jewish text Tanna de b'Eliyahu 9 puts it, the divine Spirit rests on each person, Jew or gentile, male or female, "in accordance with deeds."

AND NOW?

The Gospels' force is to encourage us to reconsider ethnicity and geography, particularism and universalism. When we see Gerasa, or the Decapolis, will we think of tombs and blood and scars, or will we recall a man proclaiming what Jesus did for him? Do we think of two thousand pig carcasses floating in the water, or four thousand people eating fish and bread on a hillside? For citizens of the United States, the same questions can be posed with regard to Germany and Korea, Vietnam and Afghanistan, and many, many more. What images do these places evoke for us, and how might new stories change the picture?

Mark's depiction of the Syrophoenician woman and her interaction with Jesus helps us ask questions about resource allocation: Should funding go first to the "children" and then to the "dogs," or are we all children in need? The story helps us get beyond the tendency to ratchet up violence, or repay insult with insult, and move to a place where everyone can benefit. It shows that "great men" are capable of changing their minds, and tenacious, desperate women are capable of helping them, forcing them, to change. And it shows the strength required to absorb an insult rather than to give up or to punch back. The life of a child is more important than honor, a point that helps to counter today's concerns for toxic masculinity, whether in the schoolyard or in the boardroom.

When Jesus tells the Samaritan woman that she worships what

she does not know and that "salvation is from the Jews," he makes the case that people should not sacrifice their beliefs for the sake of interreligious harmony. And yet, the woman does not explicitly state she agrees with him. Instead, she notes that the Messiah will reveal the truth. Jesus then insists that he is the Messiah. She leaves the question open, "He cannot be the Messiah [Greek: *christos*], can he?" (John 4:29). The last reference to her is John 4:42, "To the woman they were saying, 'No longer on account of your speech it is that we believe; for we ourselves have heard and we know that this one is truly the savior of the world." She does not affirm their claim. I like to think of the woman as returning to the well and thinking, This is *our place*, that *our ancestor* Jacob gave to Joseph, where *we worship* and where over the centuries *we will still worship*.

Putting truth claims off to the inbreaking of the kingdom of God is not a bad move. Samaritans who were still worshiping on Mount Gerizim did this. Jews who did not join the movement around Jesus did this. John's prediction of the unification of the two groups in spirit and truth has not happened. Given the various empires—Greek, Roman, Christian, Muslim, Ottoman, British—that have occupied the land where the Jews and the Samaritans still remain, and remain attached to the sites where their temples stood, calls into question the surety with which biblical predictions should be assessed. They also help us to see why, in so many cases, including the Middle East, the question of land is not just a matter of spirit and truth; it is also a matter of stone and soil.

When I was in elementary school, we were taught that the United States was a melting pot of people and cultures. John's Gospel opts for the melting pot, where all worship together in spirit and truth, where Samaritan worship is dismissed and Samaritan geography is now to be associated not just with Jacob's well, but with what Jesus did there.

Today we, or at least many of us, find the metaphor of the melting pot unhelpful, since the melting pot waters down distinct flavors, distinct identities. The metaphor shifted to salad bowl, with each flavor, each color and texture, making its own contribution. Whatever the best metaphor to use, I'm more concerned that we recognize what is at stake in the preservation of identity, what is evoked when we speak of particular people from particular locations, what happens when the call to a universal religion oppresses people who have different theologies and practices, and what can be gained when we contact each other.

CHAPTER 4
HEALTH CARE

SEVERAL YEARS AGO, I attended a conference on the historical Jesus sponsored by a Baptist seminary. The faculty and students were warm and welcoming, the local coffee was superb, the conversations about the Gospels were of high caliber. During one panel on Jesus's incarnation and resurrection, I suggested that both the incarnation (the idea that the divine takes on flesh, *carne*) and resurrection (the idea that Jesus rose bodily from the dead as opposed to being a ghost) meant that for the Gospels, the body, the *flesh*, is important. Therefore, the Gospels suggest that we should care for the body.

One fellow from the audience responded, "So, your point is that we should support Obamacare?" His tone suggested that such support was, well, un-Christian. I had not been thinking about the Affordable Care Act; I had been thinking about a friend in Nashville who had just entered hospice.

The Bible prompts us, or at least it prompts me, to think about disease and healing, doctors and diagnoses, impairment and disability.[1] While it points to various health-care providers—spouses, children, siblings, parents, slaves or servants, families, local villages, religious institutions, governmental authorities, etc.—it also reports that medical costs can reduce people to penury, as attested by the woman, hemorrhaging for twelve years, who had "spent all that was hers" (Mark 5:26 // Luke 8:43) on physicians.

For skeptics, accounts of miraculous healing are fairy tales, or opiates that dull logic and rationality. At best they are metaphors designed to indicate how Jesus inaugurates the messianic age, since in his synagogue sermon in Nazareth, he proclaims himself anointed "to give sight to the blind" (Luke 4:18). I think they do more.

Accounts of tumors shrinking, paralyzed people walking, and heart disease disappearing surface in appeals for the canonization of Roman Catholic saints, in evangelical healing services, and in personal testimonies (I have heard many). An internet search for "miraculous healing" yielded more than seventeen million results. Some writers attempt to explain spontaneous remissions by "genomics" since "therapies used in integrative medicine such as diet, exercise, meditation, stress management . . . all have the potential to actually turn on or off the genes for chronic diseases such as diabetes, heart disease and cancer."[2] Even skeptics admit that prayer can help in healing by providing the sufferer with psychological support, reducing stress and so reducing the hormones that exacerbate ailments.[3] People who have experienced unexpected recovery may use the term "miracle." Because of a bout of endocarditis, which almost killed me, I have two mechanical heart valves. My friends told me that God had answered their prayers in keeping me alive; I am more inclined to credit the health-care providers at Vanderbilt Hospital. We may both be right.

Jesus was known as a healer and an exorcist. That reputation is probably the reason he gained an audience. Standing on a rock in Capernaum and announcing "a sower went out to sow" will not draw crowds. Nor was Jesus the only healer in the neighborhood. The Gospels mention other exorcists (Matt. 12:27 // Luke 11:19), and

Acts 19:13–16 depicts, humorously, the otherwise unknown "seven sons of a Jewish high priest named Sceva" who attempted to exorcise a demon, only to have the demon respond, "Jesus I know, and Paul I know; but who are you?" The possessed man then leaps upon the exorcists, who flee "naked and wounded." Luke's audience likely would have found this example of schadenfreude hilarious. Attacks by demons that leave people wounded (the Greek is *tramatidzō*, whence "trauma") and vulnerable is not, to me, amusing.

This chapter looks at the historical context of and the teachings of Jesus and what questions they raise for what it means to heal, to promote physical and spiritual welfare. It exorcises (I couldn't resist) incorrect stereotypes that pervade readings of these texts, including the pernicious association of sickness with sin and the view that ill and disabled people are socially expendable.

Our test cases, or case studies, start with the conjoined stories of a woman suffering from vaginal or uterine hemorrhage and the dead daughter of the synagogue ruler Jairus. These narratives do more than show that Jesus can perform "mighty works," which is a better translation than "miracles" of the Greek *dynamis* (whence "dynamic"). For those who begin from a confessional position, the stories of Jesus as healer help "to address the *embodied* character of Christian faith in a way that underscores how one can experience God's care and compassion as something related to more than human spiritual welfare" (emphasis added).[4] Even if one is not a theist, the stories insist that bodies matter and that consequently health care matters. The healing narratives further show the value of agency, of familial and communal support. They finally show that free health care is a miracle.

Next is Luke's short, and less familiar, story of a man whom Jesus heals from dropsy, or edema. This narrative provides the opportunity to address how the language of sickness and cure can be helpful in treating the "diseases" often seen as of the soul rather than the body, such as greed or sloth; how physical appearance (physiognomy) and disease are related in ancient, and modern, thought; how to decouple the association of illness and disability with sin; and finally how to excise comments about the dreaded "legalism" with which Christians continue to charge Jews, here in relation to the role of healing on the Sabbath.

GENERAL COMMENTS

The constitution of the World Health Organization (WHO) defines "health" as "a state of complete physical, mental and social well-being and not merely the absence of disease or infirmity."[5] The societal concern also hints at how, where, when, and by whom disease and disability are diagnosed. What one society views as disease or disability could be seen as normal or a gift in another; diagnosis and treatment depend on context.[6]

In medical settings, personnel may refer to a patient as "the gall bladder in room 224" or "the broken arm at 3:00." Although the scriptures of Israel name impaired or diseased individuals—Naaman, whose leprosy the prophet Elisha heals (2 Kings 5; cf. Luke 4:27); Nebuchadnezzar, whose mental regression the prophet Daniel witnesses (Dan. 4:33)—the Gospels typically identify individuals by their symptoms: a hemorrhaging woman, a blind man, and so on. The WHO's interest in social well-being includes awareness that identities change. When the woman who had suffered hemorrhages no longer bleeds and the sightless man can see, both they and the people with whom they interact require new means of identification.[7]

We also need to use care with medical terms. The English language contains multiple idioms that connect physical impairment with spiritual or intellectual disability. Questions such as "Are you blind?" or "Are you deaf?" get asked when people miss our points or ignore our instructions. "What a lame comment" suggests that the remark goes nowhere. The point is not unique to English. Daniel C. Smith notes: "Plato, Galen, and the author of Luke-Acts all seem quite comfortable associating blindness with ignorance; it is a bodily difference and a loaded cultural signifier. To lack sightedness is, often enough, to fail to understand—here the linguistic slippage between the Greek *eidon* (I saw) and *oida* (I understand/I know) illustrates a point made explicit elsewhere."[8]

Jesus describes the Pharisees as "blind guides" (Matt. 15:14; 23:16, 24) and so equates blindness with ignorance if not malevolence. His famous metaphorical comment about the "blind leading the blind" (Matt. 15:14 // Luke 6:39) implies that sightless people cannot find their way, a false presupposition. In reading the Gospels, we do well to resist such metaphors.

Several years ago, during a talk for a local Church of Christ (already a miracle that a church from a relatively conservative denomination would extend an invitation), I used the term "leper" to describe one of the people whom Jesus healed. My point was about how Jesus told the man to offer the sacrifice expected for such healings (Mark 1:40–45) and thus how Jesus approved of temple sacrifice. A man in the audience stopped me, introduced himself as a dermatologist, and explained that people who have leprosy (Hansen's disease; the Greek *lepros* and Hebrew *tzara'* suggest temporary skin disfigurations) prefer not to be called "lepers," given the negative connotations of the term. I've done my best to be careful with this and other problematic descriptors.

EXORCISING FALSE VIEWS

The first stereotype is that, in Jewish thought, health is a sign of righteousness; disease or disability, a sign of sin. Second is the view that this categorization prevailed in early Judaism and that Jesus broke the connection between sickness and sin, thereby welcoming the marginalized—the blind, the deaf, those unable to walk or to speak, those suffering from skin diseases or hemorrhages—back into community. The first presumption about sin and illness has minimal support but requires nuance. The second is apologetic that uses incorrect historical reconstruction in order to make Jesus look good by making Judaism look bad. Once we diagnose and then excise the stereotypes, we are in a better position to find a better plan of care.

SIN AND SUFFERING

One popular evangelical commentary series asserts, "Jewish rabbis generally believed in a direct cause-and-effect relationship between suffering and sin (cf. the Book of Job, e.g., 4:7; *b. Sabb.* 55a). Jesus, however, while acknowledging the possibility that suffering may be the direct result of sin (cf. John 5:14), denied that such was invariably the case."[9] Sometimes it helps to look up the verses. For example, Job 4:7 asks "who that was innocent ever perished?" The book of Job indicates that these words, from Job's "friend" (friends like Job's we do not need) Eliphaz the Temanite (not a Jew), are incorrect. All people die, period. The issue is not "sin." The issue is mortality. Moreover, the book of Job insists that Job's suffering is *not* caused by sin; rather, it is a test to see whether Job will curse God. The citation to b. Shabbat 55a is to the line, "Rabbi Ami said, 'There is no death without sin and no suffering without transgression.'" The author's conclusion on what "Jewish rabbis" taught, however, is a misreading of rabbinic literature. The rest of b. Shabbat 55a *debates* Rabbi Ami's claim. As rabbinic scholar David Kraemer demonstrates, "the

Bavli [i.e., Babylonian Talmud] leads us to a complete refutation of R. Ami's view."[10] The next page, b. Shabbat 55b, adduces a number of arguments against R. Ami and concludes, "There is death without sin and there is suffering without iniquity, and this is a conclusive refutation of the opinion of Rav Ami."[11]

Finally, since early Judaism never stated that sickness was "invariably" the result of sin, the statement is wrong again in its separating of Jesus from his fellow Jews.

The Bible and later Jewish tradition recognize that illness and disability are part of the world. We see (note the metaphor!) this point most poignantly with the aged Isaac, whose "eyes were dim so that he could not see" (Gen. 27:1). Declining eyesight runs in the family, for "the eyes of Israel [i.e., Jacob] were dim with age, and he could not see well" (Gen. 48:10a). This is Jacob's second disability; wrestling at the Jabbok River, he suffered an injury that caused him to walk with a limp (Gen. 32:31). Jonathan's son Mephibosheth falls and so walks with difficulty (2 Sam. 4:4). Daniel recounts that he "lay sick for some days" as the result of a prophetic dream (Dan. 8:27). The problem is migraine, not sin. In the book of Tobit, the titular hero is blinded by bird droppings. Accidents happen. Again, sin and disability are decoupled. The list continues into the New Testament, where sin is only rarely mentioned in connection with people whom Jesus or his followers cure of demon possession, disease, or disability.

When the Bible connects sin with suffering, the context is often national. For example, Moses warns the Israelites that if they act without righteousness, they will be afflicted with "consumption, fever, inflammation, with fiery heat and drought, and with blight and mildew" (Deut. 28:22). Societies that fail to care for their most vulnerable—in biblical terms the poor, the widow, the orphan, and the migrant—are "sick" societies that will collapse. The punishments of heat and drought take on heightened meaning given climate change.

The few biblical accounts connecting disease with sin make the cause explicit. The most famous in Israel's scriptures is that of Miriam, struck with leprosy for seven days because she questioned Moses's authority (Num. 12). Numbers 12:14 notes that even though Miriam was quarantined seven days, the people did not resume their journey until the symptoms abated. They refused to leave without her. They did not, in other words, cast her out.

Another famous case of leprosy, that of Naaman, never connects the disease with sin. Nor does Naaman's leprosy prevent him from commanding the king of Aram's army (2 Kings 5:1). His story also warns against importing the stereotype that people who had leprosy were exiled or ostracized. As Myrick C. Shinall Jr. summarizes, "there is evidence in the gospels that [people with leprosy] had relatively unhindered social access. Interpretations that see the overcoming of social stigma in Jesus's healings of leprosy stem not so much from consideration of the textual evidence as from a latent tendency to construe Judaism negatively in order to make Jesus appear in a more positive light."[12]

Providing a test case from the field of disability studies, Mike Gulliver and William John Lyons query earlier scholarship that saw life as "necessarily a squalid one" for the deaf in ancient Israel. After detailing what Israel's scriptures say about deaf people, they ask, "Given the right conditions, what would have prevented deaf people in that society from being a part of a vibrant, active, communicating, signing community?"[13] The quality of an individual's life depends on familial and community support; economic resources; personal traits such as intelligence, curiosity, and tenacity; luck; and a variety of other markers. The same is true today.

Were individual suffering to be seen as prompted by sin, the Bible's repeated concern for those who suffer would make no sense. Leviticus 19:14, the same chapter that proclaims "love your neighbor as yourself," demands, "You shall not revile the deaf person or put a stumbling block before the blind person; you shall fear your God." Deuteronomy 27:18a is stronger: "Cursed be anyone who misleads a blind person on the road!"

The most famous biblical connection between disability and sin appears in John 9:2–3, where the disciples ask Jesus, "Rabbi, who sinned, this man or his parents, that he was born blind?" Jesus responds, "Neither this man nor his parents sinned; he was born blind so that God's works might be revealed in him." The question is problematic because it presumes that all congenital problems result from sin. In some instances, such as drug and alcohol use, parental behavior negatively impacts pregnancy. However, other factors also impact pregnancy. Food insecurity, chemicals in the environment, and lack of available or affordable prenatal care can also lead to congenital problems. The disciples' question is misinformed. Worse, it can lead to guilt on the part of the parents.

The answer Jesus offers is also problematic because it justifies the blindness in service to Christology. Then again, I know of many people who understand their disability as a test and their endurance as testimony to their faith. This approach follows from 2 Corinthians 12:7, where Paul mentions the "thorn . . . in the flesh, a messenger of Satan," designed to keep him from pride. To be tested or to keep from pride is not the same thing as to be punished for sin.

In another case, Jesus connects sin and suffering. In John 5:14, he tells the man whom he had healed from decades of paralysis, "Sin no more." As with any diagnosis, a case-by-case approach is a better move than presuming a connection between disability/disease and suffering. Emphysema caused by years of smoking is not the same thing as emphysema caused by alpha-1-antitrypsin deficiency.

INFERTILITY

The Hebrew term for healing, *rapha* (as in the angel Raphael, whose name means "God has healed"), first appears when Abraham prays for the healing of infertility experienced by the women of Gerar. Abraham had told the king, Abimelech, that Sarah was his sister, and the king, oblivious to their marital relationship, took Sarah into his harem. In response, God closed the wombs of the women in the king's household. The infertility alerts Abimelech that something is amiss. Discovering the deception, he condemns Abraham: "How have I sinned against you, that you have brought on me and my kingdom this great sin?" (Gen. 20:9). Abraham prays, and in response God heals (*rapha*) Abimelech, "his wife and female slaves" of infertility (Gen. 20:17).

Candida Moss and Joel Baden speak of infertility as an "invisible disability."[14] It is also one that combines major expenses with heartache: couples struggling with infertility may spend thousands of dollars for in vitro fertilization, and they find their hearts sinking at every baptism or bris or baby naming.

In the Bible numerous women suffer infertility: Sarah, Rebekah, Rachel, Mrs. Manoah (Samson's mother), Hannah (the mother of Samuel), and the Great Woman of Shunem. None is connected to sin. Other women have no children, or at least none is mentioned, and they express no distress: Dinah, Miriam, Deborah, Esther, and from the deuterocanonical literature (Old Testament Apocrypha) Judith. The Gospels offer one account of infertility. Elizabeth, the mother of John the Baptizer, was "righteous before God" and "blameless" (Luke 1:6). She was also unable to conceive, and because of her infertility she "endured reproach among people" (Luke 1:25).

From this passage, commentators conclude that childlessness "in Judaism was a misfortune, even a disgrace or a punishment for sin (see Gen 16:4, 11; 29:32; 30:1; Lev 20:20–21; 1 Sam 1:5–6; 2 Sam 6:23)."[15] The claim overstates. Misfortune, yes, as would be the case regardless of culture for a woman who wants children; feelings of personal disgrace, the same. But the issue is not sin. Luke 1:25 echoes Genesis 30:23, where Rachel, upon giving birth to Joseph, states that God has taken away her disgrace. The disgrace is her self-perception, especially given that her sister, Leah, and the enslaved cowife, Zilphah, have produced children.[16]

Second Samuel 6:23 records, regarding one of David's wives, "Michal the daughter of Saul had no child to the day of her death." The narrator leaves unmentioned *why* she had no child: had David refused to have relations with her, lest she give birth to a political rival, or had she, having come to despise David, refused him her bed? Did *she* feel that her lack of children by David was a blessing or a curse? Finally, Leviticus 20:20–21 states that adulterous relationships result in childlessness, which is not the case biologically (sperm and egg are not aware of connubial legalities) and so functions as a threat, at best. The equating of sin and infertility is therefore not a commonplace.

VISITING THE SICK

If Jews equated sickness and sin, then the mitzvah, the commandment, of visiting the sick (Hebrew: *bikur cholim*) would make little sense. Sirach 7:35 mandates, "Do not hesitate to visit the sick, because for such deeds you will be loved." The tradition ostensibly traces back to Genesis 18:1, "The LORD appeared to Abraham by the oaks of Mamre, as he sat at the entrance of his tent in the heat of the day." The verse immediately follows the account of Abraham's circumcision, so therefore God visited Abraham as he recuperated (b. Sota 14a).

In synagogues today, when congregants recite the prayer for healing, the Mi Shebeirach, they announce the names of those needing healing—whether members of the congregation, relatives, friends, including non-Jews—and then pray on their behalf. The announcement informs the congregation of who needs support; the names indicate both the people in need of healing and their families. Some Christian churches have the same system, where either during the service or in the morning bulletin the names of people in hospital or convalescing are read. Many churches will send eucharistic ministers to people unable to attend services.

In the New Testament, James 5:14–16 proposes that anyone in the congregation who is sick should call for the church elders "and have them pray over them, anointing them with oil in the name of the Lord." James asserts that the prayers of the faithful "will save the sick, and the Lord will raise them up, and anyone who has committed sins will be forgiven. Therefore, confess your sins to one another, and pray for one another, so that you may be healed. The prayer of the righteous is powerful and effective."

The passage makes several helpful points. First, if you are sick, say something. Stewing because no one called when we were ill, when we never informed anyone in the first place, is counterproductive. Second, anointing with oil is also a form of practical health care. The body is to be touched not avoided; it is to be eased with sweet-smelling ointment. Third, for the Epistle of James, the ailing body becomes not a burden but an opportunity for the community to unite. Although people were, and are, well aware that prayer does not always, even often, save—death comes for us all—they knew, and know, that prayer can be sustaining. Regarding prayer, and anointing, and visiting . . . as my mother would say, "It couldn't hurt."

HEALING, SIN, AND SALVATION

Jeremiah's prayer connects physical healing with salvation: "Heal [Hebrew: *rapha*] me, O LORD, and I shall be healed; save [Hebrew: *yasha*] me, and I shall be saved" (Jer. 17:14). In Israel's scriptures, salvation, from the root *y-sh-'*, the source of the names Joshua, Hosea, and Jesus, typically connotes being saved in this world: manumission from slavery, rescue from invasion, preservation from drought, recovery following an illness. "Salvation" was something manifest.

Salvation language also applies to sin: Tobit 12:9 states that charity "saves from death and purges away every sin"; Sirach 2:11 asserts that God both "forgives sin and saves in times of distress." While Matthew 1:21 identifies Jesus as one "who will save his people from their sins," the Synoptic Gospels frequently quote Jesus as telling someone, "Your faith has 'saved' [*sōzō*] you." Context helps us determine whether he is speaking about a medical condition, a spiritual one, or both.

Salvation from sin is more difficult to demonstrate than a healing. The question "Which is easier, to say, 'Are forgiven your sins,' or to say, 'Rise and walk around'?" (Matt. 9:5; cf. Mark 2:9; Luke 5:23) misleads, since technically both are easy to *say*. Which is easier to *prove* is a different matter. When Jesus pronounces a man's sins forgiven and then heals that man (Matt. 9:2–8 // Mark 2:3–12 // Luke 5:18–26) who had been suffering from paralysis, audiences gather that his statement about forgiveness was correct. The healing does not demonstrate the connection between sin and paralysis; it demonstrates that Jesus has the authority to forgive sin.

Rather than get bogged down in the "did Jesus heal or did he not?" debates, with conservatives affirming the historicity of the healing and liberals seeing a parable of how guilt can paralyze, we do better to ask what we can learn from the account.[17] The Gospels are christological proclamations, but they are more than that. They also tell us something about ourselves, our bodies, our support systems, and how we present ourselves to, and are understood by, those who encounter us.

WOMAN WITH HEMORRHAGES AND DYING DAUGHTER

The intertwined stories of a woman who suffered twelve years with (likely) uterine or vaginal hemorrhages and a dead twelve-year-old girl appear in all three Synoptic Gospels (Mark 5:21–43 // Matt. 9:18–26 // Luke 8:40–56). Since Mark's version is the earliest of the three, we start with Mark and note changes Matthew and Luke provide. Their interpretations show how ignorance of early Judaism leads to negative stereotyping of Jews and deformation of women's history. A corrected starting point reveals an extraordinary story of agency, trust, courage, the setting of priorities, and even new family values.

> And having gone over, Jesus [in a boat],[18] again, across, were gathered together a great crowd to him, and he was by the sea. And comes, one of the synagogue leaders, named Jairus, and seeing him, he falls to [Jesus's] feet. And he calls him, much, saying that "My daughter is about to die, so that coming, you might place the hands on her so that she is saved and lives." And he went out with him, and followed him a large crowd, and it was crushing him.
>
> And a woman being in a flow of blood twelve years, and much suffering from many physicians and having spent all that was hers, and not was she benefited, but rather into the worse, she had come. Having heard about Jesus, she, coming in the crowd, from behind, she touched his garment. For she was saying that "if I might touch, even of his garments, I shall be saved."

And immediately was dried up the spring of her blood, and she knew by the body that she had been healed from the torment.

And immediately, Jesus, knowing in himself that out of him power had gone out, turning to the crowd, was saying, "Who touched my clothes?" And were saying to him his disciples, "You see the crowd crushing you, and you say, 'Who touched me?'" And he was looking around to see the one having done this.

And the woman, fearing and trembling, knowing what had happened to her, came and fell down to him and said to him all the truth. And he said to her, "Daughter, your faith/trust has saved you. Go in peace and be healthy from your torment."

Still while he was speaking, they come from the synagogue leader, saying that "your daughter has died; why still do you trouble the teacher?" And Jesus, refusing to listen to the word being spoken, says to the synagogue leader, "Do not fear; only have faith/trust." And not did he permit any one with him to follow, except Peter and Jacob and John the brother of Jacob.

And coming into the house of the synagogue leader, and seeing the commotion and weeping and much wailing, and having entered, he says to them, "Why are you making a commotion and weeping? The child is not dead, but she sleeps."

And they were laughing at him. But he himself, casting out all, takes the father of the child and the mother and those with him, and he comes in where was the child. And seizing the hand of the child, he says to her, "*Talitha cum*," which is translated, "Girl, to you I say, rise." And immediately rose up the girl, and she walked around, for she was twelve years old. And they were amazed [immediately],[19] with great amazement. And he commanded to them much that no one should know this, and he said to give her [something] to eat.

The standard interpretation of these two healings is that they show Jesus transgressing Jewish law by touching two ritually impure people, since both vaginal bleeding and corpses convey impurity. By extension, this so-called transgressing demonstrates that Jesus trivializes or even abolishes laws concerning ritual purity. A few commentators add that the woman transgressed Jewish law by appearing in public and/or by touching a man, and thus see the story not only as dismissing purity, but also as a misogynist Jewish practice. Once we flush out this effluvium, we can see what the text might say both for antiquity and for today.

Prurient Purity Professions

The concept of ritual purity is frequently both misunderstood and deployed to score points for Jesus the social critic. Even in books having nothing to do with Jesus per se, purity nevertheless appears to show Jesus as progressive regarding women. For example, a 2022 volume addressing contemporary sexual ethics insists that "Jesus rejects the prevailing purity codes that characterized his social world and instead advocates a wholly alternative social understanding, one marked by neighbor love and compassion."[20] Sigh . . .

The pervasiveness of the purity readings is easily found by googling "Jesus and women," despite half a century at least of biblical scholars addressing incorrect views of Jesus, women, purity, and Judaism.[21]

An article available through the website of the Anglican Communion called "Promoting Women's Reproductive and Sexual Health" efficiently illustrates numerous mistakes. First, it proclaims that "according to Jewish law (Lev. 12:1–8; 15:19–30), because of her bleeding the woman was unclean which prohibited her from regular fellowship with others and worship of God. . . . [T]he taboo and discrimination attached to this disease sanctioned by Jewish law must have created psychological trauma for her."[22] This reading is not uncommon. From very good scholars come the following assertions: "because her continual hemorrhage made her ritually 'unclean,' the woman may have been as isolated socially as Jairus's daughter was separated physically by death";[23] "by deliberately touching another person she has just breached the rules regarding ritual impurity";[24] that women with irregular vaginal or uterine discharges would have been quarantined so that her *hearing* about Jesus "may reflect her ostracism from society because of ritual impurity";[25] and therefore the healing, "the touching of a ritually unclean person [transcends] Levitical purity restrictions."[26]

Speculating on her condition in the pages of *Christianity Today*, the physician L. Lewis Wall proposes that she has "what gynecologists call menometrorrhagia, heavy, irregular, and unpredictable menstrual periods" and that the "most likely reason this woman bled chronically is *anovulation:* her hormonal rhythms were badly off balance, and as a result, she was not maturing an egg in her ovary and releasing it on a regular basis." He helpfully proposes that she was also "probably anemic" and "likely chronically tired." But to make his case for how this "unclean woman" can serve as a guide for understanding, and so working to aid, fistula sufferers in Ethiopia and West Africa, he needs to understand Jesus as "deliberately violating a ritual restriction in order to perform an act of compassion."[27]

No restrictions are violated; no law is transgressed. Jesus does not reject purity laws; had he done so, he would not have sent the man healed of skin disease to the temple (Matt. 8:4 // Mark 1:44 // Luke 5:14). Rather, he restores people to states of ritual purity.[28]

Part of the problem is the failure to note purity laws concerning men. The earlier part of Leviticus 15 concerns regular male discharges, such as ejaculation, which also convey impurity. Given that men were likely to ejaculate more over the course of a lifetime than women were to menstruate, coupled with late-onset menarche, frequent pregnancies, long periods of lactation, and early-onset menopause, I suspect men were ritually impure more often than women. I have yet to find commentators complaining about how men who ejaculated were marginalized or ostracized.

The other part of the problem is the anachronistic mapping of Levitical laws onto first-century practice. Leviticus is set in the wilderness, where the community is gathered around the ark of the covenant; it is not set in the Galilee, far from the temple, where Jews gathered in synagogues. Leviticus 12:1–8 concerns the impurity created by parturition. When Mary gives birth to Jesus and Elizabeth gives birth to John (the Baptizer), locals did not think, "Stay away, impure women!" Were impurity such a problem, the community could not celebrate, on the eighth day after their births (and continuous contact with "impure" mothers), the infants' circumcisions (Luke 1:59; 2:21).

Leviticus 15:19–30, which is more relevant to Mark's narrative, concerns vaginal or uterine bleeding. The first part, 15:19–24, on menstruation, states that anyone who touches a menstruating woman "shall be unclean until the evening," and it notes that her bed and wherever she sits will also convey impurity. The woman is not banished from the community. She is forbidden proximity to the holy, the ark, and, by extension, the temple. In Galilee, where our story is set, this is not a problem.

Leviticus 15:25–30 concerns irregular bleeding, which is the case with Mark's narrative. Again, the concern is a woman's bed and where she sits; the impurity is localized. Nothing forbids the woman from having a public presence. If appearing in public or touching other people were transgressive, then in Mark's narrative both the woman's

frequent visits to physicians and her appearance in the crowd—
without the crowd parting like the Red Sea—are incomprehensible.

The Septuagint takes a broader view of purity than does the
Hebrew. In the Greek, it is not just the bed or chair that conveys impurity; it is the woman herself. And even in this case, it is likely that
the laws regarding men with irregular genital discharges, such as
the ability to wash his hands and so not convey impurity (Lev. 15:11),
apply to the woman as well. Such touching, which is not illegal, has
only minor repercussions.

A second mistake happens when authors map onto Jewish tradition practices associated with other cultures. For example, writing from the social location of South Asia, one author proposes that
"Since [the woman] was considered polluted, maybe she was not allowed to stay in the same house with other family members but given
a space near the stable or backyard of her home. Since she was considered polluted maybe she was not even allowed to continue household
chores and hence she was considered not productive." Later, the author makes the point that "even today in Indian society . . . [i]n many
homes, women during her monthly cycle are not allowed to enter the
kitchen, sit and eat with the rest of the family or worship."

The author uses Jewish tradition as the rhetorical negative in order
both to critique local practices and to promote Jesus. The ends do
not justify the means, and the approach may well serve to inculcate
or reinforce antisemitism.

A third mistake is presuming that the woman was married and
her husband controlled her finances, even though there is the reference to "having spent all that was hers"—that is, the woman had
access to her own money. The view is common that "women in first-
century Palestine were subject to family control, restricted by rigid
rules of social conduct, and had little or no independent access to
material resources."[29] The Gospels, however, consistently provide ex-

amples of women who have access to their own funds, including the women who serve as patrons for Jesus (Luke 8:3).

Finally, the article asserts in a heading, "The courageous mother disobeying the unjust law to be healed," followed by:

> Her own unique spirituality prompted her to break the law. Her faith in God of love allowed her to touch the Rabbi and take risk to be healed. . . . [S]he asserted her rights to come to the Rabbi (Jesus) to touch him, to seek healing, even though Jewish law forbade her to do so. According to the Jewish laws of ritual on purity she should not have even ventured out into the crowd.
> . . . This story reveals that Jesus wanted to break the silence. He defied the unjust Jewish law, as mentioned in book of Leviticus that oppressed women because of their sexuality or issue concerning sexual and reproductive health.
> Being a Jewish woman she was well aware of the consequences of breaking Jewish laws as written in Torah (Jewish scripture). Maybe she would have been stoned to death. . . .

No law forbids touching, or being touched by, a ritually impure person. The laws concern what to do after the touch occurs.[30] Thus, Jesus breaks no law. Nor is he "indifferent" to purity.[31]

Judith Lieu correctly notes that purity "does not seem to be part of any of the evangelists' understanding of the story: Actual provisions for and attitudes to women in a state of menstrual impurity may have been less exclusionary than is often assumed, and . . . the issue is not one which early Christians seem to have debated the way they did regulations dealing with food and table fellowship."[32] Susan Haber demonstrates that "it is the woman's health that is the primary concern of the miracle story, and not her ritual impurity."[33] Similarly, the concern Jairus has for his daughter is not that she, as a corpse, is impure; it is that she is dead. In both cases, Jesus restores the women to ritual purity;[34] more important: he stops the bleeding (the Greek term Mark uses for the healing is that he "dried her up";[35] she will not bleed again), and resuscitates the girl.

Better Diagnoses

In healing the woman, power flows out of Jesus; he too discharges. I find helpful Mark's emphasis on the toll healing takes from Jesus's body. Jesus frequently requires downtime, alone time, to restore himself. The model is helpful for people who provide health care, which is exhausting work.

By coming up behind him, the woman is not trying to avoid stoning. She comes from behind because she is afraid, since a healer's touch can both heal and harm. She reminds us of those who enter drug trials, which may cure or kill, ease suffering or increase it. She takes a risk and should be commended for it.

Alert and aware, she keeps saying, "If I touch, even his garments, I shall be saved." She then touches his garment. For Matthew 9:20, she touches his fringes, worn by Jewish men to remind them of Torah (Num. 15:38–39).

The woman feels in her own body the cure. The torment has stopped. The bleeding has stopped. Jesus invites her to tell her story, which means articulating the details of her condition. There is no mention of shame, nor should there be; our bodies, and their infirmities, should not be sources of shame. Perhaps now that she is no longer bleeding, she will, like the man who no longer suffers from a skin condition, go to the temple and offer a sacrifice. Jesus has restored her, as he restored the man, to both health and to ritual purity.

Jesus tells her, "Daughter, your faith/trust has saved you." His address, "daughter," could be seen as infantilizing, although it has a literary function: it recollects Jairus's daughter, now dead. It may also signal her lack of children, for now she is dried up; she will always be a daughter, but she may never be a (new, biological) mother. Perhaps she has a family at home, including children, who would rejoice with her. Perhaps her ailment was the result of giving birth to those children; if so, her healing potentially frees also the father and the children from any guilt they may feel for her condition. The woman appears disconnected to a family, but nothing prevents us from imagining a familial connection, just as we can imagine one for the evangelist in Gerasa.

Unlike the demon-possessed man, the woman does not ask to be Jesus's disciple; indeed, he gives her no chance. Although he calls her "daughter" and thus sets up a relationship to him, he tells her, "your faith/trust has saved you. Go in peace and be healthy from your torment." His words create distance. Her faith or trust (Greek: *pistis*) has saved her; her own initiative saved her. "Go," he says; not "come, follow me." The Gospels do not depict Jesus as singling out a woman to join him. Finally, he commands, "be healthy from your torment," that is, do not think of yourself as a body in pain; find a new identity marked by health.

The woman had faith, or trust, not only in Jesus's medical ability, but in herself. She had the faith, the trust, to listen to her body, and to advocate for herself, and to risk censure, even death, by touching a man whose body can leak power. Free health care may be a miracle, but so is the courage to face the system and prevail.

Jairus, Wife, and Daughter

Jairus is a "synagogue leader," not a Pharisee, rabbi, or priest. Synagogue leaders are patrons; like the women in Luke 8:1–3 who provide financial support for Jesus, synagogue leaders provide financial support and, likely, some leadership role in local congregations. The word "synagogue" comes from the Greek for "gather together"; Jairus may have paid for the building and/or its upkeep, as did the centurion in Luke 7:1–10.

The title Mark uses for Jairus, *archisynagogos*, appears in the feminine and is attached to women's names in approximately twenty-five inscriptions from Greece and Asia Minor. Women not only attended synagogue gatherings, where they were not restricted to balconies or hidden behind curtains, but also served as synagogue leaders.[36]

Jairus is otherwise unknown. Attempts to connect him to the judge named in Hebrew "Jair" (the Septuagint reads Jairus) in Judges 10:3–5 yield the juxtaposition of a father with "thirty sons" to the Gospel father with one daughter.[37] The connection intimates that a single daughter is not dismissed, or considered unworthy. Our Jairus is the father of a child in need of Jesus's healing; she will be known only as "Jairus's daughter." Thus, Jesus emerges in the paternal role in both the story of the woman he calls "daughter" and the story of the dead girl.

Matthew 9:18 drops both the name "Jairus" and the synagogue connection; here the petitioner is "a ruler." For Matthew's Gospel, synagogues are mostly places to be avoided. Matthew also drops the reference to Jairus's wife. Other than Mary and Joseph—and Joseph disappears after chapter 2—there are no exemplary married couples in Matthew's Gospel. Herod Antipas and his wife Herodias use their daughter (the same term, *korasion*, describes the daughters of both Jairus and Herodias) to arrange the death of John the Baptizer. Pilate's wife, who appears only in Matthew's Gospel, cannot persuade her husband to exonerate Jesus (Matt. 27:19). The wife of Zebedee and the mother of John and Jacob asks Jesus to grant her sons prominent roles at his right and left hands in his coming kingdom (Matt. 20:21). She misses both Jesus's teaching about service and the irony of her request, for the two at Jesus's right and left will be the two men between whom he is crucified (Matt. 27:38). Matthew thus emphasizes breaks in the natal family.

The notice in Luke 8:42 that the girl was Jairus's "only daughter" connects her to the judge Jephthah's only daughter, whom he sacrifices as the result of a foolish vow (Judg. 11:34–40). Jephthah's daughter laments her virginity, meaning that she will never marry; Jairus's daughter, given her age and her connection to the woman suffering hemorrhages, would be expected to marry and bear children.

Jairus is not the only biblical parent to advocate for a child. The Canaanite/Syrophoenician woman of Mark 7:26–27 // Matthew 15:23–28 advocates on behalf of her demon-possessed daughter; a father advocates for his mute self-harming son (Mark 9:17–26). The centurion who advocates for his "boy" fits this model as well. From earlier biblical sources, the widow of Zarephath begs Elijah to heal her son (1 Kings 17:18), and the Great Woman of Shunem does the same with Elisha for her son (2 Kings 4:17–30). Some commentators find Jairus surprising because he is concerned about a daughter, but there is nothing surprising here.[38] That "people were bringing children to him [Jesus] in order that he might touch them" (Mark 10:13) shows not that Jews thought children to be nobodies and Jesus invented the Children's Defense Fund, but that both Jews and gentiles regarded children, boys and girls, as precious.[39] My point is not to ignore children who are themselves ignored; all societies have children who do not receive the love and care they should have. My point is that these children, these Jewish children in the Gospel story, are precious to their parents and caregivers. Jesus, in caring for children, is not anomalous.

Jairus does not simply ask Jesus to heal his daughter, he specifies, "place the hands on her so that she is saved and lives." At stake is not the "willingness to risk contamination";[40] Jairus wants physical contact. Perhaps he is aware of how powerful Jesus's body is. His supplication thus heightens the connections between the two stories, since the woman seeks to put her hands on Jesus, or at least on his clothes. It also may hint at Jairus's doubt: he thinks healing requires direct contact.

Jesus agrees to Jairus's request, but the woman interrupts him. By the time their interaction is completed, Jairus learns that his daughter has died. The horrific news is then accompanied by the insensitive question, "Why still do you trouble the teacher?" The messenger is more concerned about Jesus's convenience than Jairus's grief. Perhaps the messengers presume that Jesus can heal the living but not raise the dead. Jesus responds correctly by ignoring the crowd and speaking directly to Jairus.

I like to think that Jairus perseveres because he witnessed Jesus's interaction with the woman. Her testimony gives him hope.

Entering Jairus's house, Jesus takes the role of father. He gives the orders about who enters and who leaves; he addresses the child and demands she be fed. This replacement fits into the new family that Jesus is establishing. In another scene similar to the encounter between Jesus and Jairus—again a crowd surrounds Jesus—he is told that his mother and brothers and sisters are asking for him. Jesus asks, "Who are my mother and my brothers?" and then answers his own question. He looks at the people seated around him and announces, "See, my mother and my brothers. Whoever might do the will of God, this one is my brother and my sister and my mother" (Mark 3:32–35).

Jesus speaks to the daughter in Aramaic, "*Talitha cum.*" Later, Jesus will put his fingers into the ears of a deaf man and command, in Aramaic, "*Ephatah*," "Open!" (Mark 7:33–34). While the Aramaic gives a sense of verisimilitude, it also suggests to me the professional language connected to arenas such as medicine, law, and even theology. Such language can provide precision; it can also suggest arcane knowledge. By offering the translation, "Girl, to you I say, rise," Mark assures readers that Jesus is not trading in magical spells.

The notice of the girl's age, twelve, around the start of puberty, connects her with the woman who had been bleeding for twelve years. The woman, because of her ailment, was likely unable to conceive or to retain a pregnancy; the girl is about to begin or has just begun to menstruate. The attention to women's bodily functions, hinted by the age rather than being explicit, I find healthy rather than prurient. Such matters need not be kept secret, let alone be regarded as shameful.

Jesus, again taking the paternal role, orders that the girl be given something to eat. The command does more than demonstrate Jesus's "tenderness and realism; he knows that the little girl's body needs nourishment to recover strength."[41] It proves that the little girl is not a ghost, for ghosts do not eat. Further, it shows that a dramatic healing is not the end of the story. Care continues. And caregivers continue to provide it.

The ending of this narrative prompts me to wonder: Has someone provided food for the courageous woman, or is she providing food to others? The daughter has the support of her parents; who is in the woman's support network, or in whose network does she provide support? Should the woman and the daughter meet, what memories would they share, and how would they pay their healings forward?

Even more: we can read their stories as presaging the Passion.[42] Like the woman, Jesus is scourged and will bleed; like the child, he will die, be raised, and even, according to Luke and John, ask for something to eat. It is easy to see his death foreshadowed by John the Baptizer's execution, but rarely is the cross connected with stories of women's suffering and women's bodies.

THE MAN WITH DROPSY

Jesus states, "Those who are well have no need of a physician, but those who are sick" (Matt. 9:12). He is speaking not of ailments or disability, but of what might be considered soul sickness. "Those who are sick," in context, refers to "sinners and tax collectors" (Matt. 9:11). The metaphor offers an intriguing way of diagnosing and responding to both the classical seven deadly sins (pride, greed, wrath, envy, lust, gluttony, and sloth) and their updated counterparts, which have been variously enumerated. Options (you can pick your top seven) include racism, sexism (and related issues: homophobia, transphobia, etc.), ecological degradation, selfishness, insider trading, bullying, sexual harassment/sexual violence/domestic violence/rape, exploitation, tax evasion, ableism, conspicuous consumption, gossip, and the ever-popular idolatry (worshiping money, beauty, power, popularity, youth, etc.). To understand such behavior as illnesses or ailments and find appropriate treatments might be more helpful than condemning, shunning, or ignoring the problems.

Jesus's encounter with a man suffering from dropsy, or edema (Luke 14:1–6), offers the opportunity to discuss how symptoms of sin (variously defined) can be treated rather than ignored. It can also show how sin (again, variously defined) can create physical symptoms and how physiognomy, the determination of a person's character on the basis of physical appearance, can be not only misleading, but also harmful.

This narrative also raises historical and practical matters, from the incorrect connection of Pharisees with legalism to the broader question of the relationship of the Sabbath to healings.

> And it happened when he came into the house of a certain ruler
> of the Pharisees, on Shabbat, to eat bread, and they themselves

were watching him carefully. And behold, a certain person who
had dropsy was there in front of him. And answering, Jesus said
to the lawyers and the Pharisees, saying, "Is it permitted on the
Sabbath to heal [Greek: *therapeuō*, whence 'therapy'] or not?" And
they remained quiet. And taking hold, he healed him and loosed
[i.e., sent him away].

And to them he said, "Which of you, a son or an ox into a well
will fall, and not immediately will you raise him on the day of the
Sabbath?"

And not were they able to answer back to these matters.

Dropsy

Dropsy (more commonly called "edema") is swelling created by ex-
cess water in the body. The term comes from the Greek *hydrops*, related to *hydro*, "water." Again, mistaken readings tend to confound
diagnosis and therefore treatment; for example, "if his edema was
so obvious as to be noticed, he would be regarded as impure because
of the Levitical strictures concerning 'swellings' that were associated
with leprosy (Lev 13:2)" or "the man is an impure, dishonored, marginalized person, which situates him among those identified as 'the
poor, the crippled, the lame, and the blind' (14:13, 21)."[43] Leviticus 13:2
mentions swellings that *become* symptomatic of a dermatological
condition. This fellow's presence at a banquet hosted by Pharisees
either means that Pharisees did not care about ritual purity (unlikely)
or that he is neither marginalized nor ostracized. Nor should we see
people who lack economic resources, who are unable to walk or see or
hear, as dishonored or marginalized. Some surely were; others, such
as the majority of the people in the Gospel narratives, are embedded
in familial and community systems of support. Such stereotyping
disempowers people who are poor and disabled, robs them of agency,
makes them objects of pity, and so is the source of the dishonor.

Rabbinic sources mention edema with the Greek loanword *hydro-kan*. In no case do they find problems with either ritual purity or social marginalization. B. Eruvin 41b notes that three types of people who appear to be in good health are liable to die suddenly: a person suffering an intestinal illness, a woman giving birth, and a person with edema. Such individuals are to be cared for, not ostracized.

More relevant for our text, b. Shabbat 31a comments on those experiencing edema and then moves to the question of physiognomy, that is, judging character by appearance. Here is one example from an extended discussion among several rabbis about Rabbi Abaye, who displays symptoms of edema. His friend Rava announces that the symptoms were not caused by sin; rather, because Abaye fasts constantly, his edema is the result of hunger. Then Rava succumbs to the same symptoms of swelling. Since he did not starve himself, did not sin, and was efficient at moving his bowels (one finds all sorts of comments in the Talmud), the edema must have been caused by pressure from others to continue teaching about Torah in the classroom and so not getting to the chamber pot on time. The rabbis are aware that edema can be associated with sin, but they tend to bring the discussion into medical, and sometimes humorous, rather than theological realms. Nothing here of marginalization, dishonor, or ostracism.

Luke takes the story in the direction of Greek and Roman thought. Ancient writers from Ovid to Seneca and Plutarch associated dropsy with greed. From this perspective, the fellow with dropsy is rich and self-indulgent, and his body reflects his conspicuous consumption.[44] Ovid, speaking of the "frantic lust for wealth," writes, "So he whose belly swells with dropsy, the more he drinks, the thirstier he grows. Nowadays nothing but money counts; fortune brings honours, friendship; the poor man everywhere lies low" (*Fasti* 1.215–16). Horace makes the same point: "If you were troubled by thirst that no water could quench, you would tell your doctor about it; then if, with possessions amassed you feel only cravings for more, would you fail to take counsel with someone about it?" (*Epode* 2.2.146–49).[45] Luke expected readers to understand the clues: dropsy, seen as "a consequence of sumptuous dining belongs to the conventional criticisms of the extravagant banquet of the upper classes."[46]

When Jesus "loosed" the fellow from dropsy, we can imagine that he also loosed him, freed him, from greed. Perhaps in encountering Jesus, he found admiration for a man who was more interested in divesting than consuming. Perhaps he found, in Jesus's power to heal, an opportunity to reconfigure his life just as Jesus had helped him to regain a healthy body. This man, like the woman with the hemorrhages or the formerly possessed man in Gerasa, will now have to form a new identity. By healing the man, Jesus gives him a do-over.

Several additional lessons can be taken from this account. The first is that our diet can kill us. It is not "what goes into the mouth that defiles a person" (Matt. 15:11, 17; cf. Mark 7:15, 18) in terms of ritual purity, but what goes into the mouth can create physical problems.

Second, the ancient association of dropsy with insatiability suggests to me the scourge of addiction, where one pill, one hit, one drink, is never enough. What is the long-term care needed to prevent the symptoms from recurring? Mark's narrative suggests the possibility of treating addiction on the medical level and calling it an illness rather than on the theological level and calling it a sin. Yes, the symptoms of addiction not only hurt the individual; they hurt that individual's family and community. And yes, such hurting requires atoning and restitution, and it may require forgiveness by others. Step 8 in the twelve-step program of Alcoholics Anonymous has the alcoholic make a list of the people they have harmed and be "willing to make amends to them all"; and step 9 has them make "direct amends to such people wherever possible, except when to do so

would injure them or others."[47] But to call the problem a "sin" threatens to create both shame and guilt, and both feelings can lead to
more problems, and feelings of hopelessness. Treatment—whether
through groups such as AA or in-patient care or medication—in a
nonjudgmental setting is more likely to effect a cure than shunning,
condemning, or damning.

Third, a point the Gospels emphasize, is that we are known by
the people with whom we break bread. Luke 14 goes on to depict
Jesus as lecturing the Pharisee and his companions on not seeking
the premier seats at banquets and on extending invitations to people
who would be unable to reciprocate (and, ideally, on making them
feel welcome rather than embarrassed). Such instruction can be
understood as prescriptions for the fellow with dropsy. To prevent
greed from returning, be generous, do not seek opportunities for
self-aggrandizement, open your table to others, and be happy to join
them regardless of the setting or the menu.

Finally, bodily swellings—such as edema, or lymphedema, or, in
my case, a massive edema on my leg caused by the combination of
being on blood thinners and banging my knee on a bedpost—should
not be taken as signs of sinfulness. Judging a person by appearances,
although common in antiquity and even today, is shallow. This is
especially the case today with obesity, which has taken the place of
dropsy in being associated with greed or sloth or indulgence. The
text can therefore serve as a warning: diagnosing without training is
as dangerous as judging without evidence.

Sabbath Healing

The healing of the man suffering from edema extends, in Jesus's table
conversation, to the matter of healing on the Sabbath. Jesus asks
the dinner guests, "Which of you, a son or an ox into a well will fall,
and not immediately will you raise him on the day of the Sabbath?"

Commentators then rush to find examples in Jewish sources that permit the animal or child to suffer so that they can present Jesus as disrupting legalism. The Cairo Genizah copy of the Damascus Document associated with the Dead Sea Scrolls advises that should a beast fall into a cistern or pit on the Sabbath, one should not lift it out (11.13–17). There is nothing here about a child; nothing here about general practice. Jesus's question *presumes* that Pharisees, known for making the mitzvot easier to follow, would agree that hoisting the ox, or the son, is the appropriate move.

Although commentators also note the "consistent forbidding of anything resembling healing on the Sabbath" and cite, for example, b. Shabbat 18a, 53b, 75b, 108b, 111a, 128a, 140a, and 147–48a, again, the verses are often taken out of context or are overread.[48] B. Shabbat 18a states, "one may place an eye salve on the eye and a bandage smeared with cream on a wound on Shabbat eve at nightfall, and the wound may continuously heal all day long on Shabbat." B. Shabbat 53b permits using oil and removing scabs on the Sabbath, and so on. Midrash Tanchuma, Lech Lecha, reads, "Thus did our masters teach us: Whenever life is endangered, the Sabbath is superseded. For example, circumcision and its healing supersede the Sabbath." The same document insists:

> One who has pain in his mouth may take medicine for it on the Sabbath because his soul is endangered, and whenever the soul is endangered the Sabbath is set aside. The law states: One may profane a Sabbath in order to observe many Sabbaths. Whence do we know this? R. Eliezer said: This may be logically deduced from the fact that if circumcision, which concerns only one of man's limbs, sets aside the Sabbath, then surely it is right that a serious illness, which threatens a man's entire body, should set aside the Sabbath.[49]

The rabbis use the same logic that Jesus uses: from the lesser to the greater.[50] Indeed, in the Gospel of John, Jesus asks his Jewish opponents, "If a man receives circumcision on the Sabbath so that will not be loosed [i.e., broken] laws of Moses, are you angry with me because I healed a man's whole body on the Sabbath?" (John 7:23).

The story in Luke 14 ends with the guests unable to answer Jesus's question about the ox or the child in the well, because they know its import: it leads to the question of what work should be permitted, indeed encouraged, on the Sabbath and what should be left for the next day. Such matters required discussion, then and now. More, Jesus does not himself provide an answer since Jesus in this passage does no "work": he does not apply medication; he does not drain the fluid. Luke laconically notes, "taking hold, he healed him and loosed."

What are the lessons for those of us with more limited, more mundane abilities? Here are several questions the story raises with which we can wrestle. First, to what extent are the others at this banquet enablers? I have witnessed on more on than one occasion people who, perceiving themselves to be hospitable, encourage people who are clearly full to continue to eat, or tell people known to be vegetarian that "a little piece of bacon won't hurt," or place a piece of cake before someone who has diabetes. Such moves are comparable to putting a drink in the hands of an alcoholic.

Second, to what extent are social lives premised on expensive food and drink, with each host attempting to outdo the previous meal? Here also surfaces the problem of reciprocation, when one cannot repay in kind for the expensive wines or the gourmet food. How do we welcome others when class differentials get in the way?

Third, when do medical professionals have a day, or an hour, of rest? The dinner guests are silent, since there is no good, let alone consistent, answer to the import of Jesus's question regarding what can or cannot be done on the Sabbath. Yes, one can, and should, save

a life on the Sabbath. For a person suffering from addiction, for anyone who is suffering, any moment is a moment when life might be
saved (cf. the rabbinic comment about a person with *hydroken* who
might, at a moment's notice, die). Therefore we must ask: What constitutes "saving a life"?

To conclude that "Jewish tradition" is bad because it insists on
Sabbath rest is a cheap reading that does not address how communities provide care. Some of my students have presumed that Jews
would allow someone to bleed to death on the Sabbath rather than
provide medical care: this is how Gospel texts lead to distorted views.
The proof text for saving a life is Leviticus 18:5, "And you will guard
my statues and my judgments, which if a person does, he will live
in/by them"; b. Yoma 85b, glosses, "and live in/by them, and not that
he should die by them." This is why the Maccabees decided, after
Jews refused to take up arms on the Sabbath and so allowed themselves to be slaughtered, to do the work of fighting on the Sabbath in
order to save lives (1 Macc. 2:34–41). How, then, do we balance our
lives, especially if we work in health care, or the military?

Questions of Sabbath rest are particularly acute in our technolog-
ical world. Jesus did not address the internet or social media. Luke 14
raises questions of what we should, or should not, do on our day of
rest. Answers are not easy, for any action—a response to an email, a
correction to a bigoted social media post, a comment on a student's
paper—might turn out to be lifesaving.

Fourth, how do we decouple physical symptom and moral
judgment?— a question that already begins with the tendency of
children to mock rather than to befriend people who "look different" from the majority. The problem can be especially acute with
children, and adults, who are obese, have skin diseases, and have
health concerns associated with the more intimate parts of the body.

Fifth, this is not the first time we have seen Jesus touch someone experiencing impairment or disability. He touches the man with a skin disease; he touches the corpse of Jairus's daughter; he touches a deaf man's ears and a blind man's eyes. To touch a person whose condition might prompt disgust or fear is to recognize the humanity beneath the disability. And that is something to celebrate.

Finally, as Catherine Hezser points out: "The very fact that Christians stressed miracle healing may have averted rabbis from presenting themselves in a similar way. In general, rabbis did not claim charismatic powers; their authority was based on Torah knowledge."[51] Given the overlap, then and now, among the categories of miracle, medicine, and magic (in general, medicine and magic come at a cost; miracle comes for free), and given the authority charismatic leaders claim, the rabbis are wary of what we today would call "faith healers." I am similarly wary of faith healers and charismatic leaders. Should we read the healing narratives as endorsing alternative medicine and nonprofessional practitioners? Should we read them as suggesting hope that, at some point, healing will come? Or do they serve as warnings: use whatever faith you have, but also use the best health care available.

AND NOW?

The biblical text recognizes the pervasiveness of illness, and it mandates care for those who are ailing. It does not generally blame individuals for their diseases and disabilities, be they fever or leprosy, aberrant behavior, deafness or blindness, or infertility. Rather, the impaired are under divine protection, just as are the widow, the orphan, the poor, and the stranger.

In his Parable of the Sheep and the Goats, Jesus teaches, "I was sick and you took care of me" (Matt. 25:36). In no case does the text speak to the responsibility of the government to care for the sick.

That was the role of the individual, the family, friends, and organizations such as synagogues.

By telling stories of sickness and healing, the Bible calls attention to matters, and to people, that many of us today would rather overlook. By speaking of individual initiative and advocacy, of the fact that illness comes to wealthy and poor, men and women, children and adults, and of the economic costs of health care, the texts insist that we pay attention, and then do our part to alleviate the suffering. If we were to do so, that would be a miracle.

CHAPTER 5
FAMILY VALUES

FOR TWELVE YEARS I served as the founding director of Vanderbilt Divinity School's Carpenter Program in Religion, Gender, and Sexuality. The program brought into conversation people who clashed over topics such as abortion, women's ordination, religious affirmation, LGBTQIA+ people, responses to sexual abuse by clergy, and so on. What the Bible says, or doesn't say, about such issues was often at the heart of the conversation.

Because the Bible has become weaponized in the culture wars, the program sought to disarm the conversation. There's an old saying that the Bible should be a rock on which one stands rather than a rock thrown to do damage. There are even older sayings about loving the neighbor, loving the "not us," and everyone being in the divine image and likeness.

As far as the fraught topics of abortion and same-sex relations: Jesus does not speak about either. On the other hand, he forbids divorce and remarriage, which at the moment are not part of new legislative packages. He commends men who, eschewing paternity, make themselves eunuchs (today we would call this gender reassignment surgery), which is a matter of legislation. When he encounters a woman caught in the act of adultery, which is sometimes a matter of public disapproval, he refuses to condemn her.

This chapter addresses Jesus's comments on issues that today we might call "family values": divorce and remarriage (he was not in favor), the eunuch statement (he was in favor, metaphorically speaking), and adultery (he was very not in favor) to see how his teachings fit into their own cultural context, and how they might speak to people today. In all these cases, Jesus is not setting long-term social policy; rather, he is anticipating the imminent end of the world and so sets behavior accordingly.

Jesus forbids divorce. The problems, and so the needed discussion, concern what to do when marriages fall apart, whether because of domestic abuse, infidelity, or disease (from dementia to various forms of addiction) or even when couples find their interests and values so divergent that there is no longer life in the relationship. Jesus's comments on divorce help us to think about the circumstances under which marriage and divorce take place, what happens when theological disagreements disrupt marital harmony, and the role of the extended family and community in supporting marriages as well as supporting people going through divorce.

The eunuch statements in Matthew 19 help in defining male and female roles. If to be "a man" is to be a husband and to father children and to be a woman is to be a wife and mother, what happens when virginity and celibacy prove to be the desired way of life? Jesus approves of those who "make themselves eunuchs"—castrate themselves (whether removing the penis, the testicles, or both; the term in Greek refers to various permutations)—for the sake of the kingdom of heaven. Such views inform political debates about gender-affirming care, changing a gender on a driver's license or passport, and even the use of preferred names and pronouns.

Finally, the story in John 8 of the "woman taken in adultery" helps us in approaching infidelity. These questions include how one judges, or whether one should judge, when all the facts are not in evidence; who has the right, or responsibility, to forgive; and what should be the response of family, community, and/or state to such a personal matter as adultery, given that this private act can have broader implications. By addressing such matters and more, the Gospel accounts prompt us to start the conversation rather than to cancel those who find such discussions necessary.

DIVORCE, REMARRIAGE, AND "FAMILY VALUES"

Many Christians are taught that Jesus speaks against divorce because of a social problem, even as a way of protecting women. This approach is based, once again, on an erroneous view of Jewish divorce practices. Here we start with how first-century CE Jews variously viewed divorce, what Jesus says about marriage and family, and why Jesus may have come down so firmly, indeed "radically" (among the few times this term is appropriate), on the subject.

Most first-century Jews accepted divorce, because Deuteronomy 24:1 sanctions it; here is a very literal translation of the Hebrew: "When will take a man a woman and marry her, and it will be that if not does she find favor in his eyes because he found in her a matter of nakedness [i.e., something objectionable], and he writes for her a book of cutting off [i.e., a document of divorce], and he gives [it] into her hand, and he sends her from his house . . ." The text continues by prohibiting the divorced wife from returning to her first husband if, after the divorce, she married someone else. The divorce procedure thus serves as the pretext for the more important point, which is forbidding remarriage to a first husband after sexual relations with a second.

The scriptures of Israel record no incidents of divorce, although prophetic texts use divorce as a metaphor for God's relationship to Israel. Isaiah 50:1 depicts God asking, "Where is your mother's certificate of divorce with which I put her away?" The voice is that of the people in Babylonian exile, who regard themselves as separated from God. Jeremiah 3:1 uses the same motif: alluding to Deuteronomy 24:1, the prophet casts Israel as the divorced wife who left her husband, left God, had relations with others, and now seeks to return. In both cases, the prophets comfort Israel. Separation leads to reconciliation.

Malachi 2:16a reads, "For I hate divorce, says the LORD, the God of Israel." However, the fragment 4Q12 from the Dead Sea Scrolls reads this same verse as saying, "If you hate [your wife], divorce," and other ancient versions follow this more liberal reading. For some, then and now, divorce was a tragedy; for others, a necessity.

Although Deuteronomy presumes that men can divorce wives, it says nothing about a woman's right to divorce her husband.[1] In antiquity, Jewish women could and did divorce. The Elephantine papyri, a cache found on an island near what is today the Aswan Dam in Egypt, yielded fifth-century BCE documents indicating this possibility. One marriage contract reads: "And if Jeh[oi]shm[a] hate her husband Ananiah and say to him, 'I hate you, I will not be your wife,' silver of hatred is on her head; her *mohar* [bride price] will be forfeit. She shall place upon the balance scale and give her [hus]band Anani silver, seven [and a half] shekels, and go forth from him with the rest of her money and her goods and her property. . . . He shall give [them] to her on [one] day at one stroke and she may go to her father's house."[2] The marriage contract (Hebrew: *ketubah*) functions as a prenuptial agreement guaranteeing the wife economic support in the marriage and, in the case of divorce, remuneration. A properly written *ketubah* would make divorce financially prohibitive, and rabbinic literature suggested that it did serve as a deterrent against men divorcing their wives.[3]

The Dead Sea Scrolls appear both to prohibit polygamy and to restrict divorce. The Damascus Document labels fornication as "taking two wives in their lives, even though the foundation of creation is 'male and female he created them.'"[4] The related fragment 4Q271.3 reads, "Let no man bring [a woman into the hol]y [covenant?] who has had sexual experience, [whether] she has such [experience in the home] of her father or as a widow who had intercourse after she was widowed." From this text, Aharon Shemesh concludes, "sectarian *halakhah* outlawed remarriage subsequent to divorce as long as the former spouse was still living."[5] The limitations apply to both wives and husbands.

In the Roman Empire, divorce was easy to procure by either the husband or the wife; the major problem was the return of the wife's dowry. Nevertheless, divorce carried some stigma: "Husbands who divorced wives deemed faultless or fruitful particularly were thought to be in the wrong, but it is wives divorcing their husbands who were more likely to be censured."[6] Such women who divorce their husbands find their way into the New Testament and the writings of Josephus.

In Mark 10:11–12, Jesus instructs, "Whoever divorces his wife and marries another commits adultery against her, and if *she divorces her husband* and marries another, she commits adultery" (emphasis added). Matthew and Luke, editing Mark, omit the possibility of a woman's divorcing her husband. While Mark may have included women's right to divorce for a gentile readership,[7] it is equally possible that Jesus, aware of Jewish women obtaining divorce, forbade divorce regardless of who initiated it. Some commentators take this restriction as an egalitarian move, in that neither men nor women can divorce, but I tend to think of egalitarian moves as extending rather than restricting rights. Nor does this restriction help women in violent, loveless, or broken relationships.

Jewish women did divorce. Describing the arrest and subsequent beheading of John the Baptizer, Mark records that Herod Antipas imprisoned John "because of Herodias, the wife of Philip his brother, because he [Herod] had married her. For John had been saying to Herod, 'It is not permitted to you to have the wife of your brother'" (Mark 6:17–18; see also Matt. 14:1–12; Luke 3:19). The background: Herodias, sister of King Agrippa I (see Acts 23) and granddaughter of Herod the Great, divorced her husband in order to marry Antipas. For the Baptizer, the issue was not divorce; it was incest, since Torah forbids a woman being married to two brothers while both are alive (Lev. 18:16, "You shall not uncover the nakedness of your brother's wife"; cf. Lev. 20:21). Josephus, more plausibly, has Antipas executing John as a preemptive strike, lest John encourage his followers to rebel (*Antiquities* 18.116–19).

Josephus also mentions other Herodian women who divorced their husbands. In *Jewish Antiquities* he records that Herod the Great's sister, Salome, divorced her husband Costabarus, "not according to Jewish laws" (15.259). He describes how the daughter of King Agrippa I and sister of King Agrippa II, Berenice, who appears in Acts 25, left her husband Polemo, king of Sicily, and how Berenice's sister Drusilla, who appears in Acts 24:24, separated from King Azizus of Emesa; a third sister, Mariamne, left her husband Julius Archelaus (*Antiquities* 20.143–47). Josephus insists, repeatedly, that an action is against the law, suggesting that what Josephus describes is apologetic designed to make Jewish practice look moral, and patriarchal, for his Roman, gentile audience.

The rabbis agree that divorce is legal; they disagree over the grounds. Among their debates is discussion of Deuteronomy's vague wording, "a matter of nakedness" or "something objectionable." In

m. Gittin 9.10, two rabbinic schools of thought disagree. According to the House of Shammai, a man may not divorce his wife unless he discovers she has engaged in forbidden sexual intercourse; the rationale is one reading of Deuteronomy 24:1, "because he has found in her a matter of nakedness." Disagreeing, the House of Hillel responds that a man can divorce his wife for such minor infractions as burning or oversalting his food. The justification is the same verse, since "a matter of nakedness" can refer to "something unseemly." Rabbi Akiva concludes that divorce is permitted even if the husband finds a prettier woman, based on the line from the same passage in Deuteronomy, "if not does she find favor in his eyes." At this point, I am not happy with Rabbi Akiva.

The House of Shammai is restrictive; the House of Hillel is no-fault. The Talmud then debates both positions. B. Sanhedrin 22a quotes Rabbi Eliezer in response to Akiva: "Whoever divorces his first wife, the very altar sheds tears for him" (see Mal. 2:16). Sifre Numbers, in discussing a husband who accuses his wife of adultery (Num. 5), limits divorce to adultery and states that there must be witnesses to the act, a requirement unlikely often to have been met.[8]

The rabbinic texts, which are all later than the time of Jesus, sometimes allow women to divorce. Among the legitimate reasons for divorce is a husband "afflicted with boils, or who has a polypus [understood to be bad breath], or who collects [dog excrement], or a coppersmith, or a tanner" (m. Ketuvim 7.10). The Jerusalem Talmud develops these points, which concern situations in which the woman finds her husband intolerable, whether because of the stink of his job or the stink of his body. The rabbis then extrapolate: "If a husband can be compelled to divorce his wife simply because he has bad breath, should he not be compelled to divorce his wife if he puts her in mortal danger by beating her?" (y. Gittin 9.9, 50d).[9] Other cases include the husband's refusal to give his wife economic support (b. Ketubot 47b–48a) and his refusal to have sexual relations with her (b. Ketubot 63a).[10] B. Yevamot 65b records the case of a woman who successfully requested a divorce since her husband was infertile.

Because rabbinic Judaism ended the possibility of women obtaining divorce, with these few exceptions, the tragedy of the *agunah*, the "chained woman," developed. While secular divorce is possible to this day, should a Jewish man refuse to give his Jewish wife the divorce certificate (*get*), she cannot remarry in a Jewish setting; should she remarry and have children, the children are considered illegitimate. Recalcitrant husbands who refuse to divorce their wives have been shamed, financially incentivized, even jailed. Organizations such as ORA and the International Coalition for Agunah Rights (ICAR) fight for women caught in this intolerable situation.[11]

This quick survey yields several points relevant to discussing Jesus's view of divorce. First, there is no evidence that Jewish men were cavalierly divorcing their wives for oversalting their dinner or other trivial matters. Rabbinic literature concerns legal possibilities, not what people are doing. Second, because of the *ketubah*, the marriage contract, divorce was financially prohibitive. Third, first-century Jewish women had the right to divorce their husbands. Fourth, the gradual liberalization of the divorce laws in rabbinic literature suggests that at the time of Jesus, divorce was relatively rare. In a conservative setting, Jesus moves further to the right. Finally, as all the literature indicates, divorce was a contested issue for Jews in Galilee and Judea.

In forbidding divorce, Jesus was neither protecting the rights of women nor engaging in social engineering. His reasons for forbidding divorce are based on his understanding of scripture and his idealized, utopian view of human potential.

Jesus's Family Values

It is not surprising that Jesus was asked about divorce, and not only because first-century Jews had different ways of interpreting the Deuteronomic legislation.[12] Jesus would have been questioned given his distinctive family values.

One of the more notable aspects of both Jesus's entourage and those who benefit from his healing is their unmarried status. Of all the women the Gospels mention, only one wife, Jairus's wife (the mother of the dead daughter discussed in Chapter 4), appears together with her husband (Mark 5:40 // Luke 8:51), and she disappears from Matthew's retelling. Otherwise, husbands are deserted or ignored. Matthew depicts Mrs. Zebedee, the mother of the apostles Jacob (James) and John, as following her sons into the movement (Matt. 20:20; 27:56), but Zebedee remains in Galilee with his boats and his hired men. Luke 8:3 locates "Joanna, the wife of Herod's manager Chuza," among Jesus's patrons, but Chuza has not joined her. Jesus heals Peter's mother-in-law, but no reference is made either to her husband or to Peter's wife. Even at the wedding in Cana (John 2:1–10), where John reports that Jesus turned water into wine, we never meet the bride and groom. John may have included the story in part to show that Jesus, known for separating families, was not averse to marriage.

Gospel "family values" lean less toward upholding heterosexual marriage with children than toward what anthropologists call "fictive kinship systems"—a family configured not on biology or marriage, but on voluntary loyalty to a person or cause. Fictive kinship groups include sororities and fraternities, sisters in convents and brothers in monasteries. In such systems, the natal family takes at best a subordinate status. Here are two of several examples that would have caused people to wonder: If Jesus separates husbands and wives, what does he think about divorce?

First, Matthew 10:34–37 has Jesus quote Micah 7:6 on the disintegration of the household:

> Do not think that I have come to cast peace upon the earth. Not
> have I come to cast peace but a sword. For I have come to turn a
> person against his father, and a daughter against her mother, and
> a bride against her mother-in-law. And enemies of a person are his
> members of his household. The one loving father or mother over
> me not is of me worthy, and the one loving son or daughter over
> me is not of me worthy.

Luke 12:52 intensifies the statement by adding, "For there will be from now five in one household divided, three against two and two against three." In Luke 14:26, Jesus states, "Whoever comes to me and does not hate his own father and mother and wife and children and brothers and sisters, still even his own self [*psyche*], not is able to be my disciple."

Second, Jesus praises those who leave homes and families. In the context of Jesus's forbidding divorce, Peter announces, "Look, we have left all and followed you" (Mark 10:28 // Matt. 19:27 // cf. Luke 5:11, 28). Jesus responds, "Amen, I say to you, there is no one who has left house brothers or sisters or mother or father or children or fields for my sake and for the sake of the good news [*euangelion*], who will not receive a hundredfold now in this time houses and brothers and sisters and mothers and children and fields, with persecutions, and in the age, the one coming, eternal life" (Mark 10:29–30 // Matt. 19:29). To the list of those left behind, Luke 18:29 adds "wife." Luke thereby limits following to men; women serve as patrons (Luke 8:1–3), but they remain householders and thus provide for the men who have left their homes.

Jesus separates families and replaces them with a new family oriented around him. But he did not want his married followers to divorce. Jesus recognizes the practice, but he finds it "acceptable only for morally disreputable people who could not commit to the ideal life of eternal marital relations."[13]

In asking him about divorce, the Pharisees are "testing" Jesus: "And coming forward, Pharisees were asking him if it is permitted for a man his wife to divorce, testing him" (Mark 10:2). Divorce was a debated question (as today, for example, is abortion). As with questions about the legality of paying the census tax, or whose wife is a multiply married woman in the resurrection, or whether a woman guilty of adultery be stoned, this question also is designed to trip Jesus up. The question about legality, of what is permitted, should have led to detailed assessment of the circumstances of the divorce, and then to legal disputation. Jesus is having none of this. Instead, he goes on the offensive by asking the Pharisees his own question:

> And he, answering, said to them, "What to you did command
> Moses?"
> And they said, "Moses permitted a book of divorce to write and
> to release."
> And Jesus said to them, "For the hardness of your heart he
> wrote to you this commandment." (Mark 10:3–5)

Jesus will instruct his disciples at Gethsemane, "Keep awake and pray that you will not come to the test; the spirit is indeed willing, but the flesh is weak" (Mark 14:38; see also Matt. 26:41). It is precisely because of "weak flesh," or "hardness of heart," that, according to Jesus, Moses allowed for the possibility of divorce. Divorce, in Jesus's view, is a concession for people unable to meet God's ideal view of marriage.

Jesus continues:

"But from the beginning of creation, male and female he made
them. On account of this, shall leave a man his father and
mother and he shall cleave to his wife. And they shall be, the two,
into one flesh, so that no longer are they two but one flesh. What
therefore God has yoked together, a person shall not remove."
(Mark 10:6–9)

Jesus uses Genesis 1:27, cited also by the Dead Sea Scrolls, to ground
his view of the permanence of marriage. According to Jesus, it is God
who "yoked" together husband and wife, and no one should remove
that yoke.

The disciples, presuming that divorce was permitted, are confused. The discussion continues:

And in the house, again, the disciples about this were asking him.
And he says to them, "The one who would loose his wife and
would marry another, commits adultery against her. And if she,
loosing her husband, marries another, she commits adultery."
(Mark 10:10–12)

For Jesus, there is ideally no divorce permitted to either the husband
or the wife, and there is no remarriage either.

In 1 Corinthians 7:10–11, Paul confirms Jesus's teaching: "To
the married I give this command—*not I, but the Lord*—that the wife
should not separate from her husband . . . and that the husband
shall not loose his wife" (emphasis added). Pastorally, Paul then
makes two concessions. First, he suggests that separation is possible: "but if she [the wife] does separate, let her remain unmarried or else be reconciled to her husband" (1 Cor. 7:11). Second, he
recognizes the problems that could arise should one spouse be a
follower of Jesus and the other not: "But if the unbelieving partner

separates, let it be so; in such a case the brother or sister [yes, he really does say 'brother or sister'] is not bound. It is to peace that God has called us" (1 Cor. 7:15).

Luke 16:18 omits Mark's comment about a wife divorcing her husband but otherwise follows the script. Matthew adapts. In both Matthew 5:32 and 19:9, Matthew creates a loophole: "anyone who looses his wife, *except on the grounds of porneia*, causes her to commit adultery, and whoever marries a divorced woman commits adultery" (emphasis added).

Porneia has a broad semantic range, including various forms of sexual misbehavior (according to current morals) and marriages forbidden by Leviticus 18:6–18, even if they were permitted under Roman law, such as Herodias marrying her brother-in-law.[14] Perhaps Matthew added the *porneia* clause to bring Jesus's saying in line with the *lex iulia de adulteriis*, the Roman law forbidding adultery, in which the husband of an adulterous wife was required to divorce lest he be accused of pimping (*lenocinium*).

I see no reason to presume that Jesus issued the *porneia* loophole and then Mark and Paul omitted it.[15] The tradition tends to move to the more liberal approach, as we see with Paul. For Jesus: no divorce; no remarriage. The question then becomes, why?

Why Forbid Divorce and Remarriage?

Some Christian commentators, uncomfortable with Jesus's prohibition of divorce and remarriage, seek a problem in Jesus's setting that the prohibition serves to correct. For example, they argue that Jewish divorce practices were "particularly unfair to women" and see Jesus as condemning "casual divorce practices in which men took advantage of wives (Mt 19:4–6)."[16] From the Roman Catholic tradition, a commentator proposes, "this provision afforded some legal protection to a woman whose husband repudiated her, in a society where it was unthinkable for a woman to live on her own."[17] One wonders how Mary and Martha managed. The general takeaway from such commentators is that "through Jesus' actions, women were emancipated from rabbinic rigidity."[18] A good thing too, since "in a patriarchal society that assumed wives to be the property of their husbands, it was extraordinary of Jesus to suggest that a woman could also be the victim of spousal infidelity."[19]

None of these explanations holds. Rabbinic legislation is later than the Gospels, and as we have seen, some rabbis restricted divorce to cases of adultery. While the Jewish system was patriarchal—husbands could take a second wife, but wives could not take a second husband—women could control their income and property. Because Pharisees were not "rigid" and neither were rabbis, Jesus does not emancipate them from "rabbinic rigidity." Were I being fussy, I would note that Jesus often is more rigid than the rabbinic sources: to the commandment against murder, he forbids anger; to the commandment against adultery, he forbids thinking about it; to a woman's desire to leave a husband who beats her and to find a husband who loves her, he forbids divorce and remarriage. As for how Jesus protects wives by siphoning off husbands to join his movement and "leave everything," commentators are silent.

A few interpreters suggest that Jesus's statement about divorce was cryptic, given that Herod Antipas killed John the Baptizer over decrying his marriage to his sister-in-law.[20] Jesus was not being cryptic, however; his statement is all too clear. No divorce, period. The problem was not an invented misogyny, for Jesus says *nothing* about preserving women's rights or about frivolous divorce legislation.

The primary rationale for Jesus's statement on divorce and remarriage is his eschatological outlook. Since the world was coming to an end, there was no reason for disciples to change their marital situations. As Paul, who has the same eschatological outlook, states: "in view of the about-to-occur calamity [i.e., impending crisis of the eschaton] . . . Are you bound to a wife? Do not seek loosing [divorce] . . . even those who having wives be as though they are not having" (1 Cor. 7:26–27, 29). Jesus is returning soon: no need for divorce, and best also to avoid sexual relations. When Paul advises his gentile congregations not to divorce, commentators rarely suggest that he is protecting women from patriarchal privilege.

Second, for Jesus and Paul, the major concern is not divorce; it is remarriage. For both Jesus, who is explicit on the point, and Paul, who thinks of the resurrected body as "spiritual" rather than "physical" (1 Cor. 15:44), resurrection does not include sexual intercourse. As Jesus states, we will become like the "angels in the heaven" who "neither marry nor are given in marriage" (Matt. 22:30; cf. Luke 20:35–36). Polygamy, or remarriage following the death of a spouse, are not problems for resurrected bodies: those bodies do not pair-bond. Similarly, Josephus talks about how in the world to come, the "revolution of the ages," the souls "return to find in chaste bodies a new habitation" (*War* 3.374–75).

Third, Jesus forbids divorce and remarriage because, as he states, that is not the way life was intended to be. He doesn't cite sociological studies; he cites Genesis: "From the beginning of creation" divorce did not exist (Mark 10:6). For Jesus, Genesis 2 supplants Deuteronomy 15. Genesis is the ideal; Deuteronomy is the concession to human weakness.

A fourth reason for forbidding divorce and remarriage relates to Jesus's view of discipleship. Jesus forbids divorce, but he also separates spouses. Being married does not require cohabiting, as couples in commuter relationships today can attest. In Luke, after Jesus makes his famous comment about how it is easier for a camel to go through the eye of a needle than for a rich person to enter the kingdom of God, Peter states, "Look, we have left our homes and followed you" (Luke 18:28). Jesus then praises those who have "left house or wife or brothers or parents or children for the sake of the kingdom of God" (Luke 18:29). He forbids divorce because divorce opens the possibility of new marriages and thus new sexual relationships. There is no reason to free either spouse in light of the impending distress.

And Now?

Anticipating the inbreaking of God's rule, Jesus forbade divorce and remarriage. Matthew added the *porneia* clause. Paul added the option of separation. We update medical textbooks and environmental laws; the Jewish tradition updates the biblical material; and Matthew and Paul update Jesus's pronouncements on divorce. Matthew 13:52 speaks of the "scribe trained for the kingdom of heaven" who takes out of his treasure box (*thesaurus*) both what is old and what is new. That is, the church adapts the teachings of Jesus in light of community needs. Today's disciples—battered spouses who will more likely see the end of their lives than the end of the world; divorced people who seek remarriage for love and companionship—may also choose to adapt.

To assess sacred texts in light of current circumstances is not selling out to the status quo. It is recognizing that the texts are not the only means of revelation, for if they were, we'd be worshiping the text—committing "bibliolatry"—rather than worshiping the one to whom the Bible points.

In the 1960s, divorce was a major topic of sermons from conservative pulpits; it was also a hot social issue as no-fault divorces became common. Then sermons turned to birth control—not a subject Jesus addressed. Then abortion. Then homosexuality, and today back to abortion.

When decisions are made—on divorce, remarriage, sexuality, etc.—in light of biblical material, exegesis is helpful: not only do we ask *what* the text says; we also ask *why*. If the *why* is based on eschatological expectation, on the goal of being perfect, or on a model of Genesis that not all people take to be historical fact, we might reconsider the *what*. And if the *what* leads not to peace or wholeness but to death, spiritual or physical, then perhaps pastoral interpretations should outweigh literal readings.

CELIBACY AND EUNUCHS

The scriptures of Israel acknowledge geriatric sex (Abraham and Sarah, Gen. 18:12), polygynous relationships (e.g., Solomon's seven hundred wives and three hundred concubines [1 Kings 11:3]), physical attraction ("May her breasts satisfy you at all times" [Prov. 5:19]), and even explicit description ("his left hand under my head, and his right hand embracing me" [Song 8:3]).

They also promote temporary celibacy, especially in relation to Holy War (1 Sam. 21:4–5; 2 Sam. 11:11) and in approaching sacred space (Lev. 22:3).[21] The single exhortation to celibacy in the Hebrew texts is Jeremiah 16:2–4, and these verses, in the context of Babylonian invasion, are a one-off. Jeremiah insists, "Do not take for yourself a wife, and not will there be to you sons and daughters in this place, because, so says YHWH about the sons and the daughters, the ones who are born in this place, and about the mothers, the ones who bore them, and about the fathers who begot them in this land, from the death [i.e., deadly] of diseases they shall die."

Then we come to the New Testament, which celebrates virginity and self-restraint. For Jesus, as we have seen, the ideal is to be like the angels in heaven, without sexual bonding. Paul states, "it is better to marry than to burn" (1 Cor. 7:9b), that is, to be consumed with lust; this is not a strong endorsement of marital relations. Paul, anticipating Jesus's return, would prefer that all followers be celibate as he is

(1 Cor. 7:7). According to Revelation 14:3b, 4a, the only ones who can "sing a new song" are the 144,000 "who have not defiled themselves with women, for they are virgins."

Times change. According to 1 Timothy 2:12–15, written in Paul's name, pregnancy and childbirth are not only commended, but incentivized. The section starts with, "I permit no woman to teach or to have authority over a man; she is to keep silent." The point runs counter to Paul's acknowledging women deacons (Rom. 16:1) and apostles (Rom. 16:7) as well as women who prophesy (1 Cor. 11:5). Granted, "woman" (*gynē*) can mean "wife," and "man" (*andros*) can mean "husband." But the passage presumes that all women will be married. It then insists that women, bearing the sin of Eve, "will be saved through childbirth, if they remain in faith and love and holiness, with self-control." The point is not salvation from maternal death. The point is that salvation depends on producing babies and then ensuring that the children are well behaved. The same letter speaks against those who "hinder marriage" (1 Tim. 4:3).

This injunction, antithetical to Paul's preferences for celibacy, may be a response to the popularity of celibacy, especially among the upper-class gentile women the letter addresses. Uninterested in marriage; cognizant of the dangers of pregnancy and childbirth; unwilling to part with their own money; familiar with accounts of the celibate Jesus, the virgin Mary, and Paul's own preferences; and seeking to be like the angels in heaven, women may have refused marriage or, if married, refused their husband's bed.

Such refusal may have been good for these women, but it was bad for the Christian minority in the pagan world. Husbands would have blamed the movement for discouraging their wives to fulfill their marital roles. Thus, 1 Timothy encourages women to marry and reproduce. While we cannot be sure this is the case, it makes sense of the change in instruction from 1 Corinthians to the Pastoral Epistles of 1, 2 Timothy and Titus; it reflects the popularity of women's celibacy seen in second-century texts like the Acts of Thecla, and it explains the odd comment about salvation by bearing children (and not, e.g., by the cross).

The norm at the time of Jesus was marriage leading to procreation, but there were outliers. Josephus (*War* 2.120–21), Philo (*Apologia pro Judaeis* 14–17), and Pliny (*Natural History* 5.15.73) mention Essenes who eschew marriage and practice continence. Regarding another Essene group, Josephus states that they marry not for pleasure but for posterity (*War* 2.161–62), and fragment 4Q270.2 from the Dead Sea Scrolls forbids intercourse with a pregnant wife.

The Mishnah, Ketubot 5.6–7, discusses voluntary celibacy and then details how often women should receive sexual satisfaction. The House of Shammai permits a man who vows not to have relations with his wife a two-week maximum; the House of Hillel, one week. The text continues: abstinence is permitted to the student of Torah who wants to study for thirty days. Developing Exodus 21:10, which mandates that a man who takes a second wife must provide the first wife with food, clothing, and "conjugal rights," the rabbis discuss how often such rights must be provided. Their suggestions include, for the independently wealthy, every day; ass drivers, once a week; camel drivers, once every thirty days; sailors, once every six months. In turn, wives can decline such advances (just as well).

B. Yevamot 63b attributes to Rabbi Eliezer the assertion, "Anyone [i.e., any man] who does not engage in the mitzvah [commandment] to be fruitful and multiply is considered as though he sheds blood." Following several other citations from Genesis commending procreation, the rabbis turn to one of their own, ben Azzai, a celibate. They note that some scholars both teach and practice, and some practice but do not teach. Yet ben Azzai, who never married, teaches the importance of procreation but does not fulfill his own teaching. Ben

Azzai responds, "What can I do? My soul yearns for the Torah, and I do not wish to deal with anything else. The world can be maintained by others who practice the mitzvah of being fruitful and multiplying."

As time went on, the more the church commended celibacy, the more Jews promoted heterosexual marriage and bearing children.

Jesus promotes the separation of families and celibacy over pro-creation. His teaching is shocking, which is exactly the type of rhetoric needed to persuade people to change their actions in light of the in-breaking of the kingdom of heaven.

Eunuchs for the Kingdom

Following the Matthean divorce saying, the disciples propose that if divorce is forbidden, "it is better not to marry" (Matt. 19:10). Otherwise put: if you can't get out of it, better not to get into it. Jesus responds:

> Not [all] hold [this] word, but those to whom it is given. For are there eunuchs who from the womb of the mother are born thus, and there are eunuchs who were made eunuchs by people, and there are eunuchs who make themselves eunuchs on account of the kingdom of the heavens. The one able to receive, [let him] receive. (Matt. 19:11–12)

This passage raises a dominant question in today's culture wars: What makes a man a "man"? What happens when a sense of self does not correspond to physical traits? Is refusing to "act like a man" to be praised, or condemned?

The term "eunuch" (Greek: *eunouxos*) indicates a male body lacking testicles, a penis, or both, whether congenitally, because of an operation inflicted by others, or by self-castration. Some eunuchs could sexually satisfy, through various means, both themselves and others. Some parlayed their physical status into positions of authority: since they would have no offspring, they could, so the presumption went, be trusted to serve others rather than guard their own family line; more, they could be trusted not to compromise women married to or "belonging to" other men (the term "eunuch" derives from the Greek *eunē*, "bed," and *exō*, "to have," suggesting oversight of the bedchamber). Some were slaves, including those forced into brothels. In the 90s CE, the emperor Domitian banned castration; in the 130s, Hadrian pronounced it a capital crime.

Eunuchs could be powerful or marginal, honored or pitied, despised or admired. Generally, they do not get good press in either pagan or Jewish sources. The self-castrating Galli who worshiped the Anatolian Mother Goddess were generally despised. Leviticus 21 states that a man who has "crushed testicles" (v. 20) cannot serve as a priest although he can eat the sacrificial offerings (v. 22). Updating Leviticus 21, Deuteronomy 23:1 states that no one with crushed testicles or whose penis is cut off can participate in the "assembly [Hebrew: *qahal*; Greek: *ekklēsia*] of the LORD." Isaiah tells King Hezekiah, "Some of your own sons who are born to you shall be taken away; they shall be eunuchs in the palace of the king of Babylon" (Isa. 39:7): the prediction of the Babylonian exile becomes visceral. Josephus says about men who have "cut away" and so have "deprived themselves of their virility" that they have an "effeminate soul" and have "changed their sex" (*Antiquities* 4.290–91); Philo agrees (*Special Laws* 1.324–25).

Yet eunuchs could also find in the Jewish tradition words of hope. Isaiah 56:3–5 proclaims, "and do not let the eunuch say, 'I am just a dry tree'" since the "eunuchs who keep my Sabbaths, who choose the things that please me and hold fast to my covenant" will have "a monument [Hebrew: *yad*, 'hand'] and a name [*shem*] better than sons and daughters . . . an everlasting name that shall not be cut off" (Yad Vashem, "a hand and a name"—indicating a concern for posterity—is the name of the World Holocaust Remembrance Center in Jerusalem). Isaiah's verses may underlie Matthew 19:11–12.

Isaiah's prediction underlies Acts 8:26–39, the account of an Ethiopian eunuch in charge of the treasury of the Candace (a title, not a proper name), the queen of Ethiopia. The officer—Jewish? gentile? Godfearer?—had come to Jerusalem to worship in the temple. We meet him reading a scroll of Isaiah in his chariot as he heads home. Suddenly, via angelic machinations, he encounters the missionary Philip running alongside the chariot (the scene is funny). Philip hears him read (silent reading was a rarity), recognizes the text, and asks, "Do you understand what you are reading?" The officer, modeling both humility and honesty, replies that he needs a guide. Then he invites Philip to join him in the chariot.

The officer was reading what we know as Isaiah 53:7 (ancient scrolls had no chapter or verse markings), about the figure we today call the "suffering servant" (the expression was coined not by Isaiah but by the German Lutheran theologian Bernhard Lauardus Duhm [1847–1928]). Philip happily explains that this servant was Jesus. The officer, delighted with the explanation, insists on immediate baptism at a pool by the side of the road. The officer, had he continued in Isaiah, or were he reading the scroll a second time, would have read the passage about "eunuchs who keep my Sabbaths."

Israel's scriptures also depict several eunuchs with heroic qualities, from Potiphar the *saris* (Gen. 39:1; the Septuagint reads *eunouchos*), who refuses to execute Joseph when his wife accuses him of attempted rape (the notice may partially explain why the wife was interested in Joseph); to Ebed-melech, who rescues Jeremiah (Jer. 38:7–13); to the chief eunuch who aids Daniel and his friends in the Babylonian court (Dan. 1:3, 7, 8–15, 18).

The question for us is what Jesus (or Matthew) suggested with the cryptic triple statement about eunuchs. I do not think, contrary to some in the early church and to some Christians since, such as the Russian Skopsi, who not only practiced castration but also advocated mastectomies for women, that Jesus was advocating self-castration, any more than I think he anticipated his followers plucking out offending eyes or lopping off offending appendages (Matt. 5:29–30 // Mark 9:43–48). These pronouncements are all of a piece, as it were. They are about controlling the body for the sake of the kingdom of heaven.[22] Jesus's hyperbolic rhetoric is consistent: If the eye offends, pluck it out; if the foot offends, lop it off; if there is a temptation to transgress a vow, don't vow at all; and if there is a temptation to adultery or to lust or to remarriage, self-castration.[23] We find similar rhetoric in the writings of Philo of Alexandria, who notes that some wise men, having been tortured, will bite off their tongues rather than betray secrets and that "it is better to be made a eunuch" than to "succumb to illicit passions" (*That the Worse Attacks the Better*, 176).

Although the eunuch statement appears only in Matthew, it is consistent with other Gospel pronouncements that undercut the importance of procreation, including Jesus's self-identification as a "bridegroom" but never a husband, his separation of families, his constructing fictive kinship groups, and the lack of any Gospel attention to his having a wife or a lover.[24] Indeed, perhaps the charge "eunuch" was thrown at him to mock his rejection of marriage and procreation. Jesus is accused of much: being a drunk and a glutton (Matt. 11:19 // Luke 7:34), working for Team Satan (Matt. 12:24 // Mark 3:22 // Luke 11:15), and/or being demon-possessed (John 8:48), but no one accuses him of sexual misconduct.[25]

Jesus was a bachelor, and the people around him, at least in the inner circle, were not paired off, whether heterosexually or homosexually. Pairing off means one's loyalty is to a partner, not to a community. In the community Jesus founds, loyalty is to him, and not to one's natal or marital relations.

As we've seen, Jesus anticipated that we would be "like the angels in heaven, who neither marry nor are given in marriage" (Matt. 22:30; see also Luke 20:34–36; Mark 12:25). That view explains his answer to the Sadducees, the party notable for their lack of belief in resurrection (as we say in biblical studies, the lack of belief in resurrection is what made them "sad, you see"), when they tested him with the question of whose wife a multiply married woman would be in the resurrection (Matt. 22:28 // Mark 12:23 // Luke 20:33). They do not care about the answer, since they do not believe people rise from the dead in bodily form. They were attempting to trap Jesus. His conclusion: in the resurrection, there is no marriage, for there is no need for pair-bonding, sexual intercourse, or children.

Among Jesus's followers are women unaccompanied by spouses. No mention is made of Mary Magdalene's male relatives; she is identified by place (Magdala or Tarichaea) or perhaps by a nickname, as "Magdala" means "tower" (Mary the Tower, as compared to Peter the Rock), not by the name of a father, spouse, or son.[26] Jesus's hosts in Bethany, Mary and Martha, have a brother named Lazarus according to John 11–12, but Luke 10:38–42 makes no mention of any male relative. Joanna, one of the patrons listed in Luke 8:1–3, is the wife of Chuza, a manager working for Herod Antipas. Luke does not mention him as a follower. The mother of the apostles Jacob (James) and John is, according to Matthew 20:20–21; 27:56, part of the movement, but her husband Zebedee is not. While the Synoptic tradition mentions that Jesus heals Peter's mother-in-law of a fever, the Gospels do not mention Peter's wife; according to 1 Corinthians 9:5, Peter has a "sister wife." The standard reading is that she is Peter's wife. The term may also indicate a spouse treated as a sister and thus a nonsexual relationship.

In Luke 11:27–28, a woman hails Jesus by calling blessed the womb and breasts of Jesus's mother. He responds, "Blessed rather

are those who listen to the word of God and keep it." The good news
here is the prioritizing of action, something within our control, over
biology/fertility, which cannot be fully controlled, as those who experience infertility well know. The statement also fits the general Gospel view that procreation is not important or necessarily desirable. In
Luke 23:29 (cf. Gospel of Thomas 79), Jesus tells the "daughters of
Jerusalem" that the days are coming when people will find blessed
not the fertile wombs or the nursing breasts, but rather "blessed are
the infertile and the wombs that never gave birth and the breasts
that never nursed." The one disability Jesus does not cure is that of
infertility.

Jesus welcomes little children and suggests that to enter the kingdom, one must be like a little child. Mark 10:13–15 (cf. Matt. 18:3;
19:13–15; Luke 18:15–17) describes people bringing children to Jesus—
to heal? bless?—and the disciples shooing them away. Jesus instructs,
"Permit the children to come to me. Do not hinder them. For of these
ones is the kingdom of God. Amen, I say to you, whoever does not
receive the kingdom of God as a child, not will he enter it." Despite the
popularity of the claim that by exhorting followers to be like children
Jesus was describing "a society of destitute beggars: unclean, degraded,
expendable people; nobodies," children are not nobodies.[27] If they
were, the numerous stories of parents and caregivers bringing their
children to Jesus make no sense. To become like a child is to recognize
dependence on others. Given biology, it is to be non-procreating. Given
cultural practices, it is to be unmarried.

And Now?

The main interpretations of Jesus's eunuch statement—when it gets
read at all—is that in Jewish contexts, eunuchs were outcasts and

that Jesus, in embracing the self-designation "eunuch," welcomes them. The first view is wrong; the second requires nuance.

Jesus's statement about self-made eunuchs is, first, shocking. So is his instruction that bread on the table is "my body that is for you" (1 Cor. 11:24), let alone John's adaptation, "Those who eat my flesh and drink my blood abide in me and I in them" (John 6:56). So was his call to hate the natal family, to forgo participating in a parent's funeral, to take a sword to family ties, to take up the cross. What sounds, or looks, unnatural or insane on the outside is both what arrests the attention and, if the speaker is trusted, demands interpretation.

One option is to embrace the comments about eunuchs and the related comments about lopping off offending limbs or plucking out offending eyes. For example, sometimes, for the sake of life, we need to cut off that which hurts us. As biblical scholar and surgeon Myrick Shinall Jr. states: "The gangrenous foot threatens the very existence of the person. Occasionally, the only way to maintain integrity is to exercise the sort of extirpation that fills the dismemberment logia."[28] To leave parts of the body behind is painful, and courageous, and often necessary.

Next, in our hypersexualized society, the Gospel tradition acknowledges that not everyone wants to marry or, if married, to reproduce. In our selfish society where focus is on the nuclear family, the eunuch statement suggests we might have some care for others in our community, not just our own family.

Third, J. David Hester proposes that in the eunuch statement, Jesus was encouraging followers to adopt the role "embodying the worst fears of masculine vulnerability and sexual transgression" and so demonstrate an "explicit rejection of the heterosexist binary."[29] I doubt Jesus thought in terms of the heterosexist binary, especially since the Jewish tradition spoke of four categories of intersex and gender-indeterminate individuals, including the *androginos* (using the Greek loanword); the *tumtum*, a person of indeterminate sexual identity; the *ay'lonit*, the female-identified person who does not display adult physical sexual maturity; and the *saris*, the "eunuch" from birth of a male who does not display adult physical sexual maturity. The texts speak of their various rights, including to marry and to inherit.

But Hester's point is worth considering: Jesus calls into question the importance of marriage and procreation, the importance of looking the way the culture would prefer (today in the West: thin, smooth skin, glossy hair); he offers alternative ways of finding honor, happiness, and meaning. The fact that he raises such challenges should encourage those who follow him to raise comparable challenges.

Next, Jesus speaks of those who were made eunuchs in the womb (perhaps a diagnosis of undescended testicles, perhaps a *saris* in the rabbinic sense). Already the text alerts us to the range of natural conditions.

We might extend these observations to the questions of gender dysphoria, of our children who are convinced that they were born into the wrong body, of the pain that they and their adult counterparts feel when they are expected to "act like a man" or "act like a woman." My trans students and trans friends attest to the enormous relief they felt when they were able to acknowledge to themselves the identity that they knew to be true, and when others acknowledged that identity as well.

Rather than go to war over whether a drag queen can read to children in a public library, or whether to make illegal someone appearing in public in clothes that do not correspond to that person's sex as assigned at birth (lest a child witness it), we do better to listen to

Jesus and recognize that gender identity, in his time as well as in ours, was fluid, that people's bodies can give a false impression of who they are (as we saw in Chapter 4 concerning physiognomy), and that refusing to abide by dominant gender constructions may be a matter of birth, or of what is done to us, or of how we see ourselves.

Finally, let's say that Jesus's opponents accused him of being a eunuch, and they did so in order to shame him. Jesus twists the insult into a badge of honor. So too did many against whom slurs were used. Defanging a term is one way to avoid the harm it causes; canceling the term is another. The Gospel again opens the conversation.

ADULTERY

In Matthew 5:27–28, Jesus repeats the commandment prohibiting adultery but also asserts, "everyone who looks at a woman with lust has already committed adultery with her in his heart." This is another example of his "building a fence about the Torah," similar to the prohibitions of anger and of oaths. The expression, which comes from the mishnaic document Pirke Avot 1.1, concerns protecting the Torah by adding guidelines. To the prohibition of murder, Jesus prohibits anger. To the prohibition against false oaths, Jesus prohibits oath-taking and insists instead that people should always be honest. Here, to the prohibition against adultery, Jesus condemns even thinking about it.

Problems emerge, however, if, to continue the metaphor, the fence is broken or the gate is open. Once the act is committed, then what? Before we come to the story of the "woman taken in adultery," with Jesus's famous line about one without sin casting the first stone, we set the context within, rather than over and against, which Jesus must be understood.

Definitions and Responses

Exodus 20:14 states, "You shall not commit adultery." The text also forbids murder, stealing, bearing false witness, and coveting, but it does not prescribe penalties. Leviticus 20:10 fills in the gap: "If a man commits adultery with the wife of his neighbor, both the adulterer and the adulteress shall be put to death." The law raises at least two problems.

First, we need to define our terms. Today, adultery usually means having a sexual relationship with someone other than one's spouse. We can debate what constitutes such a relationship. When President Bill Clinton, speaking of his relationship with Monica Lewinsky, stated, "I did not have sexual relations with that woman," he defined "sexual relations" narrowly. A strict reading of Leviticus would have found Mr. Clinton not guilty of adultery, for adultery in this context means sexual relations between a man of whatever marital status and a woman who is married or engaged to someone else. Jesus extends the language of Leviticus by suggesting that adultery can be committed against either the wife or the husband: Mark 10:11, which we discussed in relation to the question of divorce, reads, "Whoever divorces his wife and marries another commits adultery against her."

Second, we have no biblical examples of execution for adultery. David commits adultery with Bathsheba and in addition arranges the death of her husband. While the child conceived from that act died, and while the adultery's repercussions plagued David's household, capital punishment was not invoked. Hosea laments his wife's infidelity, but he takes her back rather than stones her. Proverbs 6:32 states that a man who commits adultery "is devoid of sense" (NJPS). Foolish, yes; stoning, no. The book of Susanna describes how the righteous heroine, who, contrary to so many art history classes, never gets into her bath, is accused of adultery and therefore about to be executed, but the book is fiction. In Matthew 1, Joseph suspects Mary of adultery since she is pregnant and he knows the child is not his, but he resolves to divorce her quietly. No stoning. We have seen rabbinic statements on adultery as the only action that could legitimate a divorce; were adultery a capital crime, divorce would be an unnecessary step. Further, the Mishnah, Sotah 5.1, states that an adulterous woman cannot then return to her husband, so again, that is not a capital crime.

In Mishnah Sanhedrin 7, Rabbi Eliezer ben Tzadok states, vaguely, "There was once a priest's daughter who committed adultery; they placed bundles of branches around her and burned her." The text continues: "They [the Sages] said to him, [This happened] because the court at that time was not expert." The Talmud (Sanhedrin 52b) develops the story by noting the errors of procedure and by suggesting that "a court of the Sadducees" pronounced the sentence.

The Woman Caught in Adultery

In the story of the woman caught in adultery in John 8, no one is carrying stones (that image is Hollywood, not Gospel). The scene is, rather, a test of Jesus. John 8:2–11 reads:

> And at dawn, again, he appeared in the temple, and all the people were coming to him, and sitting down, he was teaching them.
>
> And bring, the scribes and the Pharisees, a woman, upon adultery having been taken, and they stood her in the middle.
>
> They say to him, "Teacher, this woman was taken in the act of committing adultery. In the Law, to us Moses commanded such a one to stone. You, therefore, what do you say?" And this they were saying, testing him, so that they would have [something] to accuse him.

But Jesus, stooping down, with a finger was writing on the ground. And as they were remaining questioning him, he stood up and said to them, "The one without sin among you, first, upon her, should cast a stone." And again, stooping, he was writing on the ground.

And having heard, they were going out, one by one, beginning from the elders, and was left only even the woman, being in the middle.

And standing up, Jesus said to her, "Woman, where are they? Has no one condemned you?" And she said, "No one, sir/Lord [Greek: *kyrios*]. And said Jesus, "Neither do I you condemn. Go, [and] from now, no longer sin."

There are multiple problems with this account, including a complicated textual transmission, the lack of eyewitness testimony, and the missing paramour, since it takes (at least) two to commit adultery. Also missing: closure for the woman and her absent husband.

In terms of manuscript evidence, the account appears first in the fifth-century Codex Beza. The story appears in some manuscripts in John and in others in Luke, where it fits better stylistically.[30] Augustine (*De Adulterinis Conjugiis* 2.6–7) suggested that certain individuals feared that the text promoted the idea that women could commit adultery with impunity because Jesus would forgive them and so deleted the story. Ironically, Jesus never "forgives" the woman.[31]

Here we have our first moral issue. Reading the text as a model of forgiveness is popular. Scholars claim, for example, "On his own authority he unconditionally forgives a sinner," and that Jesus "opens for her 'the new life on the road of forgiveness and deliverance.'"[32] These popular readings, though well motivated, depart from what John writes. The woman does not ask for forgiveness, and Jesus says no word about forgiving her, for that would not be within his purview. The forgiveness has to be granted by the person against whom the sin was committed, the woman's husband or betrothed. God forgives sins against God, but a sin against another person must be addressed by that person.

What should the husband to do? The question is complicated by what we do not know, including the circumstances under which the marriage took place, the status of the relationship, and the reasons for the infidelity. We know nothing about the woman except that she is either married or engaged. Concerning the adultery, she may have been raped, seduced, or threatened, or she may have been the aggressor. Perhaps she was with the one man who showed her love; perhaps she had no choice. Was the man a Roman soldier and therefore not arrested? Did he run? Did he offer a bribe? Was he so socially prominent that he could do what he wanted with impunity?

Her situation, and her motives, are irrelevant to the story and to Jesus. But that does not mean they should be irrelevant to us. Adultery is complicated.

Next, does the community have a say in the forgiveness process? Do friends have a say? Should they?

The story itself is not technically about forgiveness. It is about legal procedure. Like the question about whether it is lawful to pay taxes to Caesar, or about the wife of seven brothers in the resurrection, the Pharisees' question is designed to "test" Jesus rather than pose an honest query. That term "test" (Greek: *peiradzō*) is the same word used in the "Our Father" prayer's "lead us not into temptation" and in the temptation narratives where Satan tests Jesus's fidelity as well as knowledge of scripture. The Pharisees are seeking to prod Jesus into saying something silly, unfortunate, or illegal. Were Jesus to say "go ahead and stone her," they could accuse him of violating Torah because of the lack of witnesses and so an incomplete legal process. They could accuse him of lacking in mercy. A verdict of death could also prompt the charge of sedition since, according to John 18:31, Rome had forbidden locals the right of capital punishment. Although the claim is unlikely, since Rome typically gave its subject populations autonomy in religious or private matters, it adds to the drama of the story.

Were Jesus to say "don't stone her," they could accuse him of violating the Torah or, as we see already from Augustine's comments, of approving of infidelity. In a lose-lose situation, a good move is to change the subject, which is what Jesus does.

Jesus avoids the trick question by writing on the ground. We do not know what he wrote: the sins of the others, perhaps, or the Ten Words (the Decalogue) are common guesses. Perhaps the story alludes to Jeremiah 17:13b, "Those who turn away from you will be written on the land/earth." Chris Keith suggests both that John wanted to show that Jesus was literate and that John may be alluding to Exodus 31:18, which describes the "two tablets of the covenant, tablets of stone, written with the finger of God." If Keith is correct, John is depicting Jesus both as a greater authority than Moses and as God.[33] As others have noted, more ink has been spilled over what Jesus wrote on the ground than over care for the woman.

Jesus then looks up and speaks. His statement regarding who should throw the first stone concerns Deuteronomy 13:9 and 17:7, which mandate that witnesses who testify against the accused begin the execution. If we knew we were to participate in executions, we should be more careful in our testimony or in our verdicts. What do we know for a fact versus what do we think, or guess, or presume?

The woman's accusers take Jesus's point. In attempting to trap Jesus, they trap themselves: since they cannot state that they have never sinned, they leave. They might have argued that everyone sins, which is why the system speaks of the need for atonement, and for justice, and for mercy. But that would have been their story, and John's focus is on Jesus. The opponents do not drop stones; they are not carrying them.

Finally, Jesus addresses the woman. He calls her "woman" (*gynē*), the term he uses for his mother (John 2:4; 19:26), the Samaritan woman (John 4:21), and Mary Magdalene at the tomb (John 20:13, 15). The connections among the women also point to their differences. I like to think that John is aware of the distinct circumstances in which women, and not always men, find themselves.

At the end of the story, Jesus tells the woman to sin no more. We do not know what happens next. Is she shunned by her neighbors, or do they understand what led her to the adultery and so support her? What is her husband's response? Will he, like Hosea with Gomer, or like God with Israel, take her back, or will he refuse her? Will she return to him, or will she seek divorce and move on with her life? Can we regard her, or anyone who has been unfaithful, without condemnation?

John's narrative opens numerous questions worth considering, especially given current rates of infidelity. The Institute for Family Studies reports that 11 percent of women aged eighteen to twenty-nine and 10 percent of men the same age have committed adultery.[34] The percentages then increase with age. Such questions include:

What are the circumstances that led this woman, or anyone else, into adultery? If we don't know the details, have we the right to pass judgment? Have we that right at all?

When adultery occurs, who bears the blame? Do we more easily regard women as sexual sinners, a point seen when women who cheat are regarded as "sluts" but men as "players"?

Whose business is it if the report of infidelity becomes public?

What can or should one guilty of adultery do to apologize, to regain the trust of the spouse or the community? Is public confession warranted? If so, then what?

Finally, adultery—along with homosexuality or the use of birth control or abortion, or any of the other actions related to sexuality that some traditions regard as sins—is criminalized today in a number of countries. As recently as 2022, women in Indonesia and Afghanistan found guilty of adultery were publicly whipped. In other cases and countries, family members engage in what are euphemistically called "honor killings." I do understand the problems of wanting to impose my own cultural views on people of other cultures, and yet, torture and execution are, at least in my view, of greater concern than cultural sensitivity.

AND NOW?

Divorce, celibacy, sexual indeterminacy and gender fluidity, and adultery are not only ancient issues; they are issues facing us today. The Gospel texts are invitations to conversation; better to have them now, before problems occur.

Today, it is popular to claim that Jesus is "countercultural" with the examples being that he cares about the poor, women, foreigners, and the sick. These are not countercultural views, however. Where he is countercultural, or at least in the minority, is his condemnation of divorce and remarriage, his separation of families, and his promotion of celibacy and his presenting eunuchs as models of fidelity. If the account of the "woman taken in adultery" is determined to be historical, his rejection of capital punishment is *not* countercultural, but perhaps his lack of follow-up regarding the situation may be. Instead of ignoring these teachings, which for many are at best inconvenient, we might use them to see how they help with debates today.

For example, can we read the Jesus material on divorce in light of Paul's comment in 1 Corinthians 7:15b, "It is to peace that God has called us." Can the point be extended to people who are not interested in marriage or families but do not have the option, because of confession or inclination, to become a monk, priest, or nun? Here we should also consider women who receive social disapproval for choosing a career over marriage and motherhood, or for choosing not to add to the world's population.

Given that Jesus is less interested in pair-bonding than in creating a new family of mothers and brothers and sisters, might we conclude that our interests should be better placed in supporting families than in determining who has the legal right to marry?

Can we see his comment on eunuchs in Matthew 19 as addressing intersex individuals or people experiencing gender dysphoria, and then support people, especially children and teenagers, who are suffering? I don't see Jesus as debating bathroom bills or preferred pronouns. Rather, I see him as welcoming children, of all sorts. The eunuch statements even open up the question of gender reassignment surgery. Here discussion among all stakeholders needs to precede legislation, for again, it is to peace, not to legislation, that the call is made.

In the pages of the *New York Times*, guest essayist Margaret Renkl stated concerning the legislature and governor of my home state of Tennessee, "After killing abortion rights and gender-affirming care for minors, they're now rejecting federal funds for H.I.V./AIDS prevention, targeting birth control, and going after gender-affirming care for adults too."[35] These moves are not calls to peace; they are not indicative of either love or compassion; they do not recognize Jesus's own openness to actual countercultural family values; and they are not indications of an attempt to love those with whom we disagree. As many have noted, sexual abuse is more likely to occur in a church than at a drag show.

Whatever we decide on these issues and others related to them, it helps to do the history, to recognize various interpretations, to see where the actual countercultural moves are, and to work toward peace. The Gospel verses are invitations to discussion.

CHAPTER 6
POLITICS

NUMEROUS SERMONS AND blogs present Jesus as the anti-imperial political prophet who "speaks truth to power" by condemning empire. The empire, which at the time of Jesus is Rome, comes to stand for the White House, the Kremlin, the GOP, the DNC, the Vatican, or any other institution that the interpreter finds to be oppressive and exploitative. Interpreters then deploy Jesus to promote their own views: Jesus in favor of the Second Amendment (he tells his disciples to purchase swords [Luke 22:36]); Jesus in favor of gun control ("Turn the other cheek" [Matt. 5:39]). Another set of sermons and blogs insist that Jesus is king but his kingdom "is not from this world" (John 18:36) and it is this heavenly, apolitical kingdom that he seeks, as in the prayer "your kingdom come." Whatever the political moment, Jesus becomes the hero who stands on the right side.

Several years ago, I was invited to give a talk for the Guibord Center, connected to St. John's (Episcopal) Cathedral in Los Angeles; the organizers wanted something along the lines of "For whom would Jesus vote?" The question is anachronistic; Rome was not a participatory democracy. Nor was Jesus running a democratic movement: he is not taking votes among his disciples as to whether or not they should leave the Galilee and go to Jerusalem. The only election he appears to care about concerns the "elect people" (Greek: *eklectos*) who would not be misled by "false messiahs and false prophets" who "work great signs and omens" (Matt. 24:24).

Nor, as many have noted, could he get elected to the presidency in the United States. Among the disqualifications: he belongs to no political party; he has no budget and tells one potential donor to sell all he has and give to the poor; he offers free health care; he crosses borders without worrying about visas; he hires staff with few qualifications and insufficient loyalty; he encourages men to leave their wives; he has no explicit policy on abortion; he does not include women in his inner circle; he gives away food to thousands of people, including to more than four thousand people in foreign aid; he wasn't born in the United States; he has no permanent address; he's not married but he does "love" a rich young man; he probably did not go to college or do military service; he doesn't speak English; he's got a criminal record; and he's a Jew. One might have thought that keeping company with sinners and tax collectors would have been a problem, but these days, perhaps not.

We cannot determine for whom Jesus would vote, but we can look at several statements attributed to him that concern politics, broadly defined. Again, he helps us ask the right questions.

We begin with a brief discussion of the historical context, and then, given that context, see why Pontius Pilate ordered Jesus to be crucified. Such discussion does not erase theological claims, such as the cross as related to the defeat of sin or the conquering of Satan; it does, however, counter the popular imagination that sees Jesus dying as a political revolutionary or zealot or, conversely, that sees him dying for proclaiming good news to the poor. We then turn to a few political concerns presented by the Gospels: the use of "kingdom" language; the temptation narrative in which Satan offers Jesus global rule; the famous comment regarding Roman taxes, "render unto Caesar the things that are Caesar's"; Jesus's call to "take up the cross and follow me"; and the Parable of the Sheep and the Goats.

THE CROSS AS POLITICAL SYMBOL

The Gospels report that Jesus is crucified under the inscription "King of the Jews" (Matt. 27:37 // Mark 15:26 // Luke 23:38 // John 19:19). We cannot know whether the inscription is historical or whether Mark invented it because of its ironic truth: for Mark, Jesus was, really, the (divinely appointed) king of the Jews. The inscription makes sense, historically, of the death of Jesus. Pilate sees him to be a popular leader, and the last thing Pilate wants in Jerusalem at Passover, the celebration of freedom from Egyptian slavery, is a popular leader.[1]

Jesus dies for political reasons, but not because he spoke truth to power, healed people, or promoted love in opposition to the hegemonic moral and religious beliefs of the Jews, or even because of "his option for the poor, the marginalized, and the oppressed."[2] Yet such views continue. For one example, in July of 2022 I was visiting the (Evangelical Lutheran) Church of St. Lorenz in Nuremberg, Germany, during a break from a series of lectures on the publication of *Das Neue Testament Jüdische Erklärt, Lutherübersetzung*, the German translation of the *Jewish Annotated New Testament*, which I co-edited with Marc Z. Brettler.[3] There I found a brochure, available in multiple languages. Presuming that visitors to the church had never heard of Jesus—a real possibility—the brochure explained: "Jesus was born over 2000 years ago. Until he was almost 30 years old, he lived like everyone else. Then he began to speak of God in a special way. He raised and healed people. He encouraged us to trust and pray to the loving and merciful God. Through his life he showed that every human being is equally valuable. His way of talking about

God challenged the moral and religious beliefs of his day. So he was sentenced to death at the age of 33."[4] Otherwise put, Jesus died because he challenged whatever the Jewish system was. I found this commentary appalling; so did my Christian host. From 1933 to 1938 Nazis rallied in Nuremberg. Their agenda was to get rid of not only the "moral and religious beliefs" of the Jews but the Jews themselves (okay, I am overstating, but the rhetoric of this brochure shook me). Friends in Germany who work in Jewish-Christian relations have written to the church to ask for a revision; whether the officials there change the wording of the brochure remains to be seen.

THE HISTORICAL CONTEXT

At the time of Jesus, Rome was an empire, ruled by dynastic succession and/or military coup. The military functioned primarily to support and expand the empire. Usually, Rome left governance of its colonies to client kings. That was the case in Galilee, under the rule of Herod Antipas. It was not the case in Judea.

In 63 BCE, the sons of the Jewish queen Salome Alexandra (ruled 76–67), Aristobolus II and Hyrcanus II, both claimed the throne. Each sought Rome's help, and Rome was happy to respond. One hundred years after the Maccabees had defeated Antiochus IV Epiphanes and rededicated the Jerusalem temple (164 BCE), the Roman general Pompey entered the temple and claimed it for Rome. Josephus, who describes the internecine battles in the royal household, reports, "for now we lost our liberty, and became subject to the Romans" (*Antiquities* 14.77).

In 48 BCE, Julius Caesar gave an Idumean named Antipater charge of Judea. Antipater then appointed his son Phasaelus over Judea and Herod (yes, *that* Herod, the Great) over Galilee. A few years later, the Roman Senate appointed Herod king of Judea, and in 37 BCE, Herod consolidated his control with his own military forces, including foreign mercenaries.[5]

Herod's consolidation included marrying Mariamme, a Hasmonean princess. It is possible that Jesus's mother Mary, Mary Magdalene/the Tower, Mary the sister of Martha, and Mary of Clopas, whom John locates at the cross, were all named after her, the symbol of Jewish autonomous rule. Perhaps when Mary and Joseph brought the young Jesus to Jerusalem for the pilgrimage festivals, they pointed out the Roman soldiers at the Antonia Fortress, which Herod built. Mary might have told her son about how Herod killed Mariamme's brother, the high priest, and installed a high priest he could control. This right to appoint the high priest would eventually pass to the Roman governors.

Around 4 BCE, Herod died. He had changed his will many times, and in his last days he murdered a number of his sons, which complicated the inheritance, so Rome ended up determining local rule. Dividing Herod's kingdom into three parts, Rome named his sons Herod Archelaus ethnarch over Judea, Samaria, and several coastal cities; Herod Antipas tetrarch over the Galilee and Perea; and Herod Philip ethnarch over Batanea, Trachonitis, and Paneas.

By 6 CE Judeans and Samaritans had had enough of Archelaus. After being petitioned by locals, Rome exiled Archelaus to Gaul and placed Judea, Samaria, and Idumea under direct Roman rule (see Josephus, *War* 2.117). The governors were usually elites from the equestrian rank. That is how, in 26 CE, Pontius Pilate eventually came to Judea.

In Galilee, Antipas embarked on a number of public programs to match those of his father, including rebuilding the city of Sepphoris and constructing Tiberias, named after the emperor. One popular view is that such urbanization programs worsened economic conditions: construction required higher taxes, landowners were forced from their estates because of debt, and the villages surrounding the cites became impoverished as the urban elites siphoned their resources. Commercialization replaced community. The problem: We do not know how much Antipas taxed the population. Josephus, who does discuss tax riots, mentions none in Antipas's Galilee. And while we do know that Antipas, like the other Herodians, minted his own coins, the archaeological evidence does not suggest the massive minting that would create an economic crisis.

It is also possible that construction needs added to the local economy and that producers of goods—agricultural, animal, textile, construction, ceramic—would have had increased markets. Archaeological investigations of several Galilean cities show standard-of-living increases, including more production of textiles, olive oil, and pottery as well as expansion in city size. Archaeologist Jonathan Reed finds no evidence for large-scale estates inside Galilee that used enslaved labor; nor does he see any reason to presume an increase in banditry created by people being tossed off their land.[6] People from the smaller Galilean towns may have distrusted the cities qua cities or because they rejected Antipas's rule. Some may have seen the cities as alluring rather than off-putting, with a potential generational divide.

The Gospels never depict Jesus entering the Romanized Galilean cities of Sepphoris and Tiberias; no Gospel text finds him decrying Roman statues and baths, troops, or taxes. Making the likelihood of Jesus's lack of interest in Roman culture greater is the archaeological evidence from lower Galilee: there is little Roman presence in the smaller villages around the Sea of Galilee where the Gospels locate most of Jesus's initial activity.

In lower Galilee, there is little Greek or Latin graffiti, but there are strong indications of Jewish presence: chalkstone vessels (stone does not convey impurity), *miqva'ot* (ritual baths), synagogues. Pottery imported from Judea in the south is more common than pottery made by gentile neighbors to the north. This uptick in Jewish identity markers both connects the regions of Judea and Galilee and is likely a response to Roman incursion.[7]

We have no evidence that Galilee or Judea was about to revolt against Rome in the late 20s and early 30s of the Common Era. Therefore, to read Jesus as presenting a program that countered a local powder keg violence is to invent a problem to which Jesus provides the solution. To the contrary, the presence of a popular healer and teacher in Jerusalem, Jesus, was itself the potential powder keg, which is why Pilate had him crucified.

The revolt in 66–70 CE broke out, after decades of Roman rule in Judea, not primarily because of taxation or imperial presence in the land, but because of pagan provocation: a Greek sacrificed a bird at the door of a synagogue (see Josephus, *Antiquities* 18.1). The modern analogy would be a Christian slaughtering a pig at the doorstep of a mosque in a predominantly Muslim area under Christian military rule. The upper class in Judea, weakened by the Romans who controlled the high priesthood, lacked sufficient popular support, and the response of the Roman governor, Gessius Florus, was to punish the Judean elite.[8]

If Jesus was not protesting Roman rule, Roman taxation, or Roman culture, what was the problem? The problem was the world as it was currently configured, with disease and death, poverty and sin. And for Jesus, the inbreaking of the kingdom of God was the solution, and he taught his followers to live as if they had one foot in that kingdom already.

THE KINGDOM JESUS ENVISIONED

Jesus was not interested in promoting an armed rebellion against Rome. There would be no point to do so, for in his view, God was about to enter directly into human history and right all wrongs, national, local, and personal. This view does not, however, make him apolitical. Jesus's message is highly political: it includes teaching about rulers and kings, taxes and coinage—the kingdom of God versus the kingdom of Rome.

Jesus's alternative kingdom, the one about which he teaches his followers to pray "your kingdom come" (Matt. 6:10 // Luke 11:2), is a kingdom nonetheless. Attempts to change the wording, such as "kin-dom" or "realm" or the feminine Greek term for "kingdom," *basileia*, threaten to detract from the alternative political system Jesus promotes.[9]

To pray "your kingdom come" is not, for Jesus, about parliamentary elections or presidential campaigns. No contemporary political figure is going to bring about the kingdom the prayer seeks. On the other hand, such a figure could easily today bring about the end of time as we know it, whether swiftly with nuclear weapons, or more slowly but inexorably by doing nothing about climate change. But no political figure will bring about what Jesus had in mind: a general resurrection of the dead, a final judgment, and peace on a restored earth.

Jesus eschews the title king, but he does speak about a kingdom, and that kingdom is "at hand"; his first proclamation, according to Mark 1:15, was, "The time is fulfilled, and the kingdom of God has come near; repent, and believe in the good news." The difficulty is determining the content of this "good news." At this point in Mark, the good news is *not* that Jesus will die for humanity's sins: Jesus will not speak about his death for another seven chapters, and when he does, his disciples reject the notion that he will be killed. For this "good news" to have meaning to his followers, and potential followers, it has to have an immediate referent.

The start of this good news is that this kingdom is near. To greet it, to be prepared for it, people are to repent. This means more than saying "I'm sorry" or "my bad," and it certainly means more than the common "I'm sorry, but there were extenuating circumstances." It means fixing broken relationships to the extent one can. To pray "Your kingdom come, your will be done, on earth as it is in heaven" signals that the current state of affairs is *not* the ideal. "Your kingdom come" means something other than "let's support the status quo."

STANDARDS OF RULING

In Mark 10:42, Jesus tells his disciples, "You know that the ones recognized to rule by the gentiles [*ethnos*] lord it over them, and their great ones rule over them." This is the context in which he tells them that they are to be servants and enslaved and that he himself came to serve and to give his life "as a ransom for many" (Mark 10:45). Rome ruled by might: by armies, spies, economic leverage, slavery. Jesus, informed by the scriptures of Israel, offers an alternative.

Luke 22:25b glosses the comments in Mark by having Jesus state, "those in authority over them benefactors are called." Benefactor (*eu-ergetēs*; literally, "good work[er]") is a title often accorded to kings. People in, and with, authority did (and do) good works, but their rationale may be questioned: to help people? to gain a good reputation? to solidify political authority or social status? For Luke's Jesus, the goal of discipleship is not to be known as a benefactor, a title of social status with connotations of political control and economic privilege; the goal is to serve.

Along with benefactor and king language, Jesus and the traditions about him also employ the image of the shepherd. Psalm 23 accords the title to God: "The LORD is my shepherd." In John 10:11 Jesus proclaims himself to be the "good shepherd" (cf. Heb. 13:20; 1 Pet. 2:25). The imagery is political, and it adverts to Ezekiel 34, which equates failed political leaders with bad shepherds. God tells Ezekiel, "Son of Humanity [we miss this phrase and so its connection to Jesus in translations that read the Hebrew *ben adam*, literally, 'Son of Adam,' as 'mortal'], prophesy against the shepherds of Israel" (Ezek. 34:2) for eating the fat, wearing the wool, and slaughtering the lambs rather than feeding the sheep, strengthening the weak, healing the sick, bandaging the wounded, and seeking the lost. To speak of a "good shepherd," and to regard Jesus as the ultimate good shepherd, can suggest, given the metaphor, political action. A good shepherd, a good ruler, serves, feed, heals, and seeks.

The evangelist Luke regards Jesus in this light. Luke rewrites Mark 6:1–5 to depict Jesus's opening sermon in the hometown synagogue. Jesus tells the people that he has come to bring "good news to the poor, release to the captives, recovery of sight to the blind" (Luke 4:18, paraphrasing Isa. 61:1–2). Good news to the poor is not, in ancient Jewish contexts, "you'll be rewarded in heaven." It is rather that you'll have food and shelter. Sight to the blind concerns health care. Letting the oppressed go free concerns those who are imprisoned whether because of debt or by political machinations, from Jeremiah in antiquity to people fleeing political oppression or locked up on false charges or kidnapped by terrorists today.

A NOTE ON THE TEMPTATION

Jesus's followers told stories about his battle with Satan to assure their fellow followers that they too can defeat evil by relying on God and scripture. It is also likely that Jesus himself experienced a type of temptation. Jesus speaks of visions, such as his assertion, "I watched Satan fall from heaven like a flash of lightning" (Luke 10:18). Similarly, his followers believed they saw him changed from his earthly body into a heavenly one and as conversing with Moses and

Elijah (the metamorphosis or transfiguration scene, Matt. 17:1–8; Mark 9:2–8; Luke 9:28–34; cf. 2 Pet. 1:17–18). Science may classify visions as mental or chemical glitches, but for the person who experiences them, they are real.[10] We all dream dreams.

The temptation narrative is one such vision. Mark 1:12–13 reports that, following Jesus's baptism, the spirit drove him into the wilderness, where for forty days, "he was tested [or tempted] by Satan, and was with the wild animals, and the angels served him." Matthew and Luke develop the story to depict, among other tests, the devil offering Jesus "all the kingdoms of the world," on the condition that Jesus worship him (Matt. 4:8–9; Luke 4:5–6). The vision tells us that these kingdoms *belong to Satan*. If Satan's offer is bona fide, and for the purpose of the vision it is, then all current political systems are satanic. If so, supporting such leadership means being on Team Satan, which is, at least for the Bible, the losing team. Again, Jesus advises his followers to pray "your kingdom come," because the earthly ones cannot be redeemed.

TAXATION

Mark 12:13–17 (cf. Matt. 22:15–22; Luke 20:20–26) describes one of a series of contests Jesus faces from his opponents in the Jerusalem temple:

> And they send to him some of the Pharisees and of the Herodians so that him they might trap by a word. And coming, they say to him, "Teacher, we know that truthful you are, and not is a concern to you about anyone. For not do you look to a face of people, but upon truth; the way of the God you teach. Is it permitted to give a *kensos* [i.e., a poll tax] to Caesar or not? Do we give or not give?"

And knowing of their hypocrisy, he said to them, "Why me do
you test? Bring to me a denarius so that I may see [it]."
And they brought.
And he says to them, "Of whom is this image and the epigraph?"
And they said to him, "Of Caesar."
And Jesus said to them, "The things of Caesar give over to
Caesar, and the things of God, to God."
And they were marveling over him.

The King James Version, "Render to Caesar the things that are
Caesar's, and to God the things that are God's," is typically understood
to affirm paying taxes. But the verse can also be read as implying that
since everything belongs to God, Caesar gets nothing. Exodus 9:29
proclaims "the earth is the LORD's," and Psalm 24:1 repeats the refrain:
"The earth is the LORD's and all that is in it, the world, and those who
live in it." The notion that Jesus forbade paying taxes is one way, very
early, his words were understood, for Luke 23:2 reports the charge
against him, "We found this man perverting our nation, forbidding us
to pay taxes to the emperor, and saying that he himself is the Messiah,
a king." For Luke, both charges are false.

The enigmatic line could mean "give Caesar back whatever has
his image on it," since it is idolatrous, but keep everything else. Or, we
could begin with the premise, as Warren Carter advises, that taxation is "economically sanctioned violence" that "effected status domination and psychological damage to human dignity."[11] We could see
taxes as impinging on every facet of life and tax collectors as relatively
ubiquitous—they seem to be in the Gospels, where Jesus frequently
dines with them. He is not asking these folks to give up their day
jobs, with the exception of the one tax collector. If taxes are economically sanctioned violence, we may choose to resist.

Some commentators read Jesus as affirming paying taxes to

Rome because they find here a consistency with Paul. In Romans 13:3, Paul writes to his gentile, Christ-following congregation about the "rulers" (Greek: *archontes*) who should not cause fear to one who does good works, but only to those who do evil. In Romans 13:6–7, he offers practical instruction: "You also complete the tribute, for the servants (Greek: *leitourgoi*; NRSVUE 'agents') are of God, persevering in this very thing. Pay to all the debts: tribute to whom tribute is due, tax to whom tax is due, reverence to whom reverence is due, honor to whom honor is due." The problem here is that Paul never identifies these "authorities" or "servants." As Mark Nanos argues: "Although the 'rulers' (Greek: *archontes*) in 13.3 could be imperial authorities, more likely they are synagogue rulers (Mt 23:2–3; Lk 8.41; 12.11; 14.1; 18.18; 23.13, 35; 24.20; Acts 7.27, 35; 14.5 . . .). Paul's principal concern is how non-Jews should behave among Jews."[12] Thus Paul cannot be used as a sure source for interpreting Jesus's enigmatic comment about paying taxes to Caesar.

However, the way the question is posed does provide a hint as to how Jesus initially would have been understood. His opponents, members of the Pharisaic and Herodian movements, ask whether it is permitted to give a tax to Caesar. The point is not the temple tax, and it is not taxes that go to local services. It is paying *to Caesar*. The question is a trap, as Mark indicates and Jesus knows. If he says "withhold your tax money," the Romans will kill him immediately. If he says "pay to Caesar," he opens himself up to charges either of idolatry (given what is on the coin and given where the taxes go) or of collusion (as a Roman agent).

Moreover, the apparently political question, "Is it lawful to pay the census tax to Caesar?" has theological implications. Given how Israel's scripture depicts problems with counting people, and how the poll tax is related to the numbers in the local population, one could easily have concluded that the answer is no.

Exodus 30:12 mandates that when one takes a census of the Israelites, all who are registered should give a "ransom for their lives to the Lord" in order to avert a plague that the registration could prompt. Numbers 31:48–50 makes a similar point. According to 2 Samuel 24:10, King David was appalled that he had counted the people in a census. He repents to God that by taking the census, he had sinned. The cost was enormous: seventy thousand people died because of the plague related to the registration. In its retelling of this incident, 1 Chronicles 21:1 explains that Satan prompted David to take the census.

A census determined both taxation rates and how many people could be conscripted for the military; it thus threatened the people both monetarily and physically.

Jewish tradition continues this prohibition against counting the people. One explanation for this reasons that because God promised Abraham that his descendants would be as numerous as the stars in the heavens and the sand on the shore, counting those descendants is impossible (so Gen. 32:12).

This concern for counting also has pastoral implications. A census reduces people to numbers, to commodities, to faceless bodies. Such counting marked the Holocaust; it still marks death counts in wars, disasters, and pandemics.

Jesus knows the trap of the question, and he lets his opponents know he knows: "Why me do you test?" The Greek term for testing, *peiradzō*, is, as we have seen, the same term used in both the "Our Father" prayer ("lead us not into temptation" means "do not bring us to the test") and the temptation narrative, which for Matthew begins, "Then Jesus was led up by the Spirit into the wilderness to be tested by the devil" (Matt. 4:1). To be asked to give a simple comment about taxes is a devilish test. The same point holds today. Politicians who promise "no new taxes" are likely to be liars; politicians who admit to anticipating a tax hike will have a hard time getting elected. We like simple answers; questions about taxation require details and debate.

Such questions also require attention to the money we spend. Jesus asks for a denarius, a silver coin. We've seen the denomination before: the woman who anoints Jesus's head uses perfume worth more than three hundred denarii (Mark 14:5). Now we look at the coin, for money talks in various ways. Today, many of us are living in a cashless society. We charge; we pay bills on the internet; we use digital currencies. In the time of Jesus, as well as in many societies today, coinage was propaganda. Antipas minted coins, so did Pilate, so did the emperor. The denarius depicted the image of the emperor; one had the inscription, "Caesar Augustus Tiberius, son of the Divine Augustus."[13] That would smack of idolatry on several levels: a graven image, the proclamation that a human being is divine. The obverse read *pax* (Latin for "peace") and depicted a seated woman; the inscription *pontif max* is the Latin abbreviation for Pontifex ("bridge") and Maximus. The message: peace comes from Roman rule, Roman beliefs, the Roman emperor. More, it is Rome that builds the bridges; and while bridges can suggest pluralism, or reconciliation, if Rome controls that construction, the bridge is the means by which the army colonizes.

We should also ask why Jesus asks *the questioners* for the coin, and not just any coin, but "the coin used for the tax," as Matthew explicitly says (Matt. 22:19). His opponents condemn themselves by showing it, by owning it. If they thought the coin was idolatrous, they would not have carried it. We never see Jesus himself with money: the good news to the poor is not a cash handout, but it may be a healing, an exorcism, a teaching, a dinner, a new family, compassion.

Jesus gives his answer, "The things of Caesar give over to Caesar, and the things of God, to God." His accusers, and his followers, will have to parse his meaning.

TAKE UP YOUR CROSS

That the Roman system is not the ideal form of government finds its confirmation in Jesus's teaching to take up the cross, that is, to do something that would result in crucifixion. The statement is necessarily anti-imperial. The earliest iteration of this command appears in Mark 8:34: "He called the crowd with his disciples, and said to them, 'If any want to become my followers, let them deny themselves and take up their cross and follow me" (see also Matt. 16:24; Luke 14:27). Matthew 10:38 provides a nuance, "whoever does not take up the cross and follow me is not worthy of me." Luke 9:23 provides another nuance: "If any want to become my followers, let them deny themselves and take up their crosses *daily* [literally 'according to the day'] and follow me" (emphasis added). The word "daily" helps move the sense of "challenge the government to the point of death" closer to a metaphor about self-denial. Luke strips out the initially political implications of the saying.

Taking up the cross has to be more than picking up the dry cleaning or walking the dog. It has to be more than showing up at a worship service or donating to the local food bank. Taking up the cross means challenging, for the sake of the greater good, the "powers that be," powers that can hurt, even kill.

THE SHEEP AND THE GOATS

The Parable of the Sheep and the Goats stands at the end of this chapter on politics because it associates Jesus, the "Son of Humanity,"

with the "king," who determines the fate of his followers. Here is a
literal translation of Matthew 25:31–46:

And whenever comes the Son of Humanity in his glory, and all
the angels with him, then he will sit upon the throne of his glory.
And will be gathered together before him, all the nations [or all the
gentiles; the Greek *panta ta ethnē* is the same expression found in
Matt. 28:19, the "Great Commission"]. And he will separate them
from each other, just as the shepherd separates the sheep from
the goats. And he will stand, on the one hand, the sheep at his
right, and on the other, the goats, at his left.

Then will say the king to those on his right, "Come, the blessed
ones of my Father, inherit the prepared-for-you kingdom from the
foundation of the world. For when I was hungry, you gave me to
eat, and when I was thirsty you gave drink to me, and when I was
a stranger even you gathered together me. And naked, you clothed
me, and sick/weak you visited/cared for me. And when I was in
prison even you came to me."

Then answering to him, the righteous ones, were saying,
"Lord, when did we see you hungry and we fed, or thirsty and
we gave drink? And when did we see you as a stranger and we
gathered together you, or naked and we clothed [you]? And when
did we see you sick/weak or in prison and we came to you?"

And answering the king will say to them, "Amen, I say to you,
upon as many as you have done to one of these my brothers, to
the least, to me you have done."

Then he will say even to the ones on the left, "Go you from
me, those accursed, into the eternal fire, that which has been
prepared for the devil and his angels. For I was hungry and not
did you give me to eat; I was thirsty and not did you give me to
drink. A stranger was I and not did you gather in me; naked even

and not did you clothe me; sick and in prison and not did you
visit me."

Then they will answer and they are saying: "Lord, when you did
we see hungry or thirsty or a stranger or naked or sick/weak or in
prison, and not did we serve you?"

Then he will answer to them saying, "Amen, I say to you, upon
as many as not did you do to one of these least, neither to me did
you do."

And they will go away, these, into punishment eternal, but the
righteous into life eternal.

The contours of the parable are well known to anyone who has
studied the New Testament. It determines that salvation is in fact
based on works, specifically works *not* done for the sake of reward or
reciprocity. The saved sheep do not know that in providing social services, they are doing something for the king. Debates rage over who
exactly the sheep and goats are: followers of Jesus? everyone in the
world after the second coming, when the world has proof that Jesus
is lord? just pagans and not Jews? The identity of "these least" is also
debated: missionaries, disciples, fellow followers of Jesus, anyone in
need?[14] The result—salvation based on what one does—remains the
viable reading.

We could look at the sheep and goats in terms of ancient symbolism: sheep are variously courageous, docile, obedient, and in need of
protection; goats are variously cowardly, combative unrestrained, and
promiscuous.[15] But the parable resists this type of stereotyping. The
goats are not faulted for being randy, but for refusing acts of kindness. The sheep are not saved because they are docile or obedient,
but because they do the right thing.

This type of allegorical exegesis in part explains why "for the
majority of Church history the text was *not* used as a mandate for

universal charity (i.e., all people, Christian or otherwise)."[16] The second reason is that fear of works-righteousness, especially among some heirs of Martin Luther, for whom the idea of being in a right relationship with the divine is based entirely on grace and not on anything we humans do, is paramount. But the Epistle of James (2:26) announced, "faith without works is also dead." If faith is not manifested, it is not faith.

And if the faithful want to claim that only Jesus saves—because here in this parable he reigns as king—that's fine too. But once again, it is the criteria on which he judges that make this scene so powerful.

We might also stress the idea of welcoming the stranger, the "not us," as a stranger. The point is not to convert the stranger into a fellow citizen, or a coreligionist, or someone "like us." Welcome need not mean absorption and erasure into the great whole; welcome, and hospitality, recognizes the distinction between "us" and "them," and hospitality brings honor to both parties.

Matthew finally uses the "king" language for Jesus in a way that suggests an actual king, meting out judgment to his subjects. But the king of this parable is an odd king: there is no request of tribute; there is no demand for fidelity. This king asks for no loyalty oath, citizenship papers, or birth certificates.

AND NOW?

The kingdom Jesus describes is not one gained by dynastic succession or election; it is not one that will pass away with a new campaign cycle or a change in citizenship laws. It is one where God rules, and rules justly.

Whether this divine rule is qualitatively better than what we have, or whether it is only quantitatively better, since God has more power and more resources than any human ruler, can be answered only when, or if, this kingdom of God comes about on earth. But it remains worthwhile to think about how we envision this kingdom, a question particularly pertinent to those who pray "your kingdom come." Will it be a place in which everyone worships Jesus, or will it recognize all faiths or no faith as equally valued? Will it be a place where the first will be last and the last will be first, or will it be a place of equality?

What words, what metaphors, should we use when we think about this new type of rule: Do we want to think of God as king or as shepherd, or something else entirely? Is having a "good king" comparable to having a "good father," as opposed to the rulers of both empire and household that we experience in the present? Or are the various metaphors too damaged to continue to be useful?

If we find our government to be evil, should we pay taxes or withhold them? Do we even know how our taxes are allocated? More, in this age of credit cards and digital currencies, do we even know who, or what, is depicted on our coinage? If we had the choice, whom would we put on the dollar bill or the dime, and why?

AFTERWORD

AFTERWORD,

AFTERWARD . . .

THE PARABLE OF the Sheep and the Goats returns us to other chapters in this book. For the hungry and thirsty and naked, the Gospels speak to economic issues, both responsibilities and opportunities (Chapter 1). Although the parable does not mention individuals who are enslaved (Chapter 2), we can extend its concern for those who are "in prison" to those who are not free, whether because of slavery, or debt, or what the state sees as criminal behavior, or because they have been kidnapped, or trafficked. For those who are sick and weak, the Bible speaks to the importance of health care (Chapter 4). Further, speaking of those who are "sick" reminds us also of the enslaved, who were sick, and beaten, and flayed.

When the sheep care for those who cannot care for themselves, they become the new family, based on a common ethical code (Chapter 5). For the migrant, the parable employs the category of stranger (Chapter 3): salvation is not based on converting this stranger to the same beliefs or politics or rituals as the person providing aid; salvation is based on care for those in need, regardless of race, ethnicity, religion, or any of those other categories that today so divide us.

For the first century, and for the twenty-first, politics (Chapter 6) cannot be divorced from questions of economics, national identity and immigration, slavery, health care, gender and sexuality, and any other facet of life. Politics helps to determine who can do what, who has access to resources, who can speak up, and who is silenced.

And so we return to the kingdom. Not the eschatological one that comes with the archangel's trumpet—it seems as if we're more likely to see the nuclear cloud or the antipodes of parched and flooded lands. And not the one that comes with sheep and goats, in any of their forms, going off to heavenly reward or hellish retribution. We've clearly made our own hell on earth, and we've found traces of that heaven as well. We don't need the end of the world to give us what we already have.

The historical Jesus, a first-century Jew, likely believed in heaven and hell. He surely believed in the God of Israel, and in Satan, the malevolent, supernatural force. He saw himself as God's agent, anointed to be the one to usher in the messianic age. He even likely saw his death as a ransom for humanity's sin.

But that was not all he saw. The Gospel of Luke records the following: Once Jesus was asked by the Pharisees when the kingdom of God was coming, and he answered, "The kingdom of God is not coming with things that can be observed, nor will they say, 'Look, here it is!' or 'There it is!' For, in fact, the kingdom of God is among you" (Luke 17:20–21). I suspect Jesus, the historical Jesus who taught and healed and argued with fellow Jews in Galilee and who died on a Roman cross in Jerusalem, said these words.

The Jewish tradition quotes Rabbi Yochanan ben Zakkai as stating, "If you have a sapling in your hand and people tell you that the Messiah has come, plant the sapling and then go and greet him" (Avot deRabbi Natan B 31). We can wish all we want for divine justice to mop up the mess we have made, and divine mercy to bring healing to the ill, home to the refugee fleeing war and poverty, bread to the hungry. Or we can follow the biblical tradition, as understood by Jesus and other Jews, and get to work on our own. It did not take the cross for him to show the importance of such action.

For "believers," these concerns about what we should do should complement the faith in the cross, the second coming, the final judgment. And for the nonbeliever or those who believe in other theologies, in justice, in righteousness, in loving the neighbor and the stranger, listening to the Jesus tradition in light of history, especially its Jewish history, should provide a prompt for a meaningful life.

We may not experience a final judgment when everyone, sheep and goats, is already a worshiper of Jesus, which is what I think Matthew has in mind. But we can take the point of the parable to heart. If we do not see the face of the divine in the face of everyone else—even if we don't believe in a god who looks like us—we should nevertheless be able to see the human face, the face we share, in everyone else. If we cannot, we are lost.

The first step may be looking in the mirror and seeing our own humanity. The next steps are to look at the faces not just of those we love, but also of those we despise, and move away from demonization.

We may never get to "love of enemy." I'm not there yet, and love of enemy is not on my bucket list. But human decency, that's attainable. The Bible helps us get there; the Jesus tradition helps us focus.

ACKNOWLEDGMENTS

The genesis of this volume was a suggestion from Mickey Maudlin that I write a book, entitled *Jesus for Atheists*, that would show how I, as someone outside the Christian tradition, found both inspiration and practical lessons in teachings by Jesus and about Jesus. As the volume began to take shape, the title increasingly seemed to me to be both too narrow and misleading. The instruction I find in the Gospel materials is of value to believers and nonbelievers, Christians, Jews, and people outside of these categories who have an interest in history, literature, ethics, and ethics. Nor did I want to exclude theists and agnostics, for whom historical studies of biblical texts should serve to enhance rather than to challenge theological commitments.

My gratitude extends to those who helped in the reformulation of the volume: Kathryn (Katy) Hamilton at HarperOne and now Convergent; Chantal Tom, Lisa Zuniga, Hanna Richards, Makenna Holford, Sarah Schoof, and Judith Curr at HarperOne; Roger Freet at Folio Literary Management; and the people at the following institutions who offered critique along the way: seminar students at Vanderbilt University Divinity School and Graduate Department of Religion, Hartford International University for Religion and Peace, and the Pontifical Biblical Institution (Biblicum) in Rome. Presentations of some of the material in this volume were given at the Pontificia Universita Gregoriana, Facoltà di Teologia/Centro "Cardinal Bea" per gli Studi Guidaici, Pontifical North American College, Pontifical University of

St. Thomas Aquinas (the Angelicum), Pontifical Beda College, Colgate University, St. Joseph's University, Washington University, St. Mary College of California, Davis and Elkins College, Young-Harris College, Campbell University Divinity School, Abilene Christian University, Oblate School of Theology, Auburn University, Borough Park Symposium V, Brigham Young University, University of Texas at Austin, David Lipscomb University, Vancouver School of Theology, University of Michigan, St. Andrews University, University of Oslo, Leo Baeck College—Sternberg Centre for Judaism, Universität-Bonn, Hood Seminary, University of Gothenburg, Seton Hill University, Perkins School of Theology, Diocesan Seminary of the Archdiocese of Łódź, University of Winnipeg, Wilson College, St. Leo University, Johnson University, McGill University, Georgetown University, Paris Lodron Universität-Salzburg, and the University of Tulsa.

Gratitude is also due to the churches and synagogue in Middle Tennessee, including Westminster Presbyterian Church, West End Synagogue, Greater Nashville Unitarian Universalist Church, Woodmont Christian Church, The Temple—Congregation Ohabai Shalom, and Belmont United Methodist Church.

Other congregations that have extended both warm welcomes and helpful suggestions include First United Methodist Church (Evanston, Illinois), Christ United Methodist Church (Salt Lake City), Congregation Agudas Achim (Austin), Temple Emanu-El Streicker Center (New York City), Guibord Center (Los Angeles), Temple B'nai Jeshurun and the Jewish-Christian Connection of Des Moines, First Church and the John P. Webster Library (Hartford, Connecticut), Central Reformed Church (Grand Rapids), Iowa Conference of the United Methodist Church, Myers Park United Methodist Church (Charlotte), Boston Avenue United Methodist Church (Tulsa), St. Mary Immaculate Roman Catholic Church (Plainfield, Illinois), St. Barnabas United Methodist Church (Arlington, Texas), Royal Oak First United

Methodist Church (Royal Oak, Michigan), Presbyterian Church of Western Springs (Western Springs, Illinois), Broadway United Methodist Church (Council Bluffs, Iowa), First Presbyterian Church of Bellingham (Bellingham, Washington), Temple Beth El and Christ Church Cranbrook (Detroit), National Cathedral (Washington, DC), St. Mark's Episcopal Church (Lewiston, Pennsylvania), Cathedral of St. Philip (Atlanta), Peachtree Road United Methodist Church (Atlanta), St. John's Episcopal Church (St. Cloud), Sisters of Sion (London, UK), Trinity Episcopal Church (Indianapolis), St. Luke United Methodist Church (Houston), Eastern Pennsylvania United Methodist Conference, First Church of Christ (Mansfield, CT), St. Stephen United Methodist Church (Charlotte), Future Church, Mt. Lebanon United Methodist Church (Pittsburgh), Lakeshore United Methodist Church (Manitowoc, Wisconsin), Church of the Palms (Sarasota), and Temple Mt. Sinai/Western Hills United Methodist Church (El Paso).

For friends who put up with me when I wanted to talk about Jesus (not all share exactly this same passion); special thanks to Lib Caldwell, Tammy and Mitch Geiselman, Mike Glenn, Scott Gilbert and Anne Raunio, Jeanne Marecek, Maria Mayo, Ann Neely, Bill and Eddy Rosen, Rubel Shelly, Rob Simbeck, and Julia Tanner.

Finally, to my family, for similar patience and for their love—Jay Geller, Sarah Elizabeth Geller, Alexander David Geller, Meg Pearce, and Florence and Milton Geller.

NOTES

INTRODUCTION: MEETING JESUS IN HIS TIME AND OURS

1. Charles Kimball, *When Religion Becomes Evil: Five Warning Signs*, rev. ed. (New York: HarperOne, 2008), 99.

2. See Amy-Jill Levine, *Short Stories by Jesus: The Enigmatic Parables of a Controversial Rabbi* (New York: HarperOne, 2007), 77–115.

3. See the careful discussion by Jessica Dawson, "Shall Not Be Infringed: How the NRA Used Religious Language to Transform the Meaning of the Second Amendment," *Palgrave Commun* 5, article 58 (2019), https://doi.org/10.1057/s41599-019-0276-z.

4. See Zeba Crook, "Collective Memory Distortion and the Quest for the Historical Jesus," *Journal for the Study of the Historical Jesus* 11 (2013): 53–76.

5. A representative sampling of "mythicist" views includes David Fitzgerald, *Nailed: Ten Christian Myths That Show Jesus Never Existed At All* (Lulu.com, 2010); Minas Papageorgiou, *Jesus Mythicism: An Introduction* (Thessaloniki, Greece: iWrite.gr, 2015); Richard Carrier, *On the Historicity of Jesus: Why We Might Have Reason for Doubt* (Sheffield: Sheffield Phoenix, 2014); Richard Carrier, *Proving History: Bayes's Theorem and the Quest for the Historical Jesus* (Amherst, NY: Prometheus, 2012); John W. Loftus and Robert M. Price, *Varieties of Jesus Mythicism: Did He Even Exist?* (Eugene, OR: Hypatia Press, 2021); John Pickard, *Behind the Myths: The Foundations of Judaism, Christianity and Islam* (Bloomington, IN: AuthorHouse, 2013); For counterarguments, see Bart Ehrman, *Did Jesus Exist?: The Historical Argument for Jesus of Nazareth* (New York: HarperOne, 2013); Maurice Casey, *Jesus: Evidence and Argument or Mythicist Myths?* (London: Bloomsbury, 2014).

6. For more on how Jews have understood these texts, see Amy-Jill Levine and Marc Z. Brettler, *The Bible With and Without Jesus: How Jews and Christians Read the Same Stories Differently* (New York: HarperOne, 2020).

7. I have become a Q skeptic. Q, from the German word for "source," *Quelle*, is a hypothetical source constructed of material found in the Gospels of Matthew

and Luke but not in Mark, such as the "Our Father" prayer and the "Beatitudes" ("blessed are the meek . . ." etc.). See discussion in Amy-Jill Levine and Ben Witherington III, *The Gospel of Luke* (New Cambridge Bible Commentaries; Cambridge: Cambridge Univ. Press, 2018). This is, by the way, the only biblical commentary of which I am aware fully coauthored by an agnostic Jew and an evangelical Christian.

8. Richard Dawkins, *The God Delusion* (Boston: Mariner, 2006), 250.

9. See the numerous articles in Joseph Sievers and Amy-Jill Levine, eds., *The Pharisees* (Grand Rapids: Eerdmans, 2021).

10. Peter Wehner, "The Forgotten Radicalism of Jesus," *New York Times*, December 24, 2020, https://www.nytimes.com/2020/12/24/opinion/jesus-christ -christmas-incarnation.html.

11. Marc Z. Brettler, Paula Fredriksen, Amy-Jill Levine, Margaret M. Mitchell, and Candida Moss, "What the *New York Times* Gets Wrong About Jesus," *Daily Beast*, December 29, 2020, https://www.thedailybeast.com/what-the-new-york-times -gets-wrong-about-jesus.

12. On replacing purity with compassion, see Marcus J. Borg, *Conflict, Holiness, and Politics in the Teachings of Jesus* (Harrisburg, PA: Trinity Press International, 1998), cited in David P. Gushee and Glen H. Stassen, *Kingdom Ethics: Following Jesus in Contemporary Context*, 2nd ed. (Grand Rapids: Eerdmans, 2016), 145. Gushee and Stassen quote Borg, approvingly, that for the Pharisees, "Their major sanction was social ostracism" (Borg, *Conflict*, 66–67). No evidence for this Pharisaic practice is provided. For historically grounded work on Pharisees, see the essays in Joseph Sievers and Amy-Jill Levine, eds., *The Pharisees* (Grand Rapids: Eerdmans, 2021). Frank J. Matera, *New Testament Ethics: The Legacies of Jesus and Paul* (Louisville: Westminster John Knox, 1996), offers the better phrasing, "The merciful compassionate, law observant Son of God" (52). On replacing purity with forgiveness, see William Herzog, *Jesus, Justice, and the Reign of God* (Louisville: Westminster John Knox, 2000).

13. Gushee and Stassen (*Kingdom Ethics*, 153) are again representative: "In a religious context in which the sick and disabled were often cast out from community or blamed as sinfully responsible for their own maladies. . . ." Countering this view are, e.g., Peter's mother-in-law, the man with the withered hand, the demon-possessed man, the bent-over woman in the synagogue, Jairus's daughter, the paralyzed man let down through the roof, the demon-possessed boy whose father asked the disciples for help, and so on. So too with gentiles, such as the centurion's son/slave and the Syrophoenician/Canaanite woman's daughter. Numerous others, such as the man with leprosy and the hemor-

rhaging woman, are never described as cast out of anything, or blamed. That the Gospels offer summary statements such as "they brought to him many who were possessed by demons, and he cast out the spirits with a word, and cured all who were sick" (Matt. 8:16) and "a demon-possessed man who was mute was brought to him" (Matt. 9:32; cf. 12:22) suggests an extensive role for caregivers. Ethics should not be based on a false image of Jesus's cultural context, an image not supported by the Gospels and contradicted by numerous other sources. See esp. Julia Watts Belser and Melanie S. Morrison, "Living It Out: What No Longer Serves Us: Resisting Ableism and Anti-Judaism in New Testament Healing Narratives," *Journal of Feminist Studies in Religion* 27.2 (2011): 153–70.

14. See John P. Meier, *A Marginal Jew: Rethinking the Historical Jesus,* Vol. 5: Probing the Authenticity of the Parables (Anchor Yale Bible Reference Library; New Haven: Yale Univ. Press, 2016).

15. See the essays in Chris Keith and Anthony Le Donne, eds., *Jesus, Criteria, and the Demise of Authenticity* (London: T&T Clark, 2012).

16. Susannah Heschel, *Abraham Geiger and the Jewish Jesus* (Chicago Studies in the History of Judaism; Chicago: Univ. of Chicago Press, 1998): Geiger, who argued that Jesus was a Pharisee, "wanted to counter the widespread anti-Judaism in contemporary German New Testament scholarship, as part of a larger effort to overcome religious and cultural objections to Jewish equality" (3–4).

17. Perhaps this is why the always interesting Bart Ehrman is writing about ancient views of the afterlife (*Heaven and Hell: A History of the Afterlife* [New York: Simon & Schuster, 2020]; *Journeys to Heaven and Hell: Tours of the Afterlife in Early Christian Tradition* [New Haven: Yale Univ. Press, 2022]; *Armageddon: What the Bible Really Says About the End* [New York: Simon & Schuster, 2023]), and the equally always interesting John Dominic Crossan is looking at the Gospel of Luke and the book of Revelation in terms of accommodation and resistance to empire (*Render unto Caesar: The Struggle over Christ and Culture in the New Testament* [New York: HarperOne, 2022]).

18. Matthew Thiessen, *Jesus and the Forces of Death: The Gospels' Portrayal of Ritual Impurity Within First-Century Judaism* (Grand Rapids: Baker Academic, 2020); Eric M. Meyers, "Purity Concerns and Common Judaism in Light of Archaeology," in Sievers and Levine, *The Pharisees*, 41–54.

19. Vered Noam, "Pharisaic Halakah as Emerging from 4QMMT," in Sievers and Levine, *The Pharisees*, 55–79.

20. Chris Keith, *Jesus' Literacy: Scribal Culture and the Teacher from Galilee* (Library of New Testament Studies; London: T&T Clark, 2011), and *Jesus Against the Scribal Elite: The Origins of the Conflict* (Grand Rapids: Baker Academic, 2014).

21. Febbie C. Dickerson, *Luke, Widows, Judges, and Stereotypes* (Womanist Readings of Scripture: Lanham, MA: Lexington Books/Fortress Academic, 2019).

22. James W. Barker, *John's Use of Matthew* (Emerging Scholars; Minneapolis: Fortress, 2015).

23. Candida Moss, *God's Ghostwriters: Enslaved Christians and the Making of the Bible* (New York: Little, Brown, forthcoming).

24. Myrick Shinall Jr., "The Social Condition of Lepers in the Gospels," *Journal of Biblical Literature* 137.4 (2018): 915–34.

25. See discussion in the Introduction to my book *The Misunderstood Jew: The Church and the Scandal of the Jewish Jesus* (New York: HarperOne, 2017).

26. Kaitlyn Radde, "Louisiana Voters Rejected an Antislavery Ballot Measure. The Reasons Are Complicated," National Public Radio, November 17, 2022, https://www.npr.org/2022/11/17/1137398039/louisiana-voters-rejected-an-antislavery-ballot-measure-the-reason-is-complicate.

CHAPTER 1: ECONOMICS

1. Jaime Lowe, "With 'Stealth Politics,' Billionaires Make Sure Their Money Talks: What Do They Actually Want?" *New York Times Magazine*, Money Issue, April 7, 2022, https://www.nytimes.com/2022/04/06/magazine/billionaire-politics.html.

2. For a good treatment of Luke's eschatological reversal, see Outi Lehtipuu, "The Rich, the Poor, and the Promise of an Eschatological Reward in the Gospel of Luke," in Tobias Nicklas, Joseph Verheyden, Erik M. M. Eynikel, and Florentino Garcia Mártinez, eds., *Other Worlds and Their Relation to This World: Early Jewish and Ancient Christian Traditions* (Supplements to the Journal for the Study of Judaism 143; Leiden: Brill, 2010), 229–46.

3. See, e.g., China Scherz, *Having People, Having Heart: Charity, Sustainable Development, and Problems of Dependence in Central Uganda* (Chicago: Univ. of Chicago Press, 2014). For general notes on how charity can be harmful, see Gregg E. Gardner, "The Problem of Charity," in his *The Origins of Organized Charity in Rabbinic Judaism* (Cambridge: Cambridge Univ. Press, 2015), 1–5.

4. See Amy-Jill Levine, *Short Stories by Jesus: The Enigmatic Parables of a Controversial Rabbi* (New York: HarperOne, 2007), on how this false view impacts the interpretation of the parables, and esp. the Parable of the Rich Man and Lazarus in Luke 16.

5. Brian McLaren, "Beyond Fire and Brimstone: Jesus' Teaching About Hell Flipped Popular Imagery of the Afterlife Upside Down—and Offered a Radical, Transformative Vision of God," *Sojourners*, February 2014, http://sojo.net/magazine/2014/02/beyond-fire-and-brimstone.

6. Amy-Jill Levine, "Quit Picking on the Pharisees!: A Prominent Jewish Scholar of the New Testament Argues That Christian Criticism of the Pharisees Is Anti-Semitic," *Sojourners*, March 2015, https://sojo.net/magazine/march-2015/quit-picking-pharisees. The subtitle is not, in fact, what I said. Jesus likely had similar problems with people summarizing his teaching.

7. Craig E. Morrison, "Interpreting the Name 'Pharisee,'" in Joseph Sievers and Amy-Jill Levine, eds., *The Pharisees* (Grand Rapids: Eerdmans, 2021), 3–19.

8. Michael L. Satlow, ed., *Judaism and the Economy: A Sourcebook* (London: Routledge, 2018).

9. See Levine, *Short Stories by Jesus*.

10. See Foundation for Intentional Community, https://www.ic.org. The system seeks to transform "Loneliness into belonging and meaning, Economic inequality into cooperative economy, Climate crisis into sustainable ecological design."

11. "Bava Metzia 38b:16," Sefaria, https://www.sefaria.org/Bava_Metzia.38b.16?lang=bi.

12. Cameron Buettel, "Frequently Abused Verses: 'What Is the Eye of a Needle?,'" *Grace to You*, June 24, 2019, https://www.gty.org/library/blog/B150914.

13. John MacArthur, *The MacArthur New Testament Commentary, Matthew 16–23* (Chicago: Moody, 1988), 202.

14. Dawn Ottoni-Wilhelm, *Preaching the Gospel of Mark: Proclaiming the Power of the Word of God* (Louisville: Westminster John Knox, 2008), 177.

15. See Richard Hicks, "Markan Discipleship According to Malachi: The Significance of μή ἀποστερήσες in the Story of the Rich Man (Mark 10:17–22)," *Journal of Biblical Literature* 132 (2013): 179–99; Michael Peppard, "Torah for the Man Who Has Everything: 'Do Not Defraud' in Mark 10:19," *Journal of Biblical Literature* 134.3 (2015): 595–604.

16. For discussion of Luke 16:19–31, the Parable of the Rich Man and Lazarus, see Levine, *Short Stories by Jesus*, 267–96.

17. Judith M. Lieu, *The Gospel of Luke: Epworth Commentaries* (1997; reprint Eugene, OR: Wipf & Stock, 2012), 101. On Luke as countering exclusion on the basis of physiognomy, see Mikeal C. Parsons, *Body and Character in Luke and Acts: The Subversion of Physiognomy in Early Christianity* (Waco, TX: Baylor Univ. Press, 2011). The two people Parsons uses as examples, the bent woman in the synagogue (Luke 13:10–17) and Zacchaeus the short tax collector (Luke 19:1–10), are not excluded because of physical characteristics. The women is not excluded from but located within the synagogue; Jesus does not welcome her "as is" but cures what he describes as being bound by Satan and so a "spirit of weakness" and I would describe as symptoms of osteoporosis.

18. Alan Sherouse, "The One Percent and the Gospel of Luke," *Review and Expositor* 110 (Spring 2013): 285–93 (286).

19. Michal Beth Dinkler, "The Thoughts of Many Hearts Will Be Revealed: Listening in on Lukan Interior Monologues," *Journal of Biblical Literature* 133 (2015): 371–97.

20. Scott F. Spencer, "To Fear or Not to Fear the Creator God: A Theological and Therapeutic Interpretation of Luke 12:4–34," *Journal of Theological Interpretation* 8.2 (2014): 229–49 (241).

21. Mikeal C. Parsons, *Luke* (Paideia: Commentaries on the New Testament; Grand Rapids: Baker Academic, 2015), 205.

22. Ryan S. Schellenberg, "Which Master? Whose Steward? Metalepsis and Lordship in the Parable of the Prudent Steward (Lk. 16.1–13)," *Journal for the Study of the New Testament* 30.3 (2008): 263–88 (265 n. 5).

23. Details in Brian C. Dennert, "Appendix: A Survey of the Interpretive History of the Parable of the Dishonest Steward (Luke 16:1–9)," in Patricia Walters, ed., *From Judaism to Christianity: Tradition and Transition* (Novum Testamentum Supplement 136; Leiden: Brill), 145–52 (146).

24. Dennert, "Appendix," 146.

25. Patricia Walters, "Honoring Thomas H. Tobin, S.J., PH.D.," in Walters, ed., *From Judaism to Christianity*, xvii–xxiv (xxii), summarizing Edmondo Lupieri, "Mamona iniquitatis: Can We Make Sense of the Parable of the Dishonest Steward?," in the same volume (131–44).

26. Fabian E. Udoh, "The Tale of an Unrighteous Slave (Luke 16:1–8 [13])," *Journal of Biblical Literature* 128.2 (2009): 311–35, suggests a lack of social status.

27. So, e.g., Arland J. Hultgren, *The Parables of Jesus: A Commentary* (Grand Rapids: Eerdmans, 2000): "One simply has to accept that they are, since he does not seek to defend himself" (149).

28. See David Landry, "Honor Restored: New Light on the Parable of the Prudent Steward (Luke 16:1–8a)," *Journal of Biblical Literature* 119.2 (2000): 287–309 (297).

29. Dieter H. Reinstorf, "The Parable of the Shrewd Manager (Lk 16.1–8): A Biography of Jesus and a Lesson on Mercy," *HTS Teologiese Studies* 69.1 (2013): 3. See also Landry, "Honor Restored," 291, and sources cited there.

30. Klyne R. Snodgrass, *Stories with Intent: A Comprehensive Guide to the Parables of Jesus*, 2nd ed. (Grand Rapids: Eerdmans, 2018), 406.

31. Brendan Byrne, *The Hospitality of God: A Reading of Luke's Gospel* (Minneapolis: Liturgical Press, 2000), 134. For other attempts to draw positive lessons from the parable, see the discussion in Dennis J. Ireland, *Stewardship and the Kingdom of God: An Historical, Exegetical, and Contextual Study of the Parable of the Unjust Servant in Luke 16.1–3* (Supplements to Novum Testamentum 70; Leiden: Brill, 1992), 8.

32. Correctly, Hultgren, *The Parables of Jesus*, 147.

33. Reinstorf, "Parable of the Shrewd Manager," 3, 5.

34. Snodgrass, *Stories with Intent*, 416: "Any attempt to treat the parable as it if were an allegory with the rich man representing God and the steward representing the disciples or some other group fails." Snodgrass reads the parable as being about eschatological urgency.

35. Hultgren, *The Parables of Jesus*, 150.

36. "Luke: God and Mammon. 16:1–13," Pumpkin Cottage Ministry Resources, Lectionary Bible Studies and Sermons, http://www.lectionarystudies.com/studyg/sunday25cg.html.

37. John K. Goodrich, "Voluntary Debt Remission and the Parable of the Unjust Steward (Luke 16:1–13)," *Journal of Biblical Literature* 131.3 (2012): 547–66, suggests that reducing the debts would serve to "enable and encourage their repayment, as well to secure the longevity of their tenants and their own long-term profitability" (553). Conversely, Schellenberg ("Which Master?," 281) states that the manager's scheme is "precisely what the agricultural manuals of Cato, Varro and Columella warn against. Since the parable makes clear the manager was acting dishonestly, the connection to debt release during periods of economic decline is not clearly relevant."

38. See, e.g., Goodrich, "Voluntary Debt Remission," 547 n. 2; Schellenberg, "Which Master?," 266.

39. Lehtipuu, "The Rich, the Poor," 236.

40. The translation and the commentary begin with my "This Poor Widow . . . (Mark 12:43): From Donation to Diatribe," in Susan Ashbrook Harvey, Nathaniel DesRosiers, Shira L. Lander, Jacqueline Z. Pastis, and Daniel Ullucci, eds., *A Most Reliable Witness: Essays in Honor of Ross Shepard Kraemer* (Brown Judaic Studies 358; Providence: Brown Univ., 2015), 183–94.

41. Mary Healy, *The Gospel of Mark* (Catholic Commentary on Sacred Scripture; Grand Rapids: Baker Academic, 2008), 254.

42. Ottoni-Wilhelm, *Preaching the Gospel of Mark*, 217.

43. See Levine, *Short Stories by Jesus*, 183–212.

44. Daniel Falk notes, "Leviticus 2:1 begins 'Anyone, when they bring a meal offering as an offering . . .' The word 'anyone' is the word for one's soul, one's self [*nefesh*; the LXX has *psyche*]. The rabbis read 'anyone' as the object of the verb: 'When one offers one's self'" (https://blogs.uoregon.edu/rel211dfalk/rabbis2_fr/).

45. Geoffrey Smith, "A Closer Look at the Widow's Offering: Mark 12:41–44," *Journal of the Evangelical Theological Society* 40 (1997): 27–36 (31).

46. Addison G. Wright, "The Widow's Mites: Praise or Lament?—A Matter of Context," *Catholic Biblical Quarterly* 44 (1982): 256–65 (256).

47. Wright, "Widow's Mites," 256.

48. E.g., Healy, *Gospel of Mark*, 253.

49. André Resner, "Widow's Mite or Widow's Plight: On Exegetical Abuse, Textual Harassment and Learning Prophetic Exegesis," *Review and Expositor* 107 (2010): 545–53 (549–50). See also Ottoni-Wilhelm, *Preaching the Gospel of Mark*, 217.

50. R. S. Sugirtharajah, "The Widow's Mites Revalued," *Expository Times* 103 (1991): 42–43.

51. See Elizabeth Struthers Malbon, "The Poor Widow in Mark and Her Poor Rich Readers," *Catholic Biblical Quarterly* 53 (1991): 589–604, esp. 596.

52. Daniel Boyarin, *Dying for God: Martyrdom and the Making of Christianity and Judaism* (Figurae: Reading Medieval Culture; Stanford: Stanford Univ. Press, 1999).

53. Gary Anderson, *Sin: A History* (New Haven: Yale Univ. Press, 2010), 172.

54. "He Gets Us Has an Agenda," He Gets Us, https://hegetsus.com/en?gclsrc=aw .ds&gclid=CjoKCQiAx6ugBhCcARIsAGNmMbik_YVyXMzIy2HFArM_6OUA nZ2TfL5c8wna9smwtXmKc9tM-ZImwqgaAuBDEALw_wcB.

CHAPTER 2: ENSLAVEMENT

1. Dale C. Allison Jr., *The New Moses: A Matthean Typology* (Minneapolis: Fortress, 1993).

2. Orlando Patterson, *Slavery and Social Death: A Comparative Study* (Cambridge, MA: Harvard Univ. Press, 1982), 299.

3. For an overview with a very helpful bibliography, see Bernadette Brooten, "Slavery," in W. Homolka, R. Kampling, A.-J. Levine, C. Markschies, P. Schäfer, and M. Thurner, eds., *Encyclopedia of Jewish-Christian Relations* (Berlin: De Gruyter, 2019–2024), https://doi.org/10.1515/ejcro.12360416.

4. My gratitude to Ted Hiebert for conversations on this topic.

5. So *The Guardian*, Gethin Chamberlain, "India Targets the Traffickers Who Sell Children into Slavery," August 4, 2012, and the first line, "Up to 200,000 children a year fall into the hands of slave traders in India, many sold by their poverty-stricken parents for as little as £11," https://www.theguardian.com/world/2012 /aug/04/india-traffickers-sell-children-slavery#:~:text=Azam%20was%20seven %20when%20his,since%20her%20husband%20deserted%20her. The problem continues, as PBS reported in 2021, "Why Slavery? Selling Children/Child Trafficking in India," December 10, 2021, https://www.pbs.org/video/why-slavery-selling -children-yevstg/.

6. Amy-Jill Levine and Marc Z. Brettler, *The Bible With and Without Jesus: How Jews and Christians Read the Same Stories Differently* (New York: HarperOne, 2020), 207.

7. Zev Farber, "Slavery in the Hebrew Bible," Bible Odyssey, https://www.bibleodyssey .org/passages/related-articles/slavery-in-the-hebrew-bible/.

8. See Catherine Hezser, *Jewish Slavery in Antiquity* (Oxford: Oxford Univ. Press, 2005); Hezser, "Slaves and Slavery in Rabbinic and Roman Law," in Catherine Hezser, ed., *Rabbinic Law in Its Roman and Near Eastern Context* (Tübingen:

Mohr Siebeck, 2003), 133–78; Hezser, "The Impact of Household Slaves on the Jewish Family in Roman Palestine," *Journal for the Study of Judaism* 34 (2003): 375–424. See also Tal Ilan, *Jewish Women in Greco-Roman Palestine* (Peabody, MA: Hendrickson, 1996): 207–8.

9. Hezser, "Impact of Household Slaves," 420–21.

10. Available at https://www.rac.org/sites/default/files/Passover%20Trafficking%20 Excerpt%20Mar%202016.pdf.

11. Herbert Robinson Marbury, *Pillars of Cloud and Fire: The Politics of Exodus in African American Biblical Interpretation* (Religion and Social Transformation 8; New York: New York Univ. Press, 2015).

12. "Faith-Based Partnerships to Combat Human Trafficking," NHTRC, National Human Trafficking Resource Center, https://humantraffickinghotline.org/sites /default/files/Faith-Based%20Partnerships%20to%20Combat%20Human%20 Trafficking.pdf.

13. Warren Carter, "Sanctioned Violence in the New Testament," *Interpretation* 71.3 (2017): 284–97 (294). For helpful studies of slavery in the Roman context, see several of the essays in David L. Balch and Carolyn Osiek, eds., *Early Christian Families in Context: An Interdisciplinary Dialogue* (Grand Rapids: Eerdmans, 2003), including Dale B. Martin, "Slave Families and Slaves in Families" (207–30); J. Albert Harrill, "The Domestic Enemy: A Moral Polarity of Household Slaves in Early Christian Apologies and Martyrdoms" (231–54); and Carolyn Osiek, "Female Slaves, *Porneia*, and the Limits of Obedience" (232–76).

14. The rhetoric changes in the Deutero-Pauline letters; see Annette Merz, "Believers as 'Slaves of Christ' and 'Freed Persons of the Lord'; Slavery and Freedom as Ambiguous Soteriological Metaphors in 1 Cor 7:22 and Col 3:22–4:1," *NTT Journal for Theology and the Study of Religion* 72.2 (2018): 95–110.

15. J. Albert Harrill, "The Dramatic Function of the Running Slave Rhoda (Acts 12.15–16): A Piece of Greco-Roman Comedy," *New Testament Studies* 46 (2000): 151–57; Kathy Chambers, "'Knock Knock—Who's There?' Acts 12.6–17 as a Comedy of Errors," in Amy-Jill Levine with Marianne Blickenstaff, eds., *A Feminist Companion to the Acts of the Apostles* (Feminist Companion to the New Testament and Early Christian Writings 9; London: T&T Clark, 2004), 89–98.

16. F. Scott Spencer, "Out of Mind, Out of Voice: Slave-Girls and Prophetic Daughters in Luke-Acts," *Biblical Interpretation* 7.2 (1999): 133–55 (149).

17. Eutychus is also the name of my hard drive: it goes to sleep; it crashes; it can be rebooted.

18. E.g., for books longer than four hundred pages and staples of New Testament study, in the index to Gerd Theissen and Annette Merz, *The Historical Jesus: A Comprehensive Guide* (Minneapolis: Fortress, 1988), "Sins" is followed by

"Sociology"; the index to Dale C. Allison Jr., *Constructing Jesus: Memory, Imagination, and History* (Grand Rapids: Baker Academic, 2010), has "Simon of Cyrene" followed by "Society of Biblical Literature"; the index to N. T. Wright, *The New Testament and the People of God* (Minneapolis: Fortress, 1991) has "Sin" followed by "Solipsism." Daniel Patte, ed., *Global Bible Commentary* (Nashville: Abingdon, 2004), despite extensive comments on Jesus as political and economic liberator, includes nothing on Jesus or the Gospels regarding slavery.

19. See Mary Ann Beavis, "Ancient Slavery as an Interpretive Context for the New Testament Servant Parables with Special Reference to the Unjust Steward (Luke 16:1–8)," *Journal of Biblical Literature* 111 (1992): 37–54 (37). This was one of the first articles to consider the import of slavery—as historical practice and literary motif—in relation to the Gospels.

20. Margaret Atwood, *The Handmaid's Tale* (Everyman's Library 301; New York: Knopf, 2006). Biblical women, called in the KJV "handmaids," who are placed, usually by wives, into the beds of their husbands in order to produce children include Hagar (Gen. 16:1), Bilhah (Gen. 30:4), and Zilpah (Gen. 35:26). The Hebrew is *shifchah*; the Greek, *paidiskē*.

21. For more hellish readings, see James N. Hoke, "'Behold, the Lord's Whore'? Slavery, Prostitution, and Luke 1:38," *Biblical Interpretation* 26 (2018): 43–67; Michael Pope, "Gabriel's Entrance and Biblical Violence in Luke's Annunciation Narrative," *Journal of Biblical Literature* 137.3 (2018): 701–10. See also Marianne Bjelland Kartzow, *The Slave Metaphor and Gendered Enslavement in Early Christian Discourse: Double Trouble Embodied* (London: Routledge, 2018), 3–11, and esp. 47–70, which details connections among Mary, Hagar, Zilpah, and Bilhah such that "Mary may resemble the female slaves of the Jewish tradition" (53). Taking this idea one step further, Mitzi J. Smith argues that Mary was a slave. See her "Abolitionist Messiah: A Man Named Jesus Born of a Doule," in Mitzi J. Smith, Angela N. Parker, and Ericka S. Dunbar Hill, eds., *Bitter the Chastening Rod: Africana Biblical Interpretation After* Stony the Road We Trod *in the Age of BLM, SayHerName, and MeToo* (Lanham, MA: Lexington Books/Fortress Academic, 2022), 53–70. The idea is not new. In 1998 Winsome Munro published, posthumously, *Jesus, Born of a Slave: The Social and Economic Origins of Jesus' Message* (Studies in the Bible and Early Christianity 37; Lewiston, NY: Edwin Mellen, 1988). See discussion in Jennifer A. Glancy, *Slavery in Early Christianity* (New York: Oxford Univ. Press, 2002), 123, 127, 175 n. 87.

22. Discussion in Hezser, "Impact of Household Slaves," 418–24.

23. Levine and Brettler, *Bible With and Without Jesus*, 285–312.

24. Harrill, "Dramatic Function," 151, and 176 n. 10, which reads, "J. Blanchard and N. L. Rice, *A Debate on Slavery Held in the City of Cincinnati, on the First, Second,*

Third, and Sixth Days of October, 1845, upon the Question: Is Slave-Holding in Itself Sinful, and the Relation between Master and Slave, a Sinful Relation? (Cincinnati: Wm. H. Moore, 1846), 336."

25. Kathryn A. Shaner, *Enslaved Leadership in Early Christianity* (New York: Oxford Univ. Press, 2018), offers multiple examples of how slaves, then and now, have been overlooked.

26. Glancy, *Slavery in Early Christianity*, 4, 9.

27. Frank J. Matera, *New Testament Ethics: The Legacies of Jesus and Paul* (Louisville: Westminster John Knox, 1996), 148.

28. Kartzow, *Slave Metaphor*, 3.

29. J. Albert Harrill, "Slavery and Inhumanity: Keith Bradley's Legacy on Slavery in New Testament Studies," *Biblical Interpretation* 21, 4–5 (2013): 506–14 (508). Harrill's brief summary of the impact of Bradley's work is a helpful primer on where studies of slavery in the New Testament have only recently gone, and, as we shall see, not in all areas.

30. Daniel B. Wallace, "Some Initial Reflections on Slavery in the New Testament," Bible.org, June 30, 2004, https://bible.org/article/some-initial-reflections-slavery -new-testament. The rest of the paragraph quotes this article.

31. For this and other examples, see S. Scott Bartchy, "Response to Keith Bradley's Scholarship on Slavery," *Biblical Interpretation* 21.4–5 (2013): 524–32 (531). Against the thesis that the enslaved in antiquity had any sense of upward mobility, for "'upward mobility' is a myth of modern capitalism," see Allan Callahan, Richard A. Horsley, and Abraham Smith, "Introduction: The Slavery of New Testament Studies," *Semeia* 83–84 (1998): 1–15 (5).

32. Keith R. Bradley, "Engaging with Slavery," *Biblical Interpretation* 21.4–5 (2013): 533–46 (540). See also his *Slaves and Masters in the Roman Empire: A Study in Social Control* (Collection Latomus 185; Brussels: Latomus, 1984), and *Slavery and Society at Rome: Key Themes in Ancient History* (Cambridge: Cambridge Univ. Press, 1994). See also I. A. H. Combes, *The Metaphor of Slavery in the Writings of the Early Church: From the New Testament to the Beginning of the Fifth Century* (Journal for the Study of the New Testament Supplement Series 156; Sheffield: Sheffield Academic Press, 1998); Peter Garnsey, *Ideas of Slavery from Aristotle to Augustine* (Cambridge: Cambridge Univ. Press, 1986).

33. Ruben Zimmermann, *Puzzling the Parables of Jesus: Methods and Interpretation* (Minneapolis: Fortress, 2015), 296.

34. Glancy, *Slavery in Early Christianity*, 47–48, 54, gives several examples, esp. regarding what scholars have seen as the improved role for enslaved women in Christian households; she then explains, in detail and with substantial primary source evidence, why such claims fail.

35. Details in Glancy, *Slavery in Early Christianity*, 83–84.

36. J. Albert Harrill, "The Psychology of Slaves in the Gospel Parables: A Case Study in Social History," *Beiträge zur Namenforschung* 55 (2011): 63–74 (63), in assessing John Dominic Crossan, *In Parables: The Challenge of the Historical Jesus* (New York: Harper, 1973; following "The Servant Parables of Jesus," *Semeia* 1 [1974]: 17–67). Again, Harrill provides a helpful summary of other work on this topic.

37. J. Albert Harrill neatly summarizes the slave imagery in the New Testament: "a careful study of the evidence shows them [slaves] to be literary characters drawn from the ideologies that supported Roman slavery" (*Slaves in the New Testament: Literary, Social, and Moral Dimensions* [Minneapolis: Fortress, 2006], 1).

38. J. Albert Harrill, "The Use of the New Testament in the American Slave Controversy: A Case History in the Hermeneutical Tension Between Biblical Criticism and Christian Moral Debate," *Religion and American Culture* 10.2 (2000): 149–86 (150). See also Jesper M. Svartvik, "How Noah, Jesus and Paul Became Captivating Biblical Figures: The Side-Effects of the Canonization of Slavery Metaphors in Jewish and Christian Texts," *Journal of Greco-Roman Christianity and Judaism* 2 (2001–2005): 168–227.

39. "Preface," in Keith Bradley and Paul Cartledge, eds., *The Cambridge World History of Slavery*, Vol. 1: *The Ancient Mediterranean World* (Cambridge: Cambridge Univ. Press, 2011), n.p.

40. Wallace, "Some Initial Reflections."

41. Osiek, "Female Slaves," 265. On the relationship of asceticism and the rejection of slavery in later Christian discourse, see Ilana L. E. Ramelli, *Social Justice and the Legitimacy of Slavery: The Role of Philosophical Asceticism from Ancient Judaism to Late Antiquity* (Oxford: Oxford Univ. Press, 2016).

42. Lucy Lind Hogan, "Commentary on Luke 7:1–10," *Working Preacher*, May 29, 2016, https://www.workingpreacher.org/commentaries/revised-common-lectionary/ordinary-09-3/commentary-on-luke-71-10.

43. Nicholas J. Schaser, "Unlawful for a Jew? Acts 10:28 and the Lukan View of Jewish-Gentile Relations," *Biblical Theology Bulletin* 48.4 (2018): 188–201 (188).

44. Hogan, "Commentary on Luke 7:1–10."

45. Theodore W. Jennings Jr. and Tat-Siong Benny Liew, "Mistaken Identities but Model Faith: Rereading the Centurion, the Chap, and the Christ in Matthew 8:5–13," *Journal of Biblical Literature* 123.3 (2004): 467–94 (468). See now Christopher B. Zeichmann, *Queer Readings of the Centurion at Capernaum: Their History and Politics* (Bible and Its Reception 5; Atlanta: Society of Biblical Literature, 2022).

46. D. B. Saddington, "The Centurion in Matthew 8:5–13: Consideration of the Proposal of Theodore W. Jennings Jr. and Tat-Siong Benny Liew," *Journal of Biblical Literature* 125.1 (2006): 140–42.

47. David Lertis Matson, "Pacifist Jesus? The (Mis)Translation of ἐᾶτε ἕως τούτου in *Luke* 22:51," *Journal of Biblical Literature* 134.1 (2015): 157–76.

48. M. Shawn Copeland, "To Follow Jesus," *America*, February 26, 2007, 10–12.

49. Beavis, "Ancient Slavery," 43; she cites, among others, Plautus, Menander, Terence, and Aesop.

50. John P. Meier, *A Marginal Jew: Rethinking the Historical Jesus*, Vol. 5: *Probing the Authenticity of the Parables* (Anchor Yale Bible Reference Library; New Haven: Yale Univ. Press, 2016), argues that the parable *must* be from Jesus, because no follower would describe Jesus's death in such a dishonorable manner. To the contrary, given the cross, this is precisely the story his followers would tell.

51. Klyne R. Snodgrass, *Stories with Intent: A Comprehensive Guide to the Parables of Jesus*, 2nd ed. (Grand Rapids: Eerdmans, 2018): "The language for mistreatment is a clear allusion to the mistreatment of the prophets" (288). Snodgrass is among many who identify these *douloi* as "servants." For the evangelists, this reading is probably correct.

52. David Buttrick, *Speaking Parables: A Homiletic Guide* (Louisville: Westminster John Knox, 2000), 159.

53. See William R. Herzog II, *Parables as Subversive Speech: Jesus as Pedagogue of the Oppressed* (Louisville: Westminster John Knox, 1994), 98–113.

54. Jonathan P. Guevara, "The Parable of the Tenants as a Sociolinguistic Medium of Agrarian Revolution," *Biblical Theology Bulletin* 52.4 (2022): 230–41 (240).

55. Jennifer Glancy, "Slaves and Slavery in the Matthean Parables," *Journal of Biblical Literature* 119.1 (2000): 67–90 (87). Snodgrass, *Stories with Intent*, states: "We can set aside those efforts that view the owner as a rich landowner who has confiscated peasant land. . . . Nothing in the parable gives any hint that the owner is a negative figure" (293).

56. Harrill, "Psychology of Slaves," 66.

57. Beavis, "Ancient Slavery," 41, citing Bradley, *Slaves and Masters*, 15–16.

58. Harrill, *Slaves in the New Testament*, 105.

59. Harrill, "Psychology of Slaves," 69, following Keith Bradley, *Slavery and Society at Rome: Key Themes in Ancient History* (Cambridge: Cambridge Univ. Press, 1994), 166; see also Glancy, *Slavery in Early Christianity*, 102.

60. Discussion in Timothy A. Friedrichsen, "A Note on καί διχοτομήσει αυτόν (Luke 12:46 and the Parallel in Matthew 24:51)," *Catholic Biblical Quarterly* 61 (2001): 258–64.

61. Bernard Brandon Scott, *Hear Then the Parable: A Commentary on the Parables of Jesus* (Minneapolis: Fortress, 1989), 209.

62. David P. Gushee and Glen H. Stassen, *Kingdom Ethics: Following Jesus in Contemporary Context*, 2nd ed. (Grand Rapids: Eerdmans, 2016), 143.

63. Harrill, *Slaves in the New Testament*, 23.

64. Glancy, *Slavery in Early Christianity*, 106.

65. John J. Kilgallen, "What Kind of Servants Are We? (Luke 17:10)," *Biblica* 63 (1982): 549–51 (550), proposes taking *achreios* as "not due a favor," that is, a thank-you. The term means "worthless" in the Septuagint of 2 Kings 6:22; Isa. 33:9; and Ezek. 17:6.

66. Beavis, "Ancient Slavery," 42.

67. A. Marcus Ward, "Uncomfortable Words: IV. Unprofitable Servants," *Expository Times* 81 (1970): 200–203 (201).

68. Ward, "Uncomfortable Words," 203.

69. Alec Hill, "Inside My Slavery," *Christianity Today* 58.6 (2014): 76–79.

70. Brian Schultz, "Jesus as Archelaus in the Parable of the Pounds (Lk. 19:11–27)," *Novum Testamentum* 49 (2007): 105–27 (105).

71. Hezser, *Jewish Slavery in Antiquity*, 275–84; Catherine Hezser, "New Testament and Rabbinic Slave Parables at the Intersection Between Fiction and Reality," in Annette Merz, Eric Ottenheijm, and Nikki Spoelstra (eds.), *The Power of Parables: Essays on the Comparative Study of Jewish and Christian Parables* (Leiden and Boston: Brill, 2023), 367–88.

72. Hezser, "New Testament and Rabbinic Slave Parables," 373, following Bruce W. Frier and Thomas A. J. McGinn, *A Casebook on Roman Family Law* (Oxford: Oxford Univ. Press, 2004), 221.

73. Snodgrass, *Stories with Intent*, 528; Arland J. Hultgren, *The Parables of Jesus: A Commentary* (Grand Rapids: Eerdmans, 2000), 274.

74. Herzog, *Parables as Subversive Speech*, 167. For an alternative reading that includes warnings to the rich, see Richard L. Rohrbaugh, "A Peasant Reading of the Parable of the Talents/Pounds: A Text of Terror," *Biblical Theology Bulletin* 23.1 (1993): 32–39.

75. Adam F. Braun, "Reframing the Parable of the Pounds in Lukan Narrative and Economic Context: Luke 19:11–28," *Currents in Theology and Mission* 39.6 (2012): 442–48 (448), following Richard Vinson. See also James C. Scott, *Weapons of the Weak: Everyday Forms of Peasant Resistance* (New Haven: Yale Univ. Press, 1987). Drawing on Scott's "Hidden Transcripts," see Allen Dwight Callahan and Richard A. Horsley, "Slave Resistance in Classical Antiquity," *Semeia* 83–84 (1998): 133–51.

76. Keith Bradley, "Resisting Slavery in Rome," in Bradley and Cartledge, *Cambridge World History of Slavery*, Vol. 1, 362–84. See also Scott, *Weapons of the Weak*.

77. Brad H. Young, *The Parables: Jewish Tradition and Christian Interpretation* (Grand Rapids: Baker Academic, 1998), 85.

78. Glancy, "Slaves and Slavery," 77, 79.

79. Hezser, "Parables and Daily Life," 10.

80. So the abolitionist Angelina Grimké argued in her 1836 book *Appeal to Christian Women of the South*: "Whatsoever ye would that men should do to you, do ye

even so to them. Let every slaveholder apply these queries to this own heart. Am I willing to be a slave—Am I willing to see my wife the slave of another—Am I willing to see my mother a slave, or my father, my sister or my brother? If not, then in holding others as slaves, I am doing what I would not wish to be one to me or any relative I have" (cited in Richard W. Fox, *Jesus in America: Personal Savior, Cultural Hero, National Obsession* [San Francisco: HarperOne, 2005], 207).

81. Harrill, *Slaves in the New Testament*, 90.
82. Carter, "Sanctioned Violence," 295.

CHAPTER 3: ETHNICITY AND RACE

1. Paula Fredriksen, *Paul: The Pagans' Apostle* (New Haven: Yale Univ. Press, 2017).
2. See details in Amy-Jill Levine, "The Good Samaritan," chap. 2 in *Short Stories by Jesus: The Enigmatic Parables of a Controversial Rabbi* (New York: HarperOne, 2007).
3. "Matthew: Chapter 18," United States Conference of Catholic Bishops, https://bible.usccb.org/bible/matthew/18.
4. "Matthew: Chapter 23," https://bible.usccb.org/bible/matthew/23.
5. For more on the problems with the notes to this text, see Amy-Jill Levine, "Nostra Aetate, Omnia Mutantur: The Times They Are a-Changing," in Elena G. Procario-Foley and Robert A. Cathy, eds., *Righting Relations After the Holocaust and Vatican II: Essays in Honor of John T. Pawlikowski, OSM* (Mahwah, NJ: Paulist, 2018), 226–52.
6. See Matthew Thiessen, *Paul and the Gentile Problem* (Oxford: Oxford Univ. Press, 2018).
7. For various views of the possibility of joining the Jewish community in the first century, see Daniel R. Schwartz, *Judeans and Jews: Four Faces of Dichotomy in Ancient Jewish History* (Kenneth Michael Tanenbaum Series in Jewish Studies; Toronto: University of Toronto Press, 2014); a shorter discussion can be found in his "Jewish Movements of the New Testament Period," in Amy-Jill Levine and Marc Z. Brettler, eds., *The Jewish Annotated New Testament*, 2nd ed. (New York: Oxford Univ. Press, 2017), 614–19.
8. Although Mark's Gospel is shorter than the other three canonical accounts of Jesus's life, the individual stories tend to be longer. This account, the longest of the exorcisms, runs to twenty verses. Shorter versions appear in Matt. 8:28–34 and Luke 8:26–39.
9. Dawn Ottoni-Wilhelm, *Preaching the Gospel of Mark: Proclaiming the Power of the Word of God* (Louisville: Westminster John Knox, 2008), 85, 90, 92.
10. See J. Duncan M. Derrett, "Spirit-Possession and the Gerasene Demoniac," *Man* n.s. 14.2 (1979): 2286–93.

11. See Hans Leander, *Discourses of Empire: The Gospel of Mark from a Postcolonial Perspective* (SBL Semeia Studies 71; Atlanta: Society of Biblical Literature, 2013), 95–108.

12. Warren Carter correctly contests the claim that Mark has no opposition to Rome in "Cross-Gendered Romans and Mark's Jesus: Legion Enters the Pigs (Mark 5:1–20)," *Journal of Biblical Literature* 133.1 (2014): 139–55.

13. Carter, "Cross-Gendered Romans," 143, and Colleen Conway, *Behold the Man: Jesus and Greco-Roman Masculinity* (New York: Oxford Univ. Press, 2008).

14. Carter, "Cross-Gendered Romans," 152, with primary sources. See also Joel Marcus, *Mark 1–8* (Anchor Yale Bible Commentaries; New Haven: Yale Univ. Press, 2002), 345. Had the pigs been castrated (so described, e.g., by Columella [*Rust.* 8.2]), the sexual slander becomes stronger.

15. Mary Healy, *The Gospel of Mark* (Catholic Commentary on Sacred Scripture; Grand Rapids: Baker Academic, 2008), 101.

16. "Self-Injury, Cutting," Mayo Clinic Patient Care and Health Information, https://www.mayoclinic.org/diseases-conditions/self-injury/symptoms-causes/syc-20350950.

17. On the mental health of queer-identifying youth, see "2022 National Survey on LGBTQ Youth Mental Health," Trevor Project, https://www.thetrevorproject.org/survey-2022/.

18. For a helpful definition of the term "queer," see "Definitions," Vanderbilt Student Affairs, https://www.vanderbilt.edu/lgbtqi/resources/definitions (accessed November 6, 2022).

19. Ottoni-Wilhelm, *Preaching the Gospel of Mark*, 89.

20. Hisako Kinukawa, "Mark," in Daniel Patte, ed., *Global Bible Commentary* (Nashville: Abingdon, 2004), 367–78 (371).

21. Giovanni B. Bazzana, *Having the Spirit of Christ: Spirit Possession and Exorcism in the Early Christ Groups* (Synkrisis; New Haven: Yale Univ. Press, 2020).

22. For approaches to Mark 5:1–20 in light of colonialism and trauma, see, e.g., Paul W. Hollenbach, "Jesus, Demoniacs, and Public Authorities: A Socio-Historical Study," *Journal of the American Academy of Religion* 49.4 (1981): 567–88; and Maia Kotrosits and Hal Taussig, *Re-reading the Gospel of Mark Amidst Loss and Trauma* (New York: Palgrave Macmillan, 2013). Numerous other works read Mark 5:1–20 and Synoptic parallels in conversation with colonial, neoliberal, and other political and cultural systems.

23. Tat-Siong Benny Liew, "Tyranny, Boundary and Might: Colonial Mimicry in Mark's Gospel," *Journal for the Study of the New Testament* 73 (1999): 7–31.

24. Christine J. Guth, "An Insider's Look at the Gerasene Disciple (Mark 5:1–20): Biblical Interpretation from the Social Location of Mental Illness," *Journal of Religion, Disability, and Health* 11.4 (2007): 61–70 (65, 65–66).

25. For discussion of Luke's representations of women, see Amy-Jill Levine and Ben Witherington III, *The Gospel of Luke* (New Cambridge Bible Commentaries; Cambridge: Cambridge Univ. Press, 2018).

26. Amy-Jill Levine, "Matthew's Advice to a Divided Readership," in David E. Aune, ed., *The Gospel of Matthew in Current Study: Studies in Memory of William G. Thompson, S.J.* (Grand Rapids: Eerdmans, 2001), 22–41.

27. Philip Wingeier-Rayo, "Jesus as Migrant: A Biblical Understanding of Immigration as a Cross-Cultural Model for Ministry," *Apuntes* 35.1 (2015): 19–32 (24).

28. David Rhoades, "Social Criticism: Crossing Boundaries," in Janice Capel Anderson and Stephen D. Moore, eds., *Mark and Method: New Approaches in Biblical Criticism* (Minneapolis: Fortress, 1992), 161.

29. So, e.g., Healy, *Gospel of Mark*, 144; William Barclay, *The Gospel of Mark*, rev. ed. (Daily Study Bible Series; Philadelphia: Westminster Press, 1975), 178 ("the word dog was in fact sometimes a Jewish term of contempt for Gentiles"); Wingeier-Rayo, "Jesus as Migrant," 25–26; and pretty much everywhere else. Jews, like gentiles, used the term "dog" sometimes to refer to actual dogs, and sometimes as an insult. It does not have a racist or ethnic connotation. For extensive contrary views, see the essays in Phillip Ackerman-Lieberman and Rakefet Zalashik, eds., *A Jew's Best Friend?: The Image of the Dog Throughout Jewish History* (Eastbourne: Sussex Academic Press, 2014). See also Geoffrey David Miller, "Attitudes Toward Dogs in Ancient Israel: A Reassessment," *Journal for the Study of the Old Testament* 32.4 (2008): 487–500.

30. Mark Nanos, "Paul's Reversal of Jews Calling Gentiles 'Dogs' (Philippians 3:2): 1600 Years of an Ideological Tale Wagging an Exegetical Dog," *Biblical Interpretation*, January 1, 2009, https://brill.com/view/journals/bi/17/4/article-p448_3.xml?language=en.

31. Quoted in Kenneth Snow, "The Bread, the Children, and the Dogs," in Ackerman-Lieberman and Zalashik, *A Jew's Best Friend?*, 113–34 (118). More examples abound in this article.

32. Rakefet Zalashik and Phillip Ackerman-Lieberman, "Introduction," in Ackerman-Lieberman and Zalashik, *A Jew's Best Friend?*, 1–11; Jay Geller, *Bestiarium Judaicum: Unnatural Histories of the Jews* (New York: Fordham Univ. Press, 2018), chap. 8, "Dogged by Destiny: 'Lupus est homo homini, non homo, quom quails sit non navit,'" 188–220.

33. Leticia A. Guardiola-Saénz, "Borderless Women and Borderless Texts: A Cultural Reading of Matthew 15:21–28," *Semeia* 78 (1997): 111. See discussion of this article in Levine, "Matthew's Advice," 23–24.

34. See Levine, "Matthew's Advice," for classical and rabbinic examples. See also Warren Carter and Amy-Jill Levine, *The New Testament: Methods and Meanings* (Nashville: Abingdon, 2013), 47–49.

35. E.g., Jo-Ann Brant, *John* (Paideia: Commentaries on the New Testament; Grand Rapids: Baker Academic, 2011), after giving negative comments concludes, "The Mishnah's references to the Samaritans probably reflect the views of Jesus' contemporaries" (83). Missing are the mishnaic comments on the permissibility of consuming food and wine prepared by Samaritans.

36. Victor Cancino, "The Samaritan Woman Who No Longer Fears Intimacy," *America*, March 8, 2023, https://www.americamagazine.org/faith/2023/03/08/samaritan-gospel-lent-244866.

37. D. A. Carson, *The Gospel According to John* (Pillar New Testament Commentary; Grand Rapids: Eerdmans, 1991), 217.

38. Alan D. Crown, "Redating the Schism Between the Judaeans and the Samaritans," *Jewish Quarterly Review* 82.1–2 (1991): 17–50 (17, abstract). See also Lawrence Schiffman, "The Samaritans in Tannaitic Halakhah," *Jewish Quarterly Review* 75 (1985): 323–50; Menachem Mor, "The Samaritans and Bar-Kokhbah," in Alan D. Crown, ed., *The Samaritans* (Tübingen: Mohr Siebeck, 1989), 19–31.

39. See, e.g., Teresa Okure, "Jesus and the Samaritan Woman (John 4:1–42) in Africa," *Theological Studies* 70 (2009): 401–18 (414).

40. Okure, "Jesus and the Samaritan Woman," 409.

41. Carson, *Gospel According to John*, 217.

42. For an alternative perspective, see Stephen D. Moore, "Are There Impurities in the Living Water That the Johannine Jesus Dispenses? Deconstruction, Feminism, and the Samaritan Woman," *Biblical Interpretation* 1 (1993): 207–27, reprinted in Amy-Jill Levine with Marianne Blickenstaff, eds., *A Feminist Companion to John*, Vol. 1 (Feminist Companion to the New Testament and Early Christian Writings; Sheffield: Sheffield Academic Press, 2003), 78–124.

43. Gen. 24:27 calls the enslaved man an *eved* (Hebrew); the Septuagint translates *pais*, "boy."

44. Sandra M. Schneiders, *The Revelatory Text: Interpreting the New Testament as Sacred Scripture* (San Francisco: HarperSanFrancisco, 1991), 134, asserts that the episode is "not an historical event in the life of Jesus."

45. See Adeline Fehribach, *The Women in the Life of the Bridegroom* (Collegeville: Liturgical Press, 1998); and Fehribach, "The 'Birthing' Bridegroom: The Portrayal of Jesus in the Fourth Gospel," in Amy-Jill Levine with Marianne Blickenstaff, eds., *A Feminist Companion to John*, Vol. 2 (Feminist Companions to the New Testament and Early Christian Writings 5; Sheffield: Sheffield Academic Press, 2003), 104–29; Andrea Taschl-Erber, "Between Recognition and Testimony: Johannine *Relecture* of the First Easter Witness and Patristic Readings," in Reimund Bieringer, Barbara Baert, and Karlijn Demasure, eds., *Noli Me Tangere in Interdisciplinary Perspective: Textual, Iconographic and Contemporary Interpretations* (Leuven: Peeters, 2016), 77–110 (94–95).

46. On Johannine biology, following Aristotle, see Adele Reinhartz, "'And the Word Was Begotten': Divine Epigenesis in the Gospel of John," *Semeia* 85 (1999): 83–103; and Reinhartz, "'Children of God' and Aristotelian Epigenesis in the Gospel of John," in R. Alan Culpepper and Jan G. van der Watt, eds., *Creation Stories in Dialogue: The Bible, Science, and Folk Traditions* (Leiden: Brill, 2016), 243–53.

47. Brant, *John*, 83. Nor does being alone with a woman mean he "invites impurity," contra Doug Olena, "John 2–3," February 18, 25, https://ltet.net/download /dougolena-john-2-3.pdf.

48. Herman Ridderbos, *The Gospel of John: A Theological Commentary* (Grand Rapids: Eerdmans, 1997), 154.

49. See Adele Reinhartz, "The Vanishing Jews of Antiquity," and other articles in "Jew and Judean: A Forum on Politics and Historiography in the Translation of Ancient Texts," *Marginalia*, August 26, 2014, https://themarginaliareview.com /jew-judean-forum/, and for earlier discussion, Amy-Jill Levine, *The Misunderstood Jew: The Church and the Scandal of the Jewish Jesus* (New York: HarperOne, 2017).

50. Schneiders, *Revelatory Text*, 138.

51. Ridderbos, *Gospel of John*, 155.

52. Carson, *Gospel of John*, 221.

53. Ridderbos, *Gospel of John*, 160.

54. Brant, *John*, 86.

55. Hyrcanus may have sought to integrate the Samaritans into Judean worship in Jerusalem; see Jonathan Bourgel, "The Destruction of the Samaritan Temple by John Hyrcanus: A Reconsideration," *Journal of Biblical Literature* 135.3 (2016): 505–23.

56. Adele Reinhartz, "The Gospel of John," in Levine and Brettler, *Jewish Annotated New Testament*, 168–218 (184). See also, in the same volume, Tal Ilan, "Gender," 611–14.

CHAPTER 4: HEALTH CARE

1. Candida Moss, "Mark and Matthew," in Sarah Melcher, Mikeal C. Parsons, and Amos Yong, eds., *The Bible and Disability: A Commentary* (London: SCM Press, 2018), 275–301, notes the "common disability studies distinction between impairment (a physiological phenomenon) and disability (a social phenomenon)" (276).

2. Carolyn C. Ross, "Miraculous Healing: The Body's Amazing Self-Healing Capacity," *Psychology Today*, December 24, 2010, https://www.psychologytoday.com /us/blog/real-healing/201012/miraculous-healing.

3. See Joan Kub and Sara Groves, "Miracles and Medicine: An Annotated Bibliography," *Southern Medical Journal* 100.12 (2007): 1273–76.

4. Jan-Olav Henriksen and Karl Olav Sandnes, *Jesus as Healer: A Gospel for the Body* (Grand Rapids: Eerdmans, 2016), 4.
5. "Constitution," World Health Organization, https://www.who.int/about/governance/constitution. The constitution was adopted in 1946 and entered into force in 1948.
6. The classic study is Michel Foucault, *Madness and Civilization: A History of Insanity in the Age of Reason*, trans. R. Howard (New York: Vintage, 1965); see also the abridged version, *History of Madness*, ed. Jean Khalfa, trans. Jonathan Murphy and Jean Khalfa (London: Routledge, 2009).
7. Concerning "Bartimaeus son of Timaeus," whose sight Jesus restores in Mark 10:46–52, "bar" is Aramaic for "son of," as in "bar mitzvah" (lit., "son of the commandment"). Mark translates the Aramaic: the man is Timaeus's son. The tradition may be punning on Plato's *Timaeus*, which describes the harmony of creation. For Mark, Jesus replaces the Demiurge who created the world.
8. Daniel C. Smith, "Accessing the Ancient Mediterranean Studies Classroom," *Ancient Jew Review*, October 24, 2022, https://www.ancientjewreview.com/read/2022/10/24/accessing-the-ancient-mediterranean-studies-classroom, citing, e.g., Plato, *Republic* 518C; Galen, *De Usu Partium* X.2.66; Meghan R. Henning, "Metaphorical, Punitive, and Pedagogical Blindness in Hell," in Jared Secord, Heidi Marx Wolf, and Christoph Markschies, eds., *Health, Medicine, and Christianity in Late Antiquity* (Leuven: Peeters, 2017), 139–52. See also Moss, "Mark and Matthew."
9. Andreas J. Köstenberger, *John* (Grand Rapids: Baker Academic, 2004), 281. The same point, in the same wording, appears in his contribution on John to *Zondervan Illustrated Bible Backgrounds Commentary*, Vol. 2, *John and Acts* (Grand Rapids: Zondervan, 2002).
10. David Kraemer, *Responses to Suffering in Classical Rabbinic Literature* (New York: Oxford Univ. Press, 1995), 185.
11. Shabbat 55b, the William Davison Talmud (Koren-Steinsaltz) at https://www.sefaria.org/Shabbat.55b.6?lang=bi&with=all&lang2=en.
12. Myrick C. Shinall Jr., "The Social Conditions of Lepers in the Gospels," *Journal of Biblical Literature* 137.4 (2018): 915–34 (915).
13. Mike Gulliver and William John Lyons, "Conceptualizing the Place of Deaf People in Ancient Israel: Suggestions from Deaf Space," *Journal of Biblical Literature* 137.3 (2018): 537–53 (537, 553). See their bibliography for additional work on disability in ancient Israel.
14. Candida R. Moss and Joel S. Baden, *Reconceiving Infertility: Biblical Perspectives on Procreation and Childlessness* (Princeton: Princeton Univ. Press, 2015), 7.
15. Joseph A. Fitzmyer, *The Gospel According to Luke I–IX* (Anchor Bible; Garden City, NY: Doubleday, 1981), 323.

16. *Lamentations Rabbah* 24 depicts Leah as doing what she can to prevent Rachel from feeling disgraced. See discussion in Jonathan K. Crane, "Who's Your Mama Now? Rachel, Leah, and Rabbinic Views on Their Procreative Possibilities," *Journal of Jewish Ethics* 3.1 (2017): 92–117.

17. Henriksen and Sandnes, *Jesus as Healer*, 25–63, summarize approaches in New Testament scholarship: "healer who did not cure diseases"; first-century psychiatrist, faith/placebo effect; cultural phenomenon.

18. "In a boat" appears in some but not all manuscripts. In this case, Jesus is not depicted as walking on water.

19. "Immediately" does not appear in all manuscripts.

20. Karen Peterson-Iyer, *Reenvisioning Sexual Ethics: A Feminist Christian Account* (Washington, DC: Georgetown Univ. Press, 2022), 28.

21. E.g., Amy-Jill Levine, "Discharging Responsibility: Matthean Jesus, Biblical Law, and Hemorrhaging Woman," in D. R. Bauer and M. A. Powell, eds., *Treasures Old and New: Recent Contributions to Matthean Studies* (Symposium Series 1; Atlanta: Scholars Press, 1996), reprinted in Amy-Jill Levine, ed., *A Feminist Companion to Matthew* (Feminist Companions to the New Testament and Early Christian Writings 1; Sheffield: Sheffield Academic Press, 2001), 70–87.

22. Moumita Biswas, "Promoting Women's Reproductive and Sexual Health," at http://iawn.anglicancommunion.org/media/192261/Biblical-Reflection-Mark-5-25-to-34-Moumita-Biswas.pdf. The article first appeared in *Samachar*, the newsletter of the All India Council of Christian Women, 2015. See also Anne Nasimiyu Wasike, "Jesus: An African Perspective," in Daniel Patte, ed., *Global Bible Commentary* (Nashville: Abingdon, 2004), 329–32: "He sets women free from ostracism, from blood-taboos, and other distorted views that are responses to women's natural physiological processes (Luke 8:43–48 and Gal. 5:1)" (330).

23. Elizabeth Struthers Malbon, "Fallible Followers: Women and Men in the Gospel of Mark," *Semeia* 28 (1983): 29–48 (46).

24. Mary Healy, *Gospel of Mark* (Catholic Commentary on Sacred Scripture; Grand Rapids: Baker Academic, 2008), 107. For additional (negative) readings of Leviticus vis-à-vis Jesus, see Hector Avalos, *Health Care and the Rise of Christianity* (Peabody, MA: Hendrickson, 1999). While offering a helpful summary of health care at the time, Harold Remus, *Jesus as Healer* (Cambridge: Cambridge Univ. Press, 1997), contextualizes Jesus as "transgressing" boundaries within Judaism, such as "when Jesus is defiled (according to Jewish tradition) by physical contact with a hemorrhaging woman (5:28; see Lev. 15:19–30) or defiles himself by taking a dead person by the hand (5:41; see Num. 19:11–13, 31:19)" (34). No law is broken or boundary transgressed.

25. Joel Marcus, *Mark 1–8* (Anchor Yale Bible Commentaries; New Haven: Yale Univ. Press, 2002), 357–58, and more recently, David F. Watson, "Luke-Acts," in Melcher, Parsons, and Yong, *Bible and Disability*, 303–32, who repeatedly details Levitical purity laws to conclude "the social isolation of this woman must have been acute" and that Jesus both "challenges the purity system that results in her exclusion" and "rejects the idea that people may defile through pollution" (313). Such comments invent problems for Jesus to resolve.

26. Marcus, *Mark*, 357.

27. L. Lewis Wall, "Jesus and the Unclean Woman: How the Story in Mark's Gospel Sheds Light on the Problem of Obstetric Fistula," *Christianity Today* 54.1 (January 2010): 48–52 (50, 52).

28. Paula Fredriksen, "Compassion Is to Purity as Fish Is to Bicycle and Other Reflections on Constructions of 'Judaism' in Current Work on the Historical Jesus," in John S. Kloppenborg with John W. Marshall, eds., *Apocalypticism, Anti-Semitism and the Historical Jesus: Subtexts in Criticism* (London: T&T Clark, 2005), 55–67.

29. Dawn Ottoni-Wilhelm, *Preaching the Gospel of Mark: Proclaiming the Power of the Word of God* (Louisville: Westminster John Knox, 2008), 98–99.

30. Charlotte Fonrobert, "The Woman with a Blood-Flow (Mark 5.24–34) Revisited: Menstrual Laws and Jewish Culture in Christian Feminist Hermeneutics," in Craig A. Evans and James A. Sanders, eds., *Early Christian Interpretation of the Scriptures of Israel* (Journal for the Study of the New Testament Supplement Series 148; Sheffield: Sheffield Academic, 1997), 121–40 (134).

31. Thomas Kazan, *Jesus and Purity Halakhah: "Was Jesus Indifferent to Impurity?"* (Coniectanea Biblica New Testament Series 38; Stockholm: Almqvist & Wiksell, 2002), 344. For similar views, see the list and discussion in Cecelia Wassen, "Jesus' Work as a Healer in Light of Jewish Purity Laws," in Isaac Kalimi, ed., *Bridging Between Sister Religions: Studies of Jewish and Christian Scriptures Offered in Honor of Prof. John T. Townsend* (Leiden: Brill, 2016), 87–104; see also her "Jesus and the Hemorrhaging Woman in Mark 5:24–34: Insights from Purity Laws from Qumran," in A. Voitila and J. Jokiranta, eds., *Scripture in Transition: Essays on Septuagint, Hebrew Bible, and Dead Sea Scrolls in Honour of Raija Sollamo* (Supplements to the Journal for the Study of Judaism 126; Leiden: Brill, 2008), 641–60, which questions whether touching clothing conveyed impurity.

32. Judith M. Lieu, *The Gospel of Luke: Epworth Commentaries* (Eugene, OR: Wipf & Stock, 1997), 68. According to Shaye Cohen, "Purity and Piety: The Separation of Menstruants from the Sancta," in S. Groomsman and R. Haute, eds., *Daughters of the King/Woman and the Synagogue: A Survey of History and Contemporary Realities* (Philadelphia: Jewish Publication Society, 1992), the "Gospel story about the woman with a twelve-year discharge, clearly a case of zabah, does not

give any indication that the woman was impure or suffered any degree of isolation as a result of her affliction" (279). Should purity in relation to menstruation, ejaculation, etc., have been of concern in the late Second Temple period, people had access to the numerous *miqva'ot* (ritual baths) found in Judea and Galilee.

33. Susan Haber, "A Woman's Touch: Feminist Encounters with the Hemorrhaging Woman in Mark 5.24–34," *Journal for the Study of the New Testament* 26.2 (2003): 171–92 (171), citing other feminist studies.

34. Purity is a tacit issue in the two stories, but it is not the major one. It goes too far to say that Mark is not here interested in purity concerns. Haber, "Woman's Touch," 173 n. 5, *contra* Mary Rose D'Angelo, "Gender and Power in the Gospel of Mark: The Daughter of Jairus and the Woman with the Flow of Blood," in John C. Cavadini, ed., *Miracles in Jewish and Christian Antiquity* (Notre Dame, IN: University of Notre Dame Press, 1999), 83–109 (91).

35. See Candida Moss, "The Man with the Flow of Power: Porous Bodies in Mark 5:25–4," *Journal of Biblical Literature* 129.3 (2010): 507–519.

36. Bernadette Brooten, *Women Leaders in the Ancient Synagogue: Inscriptional Evidence and Background Issues* (Brown Judaic Studies; Providence: Brown Univ. Press, 1982); see esp. Brooten's updated preface in the 2020 open access edition, https://doi .org/10.2307/j.ctvzpv5mr.

37. Mary Ann Beavis, "The Resurrection of Jephthah's Daughter: Judges 11:34–40 and Mark 5:21–24, 35–43," *Catholic Biblical Quarterly* 72.1 (2010): 46–62.

38. Elaine M. Wainwright, *Towards a Feminist Critical Reading of the Gospel According to Matthew* (Beihefte zur Zeitschrift für die neutestamentliche Wissenschaft 60; Berlin: Walter de Gruyter, 1991), finds Jairus's request "even more extraordinary when one realizes that the child is not a son, an heir needed for the continuation of the patriarchal family line, but rather a daughter, a young unmarried girl" (87).

39. For cultural concerns about children's bodies, esp. those of daughters, see Janine Elissa Luttick, "'Little Girl, Get Up!' (and Stand on Your Own Two Feet!): A Reading of Mark 5:21–24, 35–43 with an Awareness of the Role and Function of the Body," PhD diss., Australian Catholic University, 2017.

40. Ottoni-Wilhelm, *Preaching the Gospel of Mark*, 99. Contrast Beavis, "Resurrection of Jephthah's Daughter": "Nor is there anything particularly radical about Jesus' willingness to take the hand of a lifeless child, since touching a dead body is not wrong or unholy but may be a commendable act" (97–98).

41. Healy, *Mark*, 100.

42. Levine, "Discharging Responsibility."

43. Luke Timothy Johnson, *The Gospel of Luke* (Sacra Pagina; Collegeville, MN: Liturgical Press), 226; Stuart Love, "The Man with Dropsy," *Leaven* 6.3 (1998): 136, http://digitalcommons.pepperdine.edu/leaven/vol6/iss3/9.

44. Chad Hartsock, "The Healing of the Man with Dropsy (Luke 14:1–6) and the Lukan Landscape," *Biblical Interpretation* 21.3 (2013): 341–54.

45. Ovid and Horace cited in Love, "Man with Dropsy," 139.

46. Willi Braun, *Feasting and Social Rhetoric in Luke 14* (Society for New Testament Studies Monograph Series 85; Cambridge: Cambridge Univ. Press, 1995), 41. See also Amanda Miller, "Bridge Works and Seating Charts: A Study of Luke's Ethics of Wealth, Poverty, and Reversal," *Interpretation* 68.4 (2014): 416–27.

47. "The Twelve Steps," Alcoholics Anonymous, https://www.aa.org/the-twelve-steps.

48. Johnson, *Gospel of Luke*, 212 n. 14. The same statement and list appear in Charles H. Talbert, *Matthew* (Paideia: Commentaries on the New Testament; Grand Rapids: Baker Academic, 2010), who adds, "In m. Shabb. 22.6, it is expressly forbidden to straighten a dislocated hand or foot on the Sabbath" (152) and that "in the rabbinic tradition (b. Shabb. 128b), an animal that falls into a pit on the Sabbath is to be assisted (e.g., by feeding it or by supplying devices that would help it climb out), but it should not be lifted out" (153). The Mishnah states that a person suffering a dislocated hand or foot should not, on the Sabbath, move the limb vigorously in cold water, but washing in a typical manner is appropriate. The Talmud (b. Shabbat 148a) discusses various permutations of the Mishnah, including the option to reset the joint or to fix broken bones. B. Shabbat, a debate among third-century rabbis, also states that Torah forbids causing an animal to suffer and that this prohibition overrides any rabbinic halakhah.

49. Citations are from Sefaria, https://www.sefaria.org/texts.

50. See Nina Collins, *Jesus, the Sabbath and the Jewish Debate: Healing on the Sabbath in the 1st and 2nd Centuries CE* (Library of New Testament Studies; London: T&T Clark, 2016), 108–22.

51. Catherine Hezser, "Representations of the Physician in Jewish Literature from Hellenistic and Roman Times," in William V. Harris, ed., *Popular Medicine in Graeco-Roman Antiquity: Explorations* (Columbia Studies in the Classical Tradition 42; Leiden: Brill, 2016), 173–197 (188).

CHAPTER 5: FAMILY VALUES

1. Bernadette Brooten, "Konnten Frauen in altem Judentum die Scheidung betreiben? Überlegungen zu Mk 10, 11–12 und 1 Kor 7, 10–11," *Evangelische Theologie* 42 (1982): 65–80; Brooten, "Zur Debatte über das Scheidungsrecht der jüdischen Frau," *Evangelische Theologie* 43 (1983): 466–78.

2. Bezalel Porten, "Elephantine," in *Shalvi/Hyman Encyclopedia of Jewish Women*, December 31, 1999, Jewish Women's Archive, https://jwa.org/encyclopedia/article/elephantine. For details on the papyri, see esp. Annalisa Azzoni, *The Private Lives of Women in Persian Egypt* (University Park, PA: Penn State Univ. Press, 2013).

3. William Loader, *The New Testament on Sexuality* (Grand Rapids: Eerdmans, 2012), 50, citing t. Ketub. 12.1; y. Ketub. 8.32b–c; b. Ketub. 82b.

4. Yair Furstenberg, "The Shared Image of Pharisaic Law in the Gospels and Rabbinic Tradition," in Joseph Sievers and Amy-Jill Levine, eds., *The Pharisees* (Grand Rapids: Eerdmans, 2021), 199–219 (212).

5. Aharon Shemesh, "4Q271.3: A Key to Sectarian Matrimonial Law," *Journal of Jewish Studies* 49 (1998): 245–46, cited in Vered Noam, "Divorce in Qumran in Light of Early Halakhah," *Journal of Jewish Studies* 66.2 (2005): 206–23 (209).

6. See Thomas McGinn, "The Law of Roman Divorce in the Time of Christ," in Amy-Jill Levine, Dale C. Allison Jr., and John Dominic Crossan, eds., *The Historical Jesus in Context* (Princeton Readings in Religion; Princeton: Princeton Univ. Press, 2006), 309–22 (310).

7. Mary Ann Beavis, *Mark* (Paideia: Commentaries on the New Testament; Grand Rapids: Baker Academic, 2011), 151.

8. See discussion, with texts, in Noam, "Divorce."

9. For helpful discussion, which extends rabbinic texts into present-day Jewish practice, see Susan Weiss, "Divorce: The Halakhic Perspective," *Shalvi/Hyman Encyclopedia of Jewish Women*, December 31, 1999, Jewish Women's Archives, https://jwa.org/encyclopedia/article/divorce-halakhic-perspective.

10. Weiss, "Divorce."

11. Organization for the Resolution of Agunot, ORA, Freeing Agunot. Preventing Abuse, https://www.getora.org; Sonia Zylberberg, "International Coalition for Agunah Rights (ICAR); Shulamit S. Magnus, "Agunot," *Shalvi/Hyman Encyclopedia of Jewish Women*, last updated June 23, 2021, Jewish Women's Archive, https://jwa.org/encyclopedia/article/international-coalition-for-agunah-rights-icar. See Bernard S. Jackson, *Agunah: The Manchester Analysis*, Agunah Research Unit, Vol. 1 (Manchester: Deborah Charles Publications, 2011), and the other four volumes in this series.

12. Mary Rose D'Angelo, "Remarriage and the Divorce Sayings Attributed to Jesus," in William G. Roberts, ed., *Divorce and Remarriage* (New York: Sheed and Ward, 1990), 93, cautions that the divorce statements derive not from Jesus but from early Christian prophecy.

13. Furstenberg, "Shared Image," 212.

14. John W. Martens, "'But from the Beginning It Was Not So': The Jewish Apocalyptic Context of Jesus's Teaching on Marriage, Divorce, and Remarriage," *Journal of Moral Theology* 10.2 (2021): 5–33 (25).

15. See Richard B. Hays, *The Moral Vision of the New Testament: A Contemporary Introduction to New Testament Ethics* (San Francisco: HarperSanFrancisco, 1996), 352.

16. John Temple Bristow, *What the Bible Really Says About Love, Marriage, and the Family* (St. Louis: Chalice Press, 1994), 111; Walter A. Elwell and Robert W. Yarbrough, *Encountering the New Testament: A Historical and Theological Survey* (Grand Rapids: Baker Books, 1998), 341.

17. Mary Healy, *The Gospel of Mark* (Catholic Commentary on Sacred Scripture; Grand Rapids: Baker Academic, 2008), 196.

18. Healy, *Gospel of Mark*, 196.

19. Dawn Ottoni-Wilhelm, *Preaching the Gospel of Mark: Proclaiming the Power of the Word of God* (Louisville: Westminster John Knox, 2008), 173.

20. N. T. Wright, *Jesus and the Victory of God* (Minneapolis: Fortress, 1996), 397–98, suggests that Mark 10:10 is cryptic, given the political liability of arguing against divorce in Antipas's territory; cf. Mark 6:18, 21–29.

21. Details are efficiently presented in Martens, "But from the Beginning," 12–16.

22. For a comprehensive history of interpretation on this triplet, see Jennifer Sylvan Alexander, "Matthew's Parable of the Eunuchs," PhD diss., Vanderbilt University, 2021, http://hdl.handle.net/1803/16921.

23. See the helpful discussion by R. Jarrett Van Tine, "Castration for the Kingdom and Avoiding the αἰτία of Adultery (Matthew 19:10–12)," *Journal of Biblical Literature* 137.2 (2018): 399–418.

24. This section draws on Amy-Jill Levine, "The Earth Moved: Jesus, Sex, and Eschatology," in John S. Kloppenborg with John W. Marshall, eds., *Apocalypticism, Anti-Semitism and the Historical Jesus: Subtexts in Criticism* (London: T&T Clark, 2005), 83–96.

25. Amy-Jill Levine, "Women's Itineracy and the Criteria of Authenticity in John Meier's *Marginal Jew*," in Vincent T. M. Skemp and Kelley Coblentz Bautch, eds., *The Figure of Jesus in History and Theology: Essays in Honor of John Meier* (Catholic Biblical Quarterly Imprints; Washington, DC: Catholic Biblical Association of America, 2020), 90–113.

26. Elizabeth Schrader and Joan Taylor, "The Meaning of 'Magdalene': A Review of Literary Evidence," *Journal of Biblical Literature* 140.4 (2021): 751–73.

27. Juan M. C. Oliver, "Nobodies in Charge, Proper 18 (A)—1996," Sermons That Work, The Episcopal Church, September 1, 1996, https://www.episcopalchurch.org/sermon/nobodies-in-charge-proper-18-a-1996/. A Google search with key words "Jesus, children, nobodies" yields numerous examples.

28. Myrick C. Shinall Jr., "Dismemberment, Dualism, and Theology of the Body in the Gospel of Matthew," *Biblical Theology Bulletin* 44.4 (2014): 185–94 (193).

29. J. David Hester, "Eunuchs and the Postgender Jesus: Matthew 19.12 and Transgressive Sexualities," *Journal for New Testament Studies* 28.1 (2005): 13–40 (13).

30. For the textual tradition, see Jennifer Knust and Tommy Wasserman, *To Cast the First Stone: The Transmission of a Gospel Story* (Princeton: Princeton Univ. Press, 2019).

31. Maria Mayo, *The Limits of Forgiveness: Case Studies in the Distortion of a Biblical Ideal* (Minneapolis: Fortress, 2015; reprint Eugene, OR: Wipf & Stock, 2016), 27, 172–73.

32. Francis J. Moloney, *The Gospel of John*, Sacra Pagina Vol. 4, rev. ed. (Collegeville, MN: Liturgical Press, 2005), 262; Herman Ridderbos, *The Gospel of John: A Theological Commentary* (Grand Rapids: Eerdmans, 1997), 291.

33. Chris Keith, *The Pericope Adulterae, the Gospel of John, and the Literacy of Jesus* (New Testament Tools, Studies, and Documents 38; Leiden: Brill, 2009); see also Keith, "Manuscript History and John 8:1–8:11," *Bible Odyssey*, https://bibleodyssey.com /passages/related-articles/manuscript-history-and-john-81-811/.

34. Wendy Wang, "Who Cheats More? The Demographics of Infidelity in America," Institute for Family Studies, January 10, 2018, https://ifstudies.org/blog/who -cheats-more-the-demographics-of-cheating-in-america.

35. Margaret Renkl, "My State's Anti-Drag Campaign Is Beyond Ludicrous," *New York Times*, March 13, 2023, https://www.nytimes.com/2023/03/13/opinion/tennessee -anti-drag-laws.html.

CHAPTER 6: POLITICS

1. See Paula Fredriksen, *Jesus of Nazareth, King of the Jews: A Jewish Life and the Emergence of Christianity* (New York: Vintage, 2000).

2. Anne Nasimiyu Wasike, "Jesus: An African Perspective," in Daniel Patte, ed., *Global Bible Commentary* (Nashville: Abingdon, 2004), 329–32 (331).

3. The lectures were noting the publication of *Das Neue Testament Jüdische Erklärt, Lutherübersetzung* (Stuttgart: Deutsche Bibelgesellschaft, 2021), translation, in- cluding a few additional essays, of Amy-Jill Levine and Marc Z. Brettler, eds., *The Jewish Annotated New Testament* (Oxford: Oxford Univ. Press, 2011).

4. "Vor über 2000 Jahren wurde Jesus geboren. Bis fast zu seinem 30. Lebensjahr hat er gelebt wie jeder andere auch. Dann hat er begonnen, in besonderer Weise von Gott zu sprechen. Er hat Menschen aufgerichtet und geheilt. Er hat Mut ge- macht, dem liebenden und barmherzigen Gott zu vertrauen und zu ihm zu beten. Durch sein Leben hat er gezeigt, dass jeder Mensch gleichermaßen wertvoll ist. Seine Art von Gott zu reden stellten die moralischen und religiösen Überzeu- gungen seiner Zeit infrage. So wurde er mit 33 Jahren zum Tod verurteilt."

5. Guy D. Stiebel, "'Romani Ite Domum'—Expressions of Identity and Resistance in Judaea," in Joan Taylor, ed., *Jesus and Brian: Exploring the Historical Jesus and His Times via Monty Python's* Life of Brian (London: Bloomsbury T&T Clark, 2015), 107–12.

6. Jonathan Reed, "Reappraising the Galilean Economy: The Limits of Models, Archaeology, and Analogy," unpublished paper following his 1994 Claremont Graduate University PhD diss., "Places in Early Christianity: Galilee, Archaeology, Urbanization, and Q," which was summarized in *Archaeology and the Galilean Jesus: A Re-Examination of the Evidence* (Philadelphia: Trinity Press International, 2000). On banditry, Reed is following John Kloppenborg, *The Tenants in the Vineyard: Ideology, Economics, and Agrarian Conflict in Jewish Palestine* (Tübingen: Mohr Siebeck, 2006), 284–87.

7. Andrea M. Berlin, "Jewish Life Before the Revolt: The Archaeological Evidence," *Journal for the Study of Judaism* 36.4 (2005): 417–70. See also her "Romanization and Anti-Romanization in pre-Revolt Galilee," in Andrea M. Berlin and J. Andrew Overman, eds., *The First Jewish Revolt: Archaeology, History, and Ideology* (New York: Routledge, 2002), 57–73.

8. See Martin Goodman, "Jewish History, 331 BCE–135 CE," and Eric M. Orlin, "Revolts Against Rome," in Levine and Brettler, *Jewish Annotated New Testament*, 583–89 and 589–92, respectively.

9. John Dominic Crossan, Appendix A, "Intercultural Translation of 'Kingdom of God/Heavens,'" in *Render unto Caesar: The Struggle over Christ and Culture in the New Testament* (New York: HarperOne, 2022), 281–83. Discussion of kingdom terminology also opens to anti-Jewish nuance. David P. Gushee and Glen H. Stassen (*Kingdom Ethics: Following Jesus in Contemporary Context*, 2nd ed. [Grand Rapids: Eerdmans, 2016]) ask, "Why not abandon the old Jewish term 'kingdom of God' in favor of, for example, 'kin-dom' of God?" (17). "Kingdom of God," however, is not an "old Jewish term"; primarily found on the lips of Jesus, it appears rarely in earlier texts.

10. See Dale C. Allison Jr., *Encountering Mystery: Religious Experience in a Secular Age* (Grand Rapids: Eerdmans, 2022).

11. Warren Carter, "Sanctioned Violence in the New Testament," *Interpretation: A Journal of Bible and Theology* 71.3 (2017): 284–97 (284, 291).

12. Mark D. Nanos, "The Letter of Paul to the Romans," in Amy-Jill Levine and Marc Z. Brettler, *The Jewish Annotated New Testament*, 2nd ed. (New York: Oxford Univ. Press, 2017), 285–320 (314). See also his *The Mystery of Romans: The Jewish Context of Paul's Letter* (Minneapolis: Fortress, 1996), chap. 6, "Romans 13:1–7: Christian Obedience."

13. For additional discussion, see Crossan, *Render unto Caesar*, 9–21.

14. Options in John R. Donahue, "The 'Parable' of the Sheep and the Goats: A Challenge to Christian Ethics," *Theological Studies* 47 (1986): 3–31.

15. See Kathleen Weber, "The Image of Sheep and Goats in Matthew 25:31–46," *Catholic Biblical Quarterly* 59.4 (1997): 657–78.

16. Donahue, "'Parable' of the Sheep and the Goats," 8.